Teach Yourself VISUALLY™

W9-BUU-913

Knitting

Second Edition

Sharon Turner

WILEY

Wiley Publishing, Inc.

Praise for the Teach Yourself VISUALLY Series

I just had to let you and your company know how great I think your books are. I just purchased my third Visual book (my first two are dog-eared now!) and, once again, your product has surpassed my expectations. The expertise, thought, and effort that go into each book are obvious, and I sincerely appreciate your efforts. Keep up the wonderful work!

—*Tracey Moore (Memphis, TN)*

I have several books from the Visual series and have always found them to be valuable resources.

—*Stephen P. Miller (Ballston Spa, NY)*

Thank you for the wonderful books you produce. It wasn't until I was an adult that I discovered how I learn—visually. Although a few publishers out there claim to present the material visually, nothing compares to Visual books. I love the simple layout. Everything is easy to follow. And I understand the material! You really know the way I think and learn. Thanks so much!

—*Stacey Han (Avondale, AZ)*

Like a lot of other people, I understand things best when I see them visually. Your books really make learning easy and life more fun.

—*John T. Frey (Cadillac, MI)*

I am an avid fan of your Visual books. If I need to learn anything, I just buy one of your books and learn the topic in no time. Wonders! I have even trained my friends to give me Visual books as gifts.

—*Illona Bergstrom (Aventura, FL)*

I write to extend my thanks and appreciation for your books. They are clear, easy to follow, and straight to the point. Keep up the good work! I bought several of your books and they are just right! No regrets! I will always buy your books because they are the best.

—*Seward Kollie (Dakar, Senegal)*

Credits

Acquisitions Editor
Pam Mourouzis

Project Editor
Natasha Graf

Copy Editor
Kitty Wilson

Technical Editor
Kristi Porter

Editorial Manager
Christina Stambaugh

Vice President and Publisher
Cindy Kitchel

Vice President and Executive Publisher
Kathy Nebenhaus

Interior Design
Tai Blanche, with Elizabeth Brooks

Interior Photography
Matt Bowen

Special Thanks...

To the following companies for providing the yarn for the projects shown in this book:

- elann.com
  (www.elann.com)

- Muench Yarns
  (www.muenchyarns.com)

- Cascade Yarns
  (www.cascadeyarns.com)

- Dale of Norway Yarns
  (www.daleofnorway.com)

About the Author

Sharon Turner designs knitwear and published Monkeysuits, a line of knitting patterns for babies and children. She is the author of *Monkeysuits: Sweaters and More to Knit for Kids, Teach Yourself Visually Knitting Design, Knitting Visual Quick Tips,* and *Find Your Style and Knit It Too.* Sharon lives in Brooklyn, New York, with her husband and three daughters.

Acknowledgments

Thank you always to my dear family. For helping with the knitting, many, many thanks go to Pam Mourouzis, Natasha Graf, and my sister Lauren. Ann Cannon-Brown, of elann.com, provided many skeins of her beautiful Peruvian Collection Highland Wool for most of the swatches plus many of the yarns for the new projects. Thank you also to Kirstin Muench, of Muench Yarns for years of yarn support. My gratitude goes out to Matt Bowen for another photography job well done. Thanks to Kristi Porter for her excellent technical editing. Finally, Pam Mourouzis, Natasha Graf, Cindy Kitchel, and Christina Stambaugh worked so hard and contributed so much that this is really their book, too. Thanks to all of you at Wiley—it's always a pleasure!

Table of Contents

Table of Contents

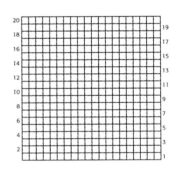

CHAPTER 7   Knitting in the Round   102

CHAPTER 8   Bobbles, Cables, and Textured Stitches   112

Table of Contents

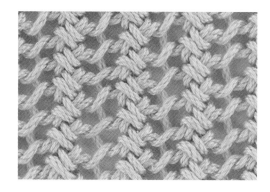

CHAPTER 11   Finishing Techniques   160

CHAPTER 12   Finishing Details   178

Table of Contents

CHAPTER 1

Introduction to Knitting

Are you ready to learn how to knit? Before you put any stitches on a needle, you need to gather materials: yarn, needles, and a few essential tools. There's such a variety of yarns and tools that it's a good idea to understand your options before you stock up on supplies.

Getting Started

Get yourself some yarn and needles and let this book walk you through the basics of knitting. By the end of the first few chapters, you will be proficient enough to create a beautiful scarf, a bag, or even a hat.

Once you begin to get into a knitting rhythm, you'll discover one of the most relaxing and satisfying of hobbies. Sitting down and taking up your knitting—the feel of soft, warm wool running through your fingers, the look of vivid color against color, the excitement of watching your fabric grow—will become one of the highlights of your day.

Grandmothers are not the only ones who know the joy of knitting. Knitting has grown so much in popularity that there are knitting groups, knitting Web sites, and pattern books geared toward knitters of all ages and sensibilities. Children and teens are knitting in after-school groups, twenty-somethings are holding knitting circles in cafes, and new mothers are celebrating the births of their babies by knitting for them.

As more people have taken up knitting, the selection of yarns and tools has grown by leaps and bounds. Walk into any yarn shop, and the riot of texture and color will overwhelm and entice you. You'll discover what seasoned knitters mean when they talk about the tremendous "stashes" of yarn hidden under their beds and in their closets.

What's also wonderful about knitting is that you can take it with you everywhere. You may even begin to look forward to time spent in the doctor's waiting room, or at your daughter's violin lesson, or on a long train ride. You won't be able to leave for vacation until you have packed a selection of knitting projects.

A hand-knit gift has extra meaning for both the person giving and the one receiving. When you knit a special hat, scarf, or baby sweater for someone, you weave your love into the fabric, and the person receiving your gift will know it and appreciate it.

It's no wonder that people have been knitting for centuries. Even now, when sweaters can be mass-produced by machine, people are still choosing to create by hand. Hand knitting is a creative outlet that satisfies the senses and soothes the nerves. It's good for you. Did you know that the rhythmic repetition of hand knitting can induce brain waves similar to those achieved through meditation? Once you learn the basic techniques that follow—and they're easy—you, too, can let your needles fly and your mind wander.

Yarn Types

Knitting yarns come in so many fibers, weights, and textures that you may be overwhelmed when you first walk into a yarn shop. You can use the guide that follows to help choose yarns.

NATURAL FIBERS

Yarns spun from animal fibers, like wool, alpaca, mohair, cashmere, and angora, are generally the warmest to wear and hold their shape well. **Wool** comes in a range of textures, from sturdy Shetlands to soft merinos. **Alpaca** is a sumptuous fiber with a lot of drape. **Mohair** is hairier than wool, and mohair-only garments have a fuzzy halo. **Cashmere** comes from goats and is buttery soft, but expensive. **Angora**, spun from rabbits, is also supple and fuzzy. **Silk** is warm, but not as elastic as wool. Garments knit in **cotton**, **linen**, **bamboo**, and **hemp** yarns are good for warm weather wear. These yarns, however, are less stretchy than wool. Sweaters knit in these fibers can lose their shape over time. Soft but strong, yarn made from **soy** has the look of silk.

Alpaca
Wool
Cotton
Mohair
Wool

SYNTHETIC FIBERS

Synthetics include **acrylic**, **nylon**, and **polyester**. These yarns are human-made and often less expensive than natural fibers. Many are machine-washable.

Acrylic
Nylon
Polyester

BLENDS

Two or more fibers can be combined and spun into one yarn; these yarns are called **blends**. Certain characteristics of a fiber can be altered by combining it with another fiber. For example, cotton can be improved in body and elasticity by being combined with wool; combining wool with alpaca or cashmere can soften it. The combinations are limitless.

Wool/llama
Cotton/acrylic
Wool/acrylic
Wool/alpaca/cashmere
Cotton/alpaca

NOVELTY YARNS

Furry, metallic, and bumpy yarns are called **novelty yarns**. These yarns work well for trims and dressy garments, and they can be doubled with another yarn for added texture and color. Novelty yarns are not recommended for beginners, as it is difficult to see stitches and mistakes in a fabric knit in novelty yarn.

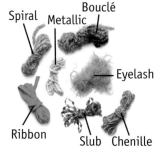

YARN WEIGHTS

Yarn weight refers to the thickness of a yarn. Yarn comes in many thicknesses and is labeled—from thinnest to thickest—as **super-fine**, **fine**, **light**, **medium**, **bulky**, and **super-bulky**. Super-fine yarns include fingering, baby, lace-weight, and many sock yarns. Fine yarns generally encompass sport weight and some baby yarns. Light yarns include double-knitting and light worsted. Medium yarns are also called worsted, Aran, or afghan yarns. Bulky refers to yarns that are labeled chunky or heavy worsted. Super-bulky yarns are sometimes called polar or roving. In general, fine yarns require thin needles, while bulky yarns require thick needles.

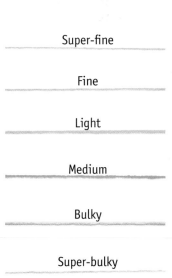

BALLS, SKEINS, AND HANKS

Yarn comes packaged in many shapes. Yarn can come in a **ball**, with a label in the center, or as a **skein**, with the label wrapped around the middle. Both balls and skeins can be knit from directly. Some yarns come in **hanks**, which look like twisted braids. You must wind a hank into a ball before using it, or it will become tangled.

Most yarns come packaged with a label, also called a ***ball band.*** Always save your ball band with your yarn, as it contains useful information regarding the yarn.

The largest print on a ball band is the yarn manufacturer's name and/or logo, and then the name of that particular yarn. Also included is the fiber content of the yarn.

The ball band also lists the weight of the ball and the yardage, or the length of yarn contained in the ball. Yarn companies assign numbers to indicate color. These numbers are not the same from one manufacturer to the next. Also listed is a *dye lot* number. Yarns are dyed in large batches, or lots, and the dye lot number refers to a particular batch of a particular color. It's important to buy enough yarn from the same dye lot for a project because color differs from one dye lot to the next.

The yarn label also suggests the size of knitting needles to use with the yarn and lists the desired gauge for that yarn when knit with those needles. Care instructions are usually shown in the form of symbols like those found on clothing labels.

Weight 100g/220 yards

Needle size:
7 = 5 st per 1"
8 = 4½ st per 1"

Col. no. 32
Lot no. 1077

fine wool yarns
Soft & Thick
Made in the U.S.A.

90% Merino Wool
5% Alpaca
5% Cashmere

Care Instructions and Symbols

It is a good idea to become familiar with the symbols used to indicate care instructions for a particular yarn. You need to know this information when it comes time to clean your hand-knit items.

Symbols using the image of a **tub** or **washing machine** indicate whether a fiber is machine- or hand-washable. Note that the symbol of the tub with an X over it means the fiber is neither machine- nor hand-washable. The triangular symbols indicate bleaching instructions.

Symbols using the image of an **iron** indicate whether a fiber can be pressed. The symbol of the iron with dots in it illustrates what temperature should be used when pressing.

Circular symbols illustrate dry-cleaning instructions. If the circle has an X through it, the fiber should not be dry-cleaned. Circles with letters in them indicate what chemicals should be used to dry-clean the fiber. The people at your dry-cleaning shop should be able to tell you what solvents they use.

MACHINE WASH TEMPERATURE	BLEACH	IRON TEMPERATURE (Dry or Steam)	DRY-CLEAN TEMPERATURE
Do Not Wash	Do Not Bleach	Do Not Iron	Do Not Dry-Clean
Hand Wash	Any Bleach (when needed)	Low	Dry-Clean, Petroleum Solvent Only (F)
Normal		Medium	Dry-Clean, Any Solvent Except Trichloroethylene (P)
Delicate/Gentle		High	Dry-Clean, Any Solvent (A)
Cool/Cold			
Warm			
Hot			

Needles and Accessories

Knitting needles come in many shapes, sizes, and materials. Try out various types to see which ones work best for you. There are also a number of accessories, but you will need only a few to start. As you complete more projects, your collection of needles and accessories will grow.

TYPES OF NEEDLES

Knitting needles come in metal, plastic, wood, and bamboo. Yarn slides easily along **metal** needles. **Plastic** needles are lightweight but can bend. **Wood** needles are beautiful and can be more expensive than metal or plastic. **Bamboo** needles are lighter and less expensive than wood needles. Some teachers recommend bamboo for beginners because the surface slows yarn from slipping off the needle.

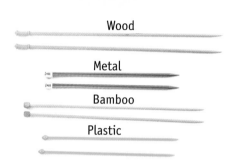

SIZES OF NEEDLES

Needle sizing can be confusing because each needle has three numbers that refer to the size. The most important number is the **diameter** of the needle shaft, which is measured in millimeters (mm). The second number, representing the **U.S. numbering system**, labels sizes ranging from 0 for the thinnest needle to 50 for the thickest needle. The third number on a needle is the **length** of the needle's shaft. This number is generally represented on the needle package in both inches and centimeters. The UK/Canadian numbering system for needles differs from the U.S. system, so it's better to buy needles based on diameter than on numbering system. The chart below shows needle size in metric as well as both U.S. and UK/Canadian numbering.

Needle Sizes					
Metric (mm)	U.S.	UK/Canadian	Metric (mm)	U.S.	UK/Canadian
2.0	0	14	6.5	10½	3
2.25–2.5	1	13	7.0	10¾	2
2.75	2	12	7.5	—	1
3.0	—	11	8.0	11	0
3.25	3	10	9.0	13	00
3.5	4	—	10.0	15	000
3.75	5	9	12.0–12.75	17	—
4.0	6	8	16.0	19	—
4.5	7	7	19.0	35	—
5.0	8	6	20.0	36	—
5.5	9	5	25.0	50	—
6.0	10	4			

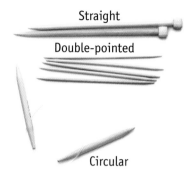

Straight

Double-pointed

Circular

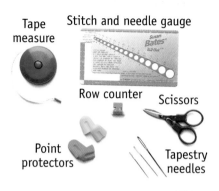

Tape
measure

Stitch and needle gauge

Row counter

Scissors

Point
protectors

Tapestry
needles

SHAPES OF NEEDLES

Straight needles, also called single-pointed needles, come in various lengths and have a point on one end and a knob on the other. **Double-pointed needles** are sold in sets of four or five. **Circular needles**, which have two points connected by a nylon or plastic cord, come in a variety of lengths and materials.

ESSENTIAL ACCESSORIES

You'll want a small pair of **scissors** and a **tape measure**. **Row counters** record rows knit. **Tapestry needles** are used for sewing knitted pieces together and darning in loose ends. **Point protectors** prevent work from slipping off the needles. A **stitch and needle gauge** measures stitch and row gauge as well as needle diameter.

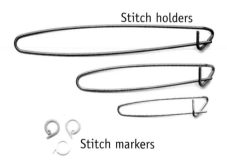

Stitch holders

Stitch markers

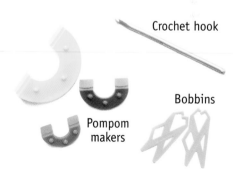

Crochet hook

Bobbins

Pompom
makers

OTHER ACCESSORIES

Stitch holders hold stitches to be worked later. Plastic-headed **knitting pins** fasten knitted pieces together before sewing. **Stitch markers** are small plastic rings used to mark a point in knitting where an increase, a decrease, or a pattern change occurs. **Cable needles** are used to hold stitches when making cables.

HANDY EXTRAS

Choose a **knitting bag** that stands open, has a smooth interior, and has pockets for accessories (watch out for Velcro fasteners—they can snag your knitting). Small amounts of yarn can be wound on plastic **bobbins**. **Crochet hooks** come in handy for making edgings and ties. **Pompom makers** are great for making thick, round pompoms.

11

CHAPTER 2

Basic Techniques

A knitted fabric is made up of many stitches. In this chapter, you will learn the basics: how to get your first row of stitches on the needle as well as how to knit and purl those stitches using a variety of methods. After you master knit and purl stitches, you will learn how to join new yarn so that you won't have to stop when your yarn runs out. Finally, you will find out how to bind off, which is what you do to remove your stitches from the needle when you're done.

Make a Slipknot

The time has come to pick up your needles and learn to knit. You need a ball of worsted weight or bulky yarn and a pair of needles in the size that the yarn's ball band calls for. When you have those things, you are ready to put your very first stitch—a *slipknot*—onto your needle. You have probably made a slipknot before, but there's a special method for putting one onto your knitting needle.

How to Make a Slipknot

① Starting about 10 inches in from the end of your yarn, make a loop.

② Pull the working yarn (the yarn coming from the ball) behind the loop as shown. Insert the needle underneath the working yarn and pull it up through the loop.

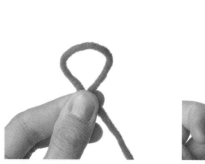 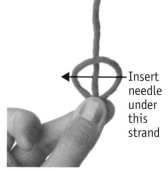

Insert needle under this strand

③ Pull the ends of the yarn so that the slipknot sits snugly on the needle.

*C*asting on* is what you do to get a foundation row of stitches on your needle so that you can start to knit. There are many cast-on methods, each with different results. Take care not to cast on too tightly, or your edge will have no elasticity.

Backward-Loop Cast-On

This method of casting on is the easiest and quickest, so it's good for beginners. It doesn't, however, create a very tidy edge. It is also referred to as the simple cast-on method.

① With the needle with the slipknot on it in your right hand and the working yarn in your left, make a loop with the working yarn, then give the loop a twist so the working yarn is on the right and the back of the loop is on the left.

② Place the loop onto the needle with your left hand and then pull the working yarn to tighten.

③ Repeat steps 1 and 2 until you have the desired number of stitches on the needle.

Long-Tail Cast-On

You may think that this method of casting on stitches looks complicated, but once you master it, it's very quick and easy. This method creates a neat, elastic edge.

1 Put a slipknot on your needle, leaving a tail that's the equivalent of 1 inch per stitch you plan to cast on plus a few more inches. (So if you plan to cast on 12 stitches, leave a tail that's about 15 inches long.)

2 Hold the yarn with the tail wrapped over your thumb and the working yarn over your forefinger, grasping both ends with your pinky and ring finger in the center of your palm.

3 Lower the needle to create a V.

NOTE: Holding the slipknot in place with your right forefinger can prevent the stitch from slipping off the needle.

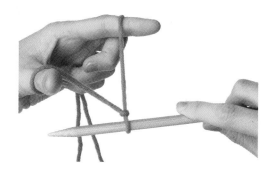

4 Insert the needle up and under the yarn that is looped around the outside of your thumb.

⑤ Move the needle to the right and
use it to grab the yarn from the
nearest side of your forefinger (a);
then pull it through the loop
around your thumb (b).

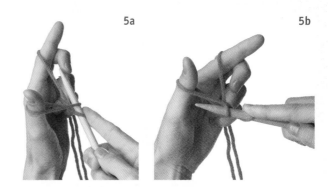

5a   5b

⑥ Once the yarn is pulled through the loop
between your thumb and needle, drop the
loops from your thumb and forefinger and pull
both ends of the yarn to tighten the stitch on
the needle.

You have just cast on 1 stitch.

⑦ Repeat steps 2–6 until you have cast on the desired
number of stitches.

Knit Cast-On

The knit cast-on produces an elegant elastic edge, so it's good for most anything—sweaters, hats, socks, and scarves, to name a few. You start with a slipknot on your left needle and then use the right needle to work the stitch as if you're going to knit it, but instead of taking it off the needle, you place the new stitch back onto the left needle.

1 Put a slipknot on your needle. Holding this needle in your left hand and the empty needle in your right hand, insert the right needle into the stitch from front to back, as if to knit.

2 Wrap the working yarn around the tip of the right needle and pull up a loop, as when knitting a stitch.

3 Do not slip the stitch off the needle. Transfer the new stitch to the left needle by inserting the left needle into the stitch then sliding the right needle out.

4 Pull the working yarn to tighten.

5 Repeat steps 1–4, placing each new stitch to the right of the previously cast-on stitch until you have the desired number of stitches on the left needle.

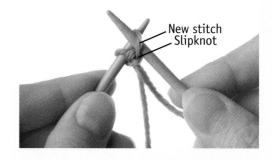

New stitch
Slipknot

Cable Cast-On

The cable cast-on is performed like the knit cast-on, except that the needle is inserted between two stitches before the loop is pulled up. It produces an attractive rope-like edge on both sides of the knitting. It is not as elastic as the knit cast-on, but is good for buttonholes and non-ribbed edgings. Use a different cast-on if you require a flexible edge.

1 Perform steps 1–4 of the knit cast-on. You should now have 2 stitches on your needle—the slip-knot and 1 new stitch.

2 Insert the right needle between the 2 stitches, and not into their loops. Wrap the working yarn around the tip of the right needle (a). Now pull up a loop, as you would when knitting a stitch (b).

2a

2b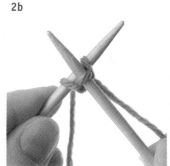

3 Leaving the initial 2 stitches on the needle, use the right needle to place the pulled-up loop onto the left needle.

4 Repeat steps 2 and 3, placing each new stitch to the right of the previously cast-on stitch until you have the desired number of stitches on the left needle.

New stitch
Slipknot

FAQ

I'm having difficulty pulling the new loop between the stitches when working the cable cast-on; it keeps slipping off the tip of the right needle on the way through. What can I do?

This can be a problem with the cable cast-on at first, particularly if you're using inelastic yarns like cottons and silks. Try replacing the right needle with a crochet hook a size or two smaller than your yarn requires.

Provisional Cast-On

You use the provisional, or open, cast-on when you want to be able to access the cast-on edge as "live" stitches to be worked later. For example, you might want to work a lacy border or add a peplum or hem to your lower edge. The provisional method is worked very much like the long-tail cast-on, only you need a length of scrap yarn—something strong yet slippery, like mercerized cotton.

In the instructional photos for the provisional cast-on, the working yarn is yellow and the waste yarn is green.

1. Cut a length of scrap yarn equal to 1" per stitch you need to cast on, plus a few inches extra. For example, to cast on 30 stitches, use a 36" length of scrap yarn. Tie the end of the scrap yarn to the end of the working yarn.

2. Holding the yarns and a needle in your right hand, hold the knot against the needle with your thumb.

3. Take the yarns in your left hand, holding them as you would for the long-tail method, with the waste yarn around your thumb and the working yarn over your forefinger, grasping both ends with your pinky and ring finger in the center of your palm.

3

4. Work as you would with the long-tail method, inserting the needle up and under the waste yarn that is looped around the outside of your thumb (a), and then move the needle to the right and use it to grab the working yarn from the nearest side of your forefinger (b).

4a

4b

⑤ Pull the working yarn through the loop between your thumb and the needle.

⑥ Drop the loops from your thumb and forefinger and pull both ends of the yarn to tighten the stitch on the needle.

You have just cast on 1 stitch.

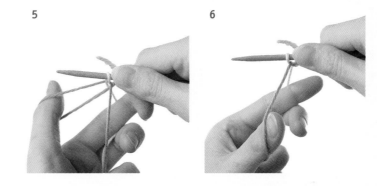

⑦ Repeat steps 4–6 until you have cast on the desired number of stitches. Then continue knitting your project with the working yarn.

⑧ When you need the stitches to be "live" again, carefully snip the waste yarn from each stitch and slip the freed stitches onto a needle as you go.

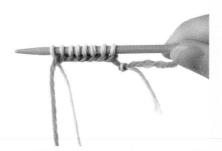

FAQ

Is there an easier way to work the open cast-on?

If working with two yarns at the same time is just too confusing, you can cast on in scrap yarn and knit a row or two. Join your project yarn and work from there. When it's time to access the live stitches at the beginning, snip and unravel the waste knitting, sliding your needle into the first row of project yarn stitches.

Hold Needles and Yarn

Some people knit holding the yarn in their right hand, which is called the *English method*, while others hold it in their left hand, which is called the *Continental method*. Try both methods and experiment to see which suits you. The most important thing is to be relaxed and comfortable.

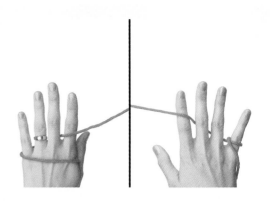

Holding Needles and Yarn for the English Method

1 Holding the needle with the stitches on it in your left hand, wind the working yarn in a loop around your pinky, under your two middle fingers, and over the forefinger of your right hand.

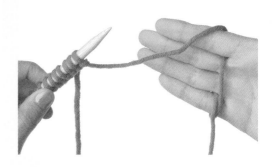

2 Hold the empty needle (called the *working needle*) in your right hand while keeping the working yarn wound through your fingers to maintain even tension.

Holding Needles and Yarn for the Continental Method

1 Holding the needle with the stitches on it in your right hand, wind the working yarn around the back of your hand, under your pinky and two middle fingers, and over the forefinger of your left hand.

2 Take the needle with the stitches on it back into your left hand, keeping the working yarn wound through your fingers to maintain even tension, and hold the working (empty) needle in your right hand.

FAQ

When I wind the yarn around my fingers as described, it feels loose and awkward. Is there another way to hold the yarn?

Yes, there are infinite ways. If it feels too loose, or if wrapping the yarn around your pinky is awkward, try wrapping the yarn over your palm instead. The important thing is to be comfortable and to have the yarn flow easily through your fingers. Many knitters make up their own way of holding the yarn.

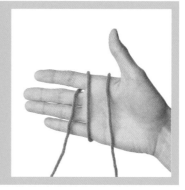

Knit: English Method

Now that you know how to cast on stitches and hold your yarn and needles, you can try actually knitting. Many knitters use the English method and hold the yarn with the right hand. (You don't have to be right-handed to use this method.)

It's a good idea to start with a small number of stitches (10–15) on your needles. You will want to count your stitches after every row to make sure you haven't dropped or added any accidentally.

How to Knit Using the English Method

1 Hold the needle with the cast-on stitches on it in your left hand and hold the working (empty) needle in your right hand, with the working yarn wound around the fingers of your right hand.

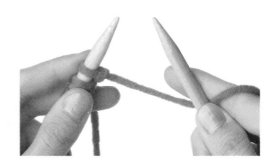

2 Holding the yarn in back of both needles, insert the right needle into the front of the first stitch on the left needle.

Your needles will form an X, with the right needle behind the left needle.

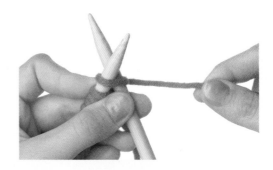

3 Holding the crossed needles between your left thumb and forefinger, bring the working yarn around the right needle from back to front (a) and then bring it down between the two needles (b).

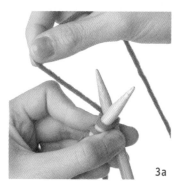

3a

3b

4 Pull the right needle toward the front, bringing the new loop of yarn you just wrapped around it through the stitch on the needle (a), and slip the old stitch off the left needle (b).

You now have 1 stitch on the right needle—your first knit stitch.

4a

4b

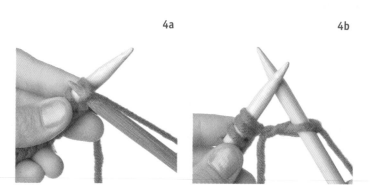

5 Repeat steps 2–4 for each remaining stitch, until all the new stitches are on the right needle.

When you have knit all the stitches from the left needle, you have completed one *row* of knitting.

6 Switch the needle with the stitches on it to your left hand and repeat steps 2–5 for each row.

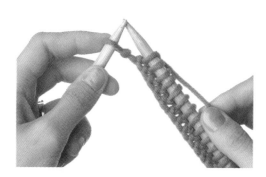

Purl: English Method

When you have mastered the knit stitch with the English method, you are ready to try the purl stitch. Purling is the opposite of knitting. You hold the needles the same way as for knitting, but you keep the yarn in front of the needles instead of at the back.

How to Purl Using the English Method

① Hold the needle with the cast-on stitches on it in your left hand and hold both the working (empty) needle and the working yarn in your right hand.

② Holding the yarn in front of both needles, insert the right needle from back to front (that is, from right to left) into the first stitch on the left needle.

Your needles will form an X, with the right needle in front of the left needle.

3 Hold the crossed needles between your left thumb and forefinger and bring the yarn behind the right needle, or between the crossed needles (a); then wrap the yarn around the right needle in a counterclockwise direction (b).

3a

3b

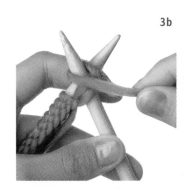

4 Pull the right needle toward the back, bringing the new loop of yarn you just wrapped around it through the stitch on the needle (a); then slip the old stitch off the left needle (b).

You now have 1 stitch on the right needle—your first purl stitch.

4a

4b

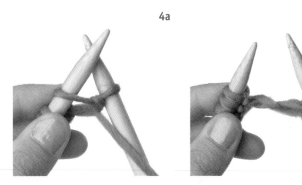

5 Repeat steps 2–4 for each remaining stitch, until all the new stitches are on the right needle.

When you have purled all the stitches from the left needle, you have completed one *row* of purling.

6 Switch the needle with stitches on it back to your left hand and repeat steps 2–5 for each row.

Knit: Continental Method

Now you can try knitting using the Continental method, in which you hold the yarn and control tension with your left hand. Don't worry if you're right-handed, though: Both right-handed and left-handed Europeans have been knitting this way for centuries.

How to Knit Using the Continental Method

① Hold the needle with the cast-on stitches on it in your left hand and hold the working (empty) needle in your right hand, with the working yarn wound around the fingers of your left hand.

② Insert the right needle into the front of the first stitch on the left needle, holding the yarn in back of both needles.

Your needles will form an X, with the right needle behind the left needle.

3 Use your left forefinger to wrap yarn around the right needle from front to back.

NOTE: This is a small, quick motion involving primarily the left forefinger. You can help it along by grabbing the yarn with the right needle at the same time.

4 Pull the right needle toward the front, bringing the new loop of yarn you just wrapped around it through the stitch on the needle (a), and slip the old stitch off the left needle (b).

You now have 1 stitch on the right needle—your first knit stitch.

NOTE: You may want to use your right forefinger to keep the wrapped strand from slipping off the tip of the needle at step 4 (a).

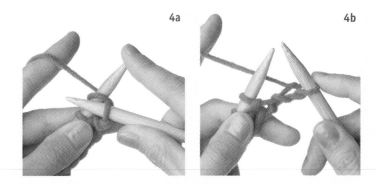

4a

4b

5 Repeat steps 2–4 for each remaining stitch, until all the new stitches are on the right needle.

When you have knit all the stitches from the left needle, you have completed one *row* of knitting.

6 Switch the needle with the stitches on it to your left hand and repeat steps 2–5 for each row.

Purl: Continental Method

When you purl using the Continental method, you hold the yarn and control tension with your left hand while holding yarn in front of the needles. This makes it easier to move the yarn from the front of the needles to the back of the needles in the same row. When you mix knitting and purling in the same row (ribbing or other combination stitches), you really see the difference.

How to Purl Using the Continental Method

1 Hold the needle with the cast-on stitches on it in your left hand and hold the working (empty) needle in your right hand, with the working yarn wound around the fingers of your left hand.

2 Holding the yarn in front of both needles, insert the right needle from back to front (that is, from right to left) into the first stitch on the left needle.

The needles will form an X, with the right needle in front of the left needle.

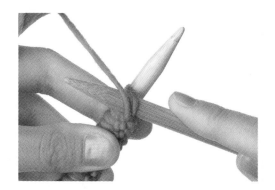

3 Use your left forefinger to wrap the yarn around the right needle from front to back, between the needles, and back to the front of the right needle.

NOTE: This is a small, quick motion involving flicking your left forefinger down, bringing the yarn between the needles and then back up, and creating a loop on the right needle.

4 Pull the right needle toward the back, bringing the new loop of yarn you just wrapped around it through the stitch on the needle (a); then slip the old stitch off the left needle (b).

You now have 1 stitch on the right needle—your first purl stitch.

NOTE: You may want to use your right forefinger to keep the wrapped strand from slipping off the tip of the needle at step 4 (a).

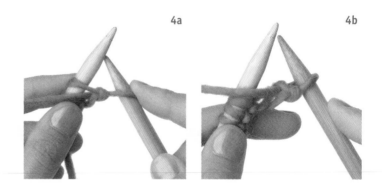

4a   4b

5 Repeat steps 2–4 for each remaining stitch, until all the new stitches are on the right needle.

When you have purled all the stitches from the left needle, you have completed one *row* of purling.

6 Switch the needle with stitches on it back to your left hand and repeat steps 2–5 for each row.

Join New Yarn

Have you run out of yarn yet? If not, there will come a time when you run out or want to change color. At that time, you'll need to know how to join a new ball of yarn.

How to Join New Yarn

AT THE BEGINNING OF A ROW

It's best to join a new ball of yarn at the beginning of a row. That way, you can sew your loose ends into a seam or an edge. When your first ball of yarn has length remaining that is less than four times the width of your knitting, it's time to change to a new ball. At that point, finish your row and cut off the old yarn, leaving a 6-inch tail.

1 Tie a 6-inch end from your new ball snugly onto the tail of the old yarn.

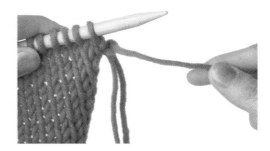

2 Taking care not to confuse the new working yarn with the tied end, work across the row as usual.

NOTE: When you finish your project, you can untie the knot and weave in the ends to hide them.

IN THE MIDDLE OF A ROW

Sometimes you have no choice but to join a new yarn in the middle of a row—like when you're knitting in the round or working on a color pattern that changes in the middle of a row. Make sure you have at least 6 inches of the old yarn left to weave in later and that the tail of the new yarn is at least 6 inches long.

① Work the next stitch using the new yarn; knit if it should be a knit stitch or purl if it should be a purl stitch.

② After you complete the row, tie the two ends together somewhat loosely so that they don't become unraveled.

NOTE: When you finish your project, you can untie the knot and weave in the ends to hide them.

How to Splice New Yarn

Splicing works with yarn that is made up of more than one strand of fiber twisted together. It works well for mid-row joins and doesn't create a knot in the back, but it takes some skill to master.

① Untwist the ends of the old and new yarn for 3 inches; divide the plies into two clumps for each yarn.

② Twist one clump of strands from the old yarn together with one clump of strands from the new yarn. Continue working the row as usual with the new yarn. You can weave in the loose plies later.

33

Slip a Stitch

Knitting instructions sometimes tell you to slip a stitch. This usually means you move the stitch from the left needle to the right needle, without knitting or purling it. Slipped stitches are often used in decreases, textured stitch patterns, heel flaps, and edge stitches. You also slip stitches when you need to simply transfer stitches from one needle type to another. Stitches can be slipped *knitwise* or *purlwise.*

How to Slip a Stitch Knitwise

When you slip a stitch knitwise, leave the working yarn at the back, as you do when knitting, unless the pattern specifies otherwise. Slipping a stitch knitwise twists the stitch; so knitting instructions usually specifically state to slip the stitch knitwise if that is required.

1 Insert the right needle from front to back (knitwise) into the next stitch on the left needle.

2 Without knitting the stitch, slip it from the left needle to the right needle.

How to Slip a Stitch Purlwise

When you slip a stitch purlwise, leave the working yarn at the front, as you do when purling, unless the pattern specifies otherwise. Slipping a stitch purlwise maintains the proper placement of the stitch on the needle. If knitting instructions do not indicate how to slip the stitch, you should slip it purlwise.

1 Insert the right needle from back to front (purlwise) into the next stitch on the left needle.

2 Without purling the stitch, slip it from the left needle onto the right needle.

Sometimes you want to knit with two strands of yarn at the same time: Your knitting pattern might call for it, or you might want to substitute a double strand of a thin yarn that you have on hand for a thicker yarn required by a particular pattern. It's easy to do.

How to Knit with a Double Strand of Yarn

If you have only one ball of the yarn you want to knit double, you can pull ends from both the inside of the ball and the outside and hold them together; or you can wind the yarn into two balls and hold together a strand from each ball. When you knit with a double strand of yarn, you do everything—casting on, knitting, and purling—as you would with a single strand of yarn, only you hold both strands together as if they're one and knit or purl both strands at the same time.

TIP

Make Your Own Marls and Blends

By knitting with a double strand of yarn, you can create or enhance yarn. For example, you can combine two or three strands of different-color yarns to create your own marled yarns. Just remember that you'll need larger needles than the single yarn calls for, and you'll definitely want to measure your gauge (see page 95).

Also, many thin novelty yarns are great for accenting a plain yarn. For example, a lace-weight mohair can add a warm halo and body to basic wool, metallics add sparkle, and eyelash yarns create a fun fuzzy accent.

Bind Off

B_inding off_ is what you do when you want to get your stitches off the needle permanently, without allowing them to unravel. You may bind off at the very end of a project to finish it, or you may shape your garment's armholes or neck by binding off a few stitches here and there. New knitters often bind off so tightly that the finished edge has no elasticity. If your bound-off edge seems too tight, try using a larger needle to bind off than you use to knit the fabric.

How to Bind Off Knitwise

This method is the most frequently used, and it is the easiest bind-off. You use it to bind off knit stitches. Remember to keep it loose.

1 On the bind-off row, knit until you have 2 stitches total on the right needle; then insert the left needle into the front of the first stitch knit on the right needle (that is, the rightmost stitch).

2 Pull the first stitch over the second knit stitch and off the right needle.

You have bound off 1 stitch _knitwise_, and you have 1 stitch on the right needle.

3 Repeat steps 1 and 2 until you have bound off the desired number of stitches.

4 Cut the working yarn, leaving a long enough tail to weave in later, and pull it through the last loop on the needle.

1

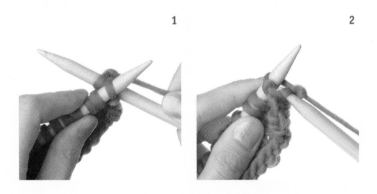

2

3

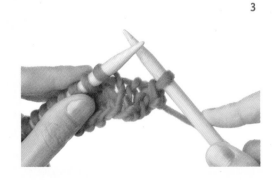

How to Bind Off Purlwise

This method is just like the knit bind-off, except you purl instead of knit. You use it to bind off purl stitches.

1 On the bind-off row, purl until you have 2 stitches total on the right needle; then insert the left needle into the front of the first stitch purled on the right needle (that is, the rightmost stitch).

2 Pull the first stitch over the second purled stitch and off the right needle.

You have bound off 1 stitch *purlwise,* and you have 1 stitch on the right needle.

3 Repeat steps 1 and 2 until you have bound off the desired number of stitches.

4 Cut the working yarn, leaving a long enough tail to weave in later, and pull it through the last loop on the needle.

1

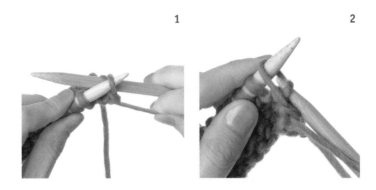

2

3

FAQ

What do I do when I have bound off all stitches and have only 1 left on the right needle?

When you have completed your bind-off and you have only 1 stitch remaining on the right needle, cut your working yarn, leaving a tail at least 6 inches long. Thread this tail through the last stitch and pull tight.

Bind Off *(continued)*

How to Bind Off in Pattern

Binding off in pattern means continuing your stitch pattern and binding off simultaneously. Your finished project will have a refined look, and your ribbings will remain elastic. As an example, here is how to bind off in seed stitch (see page 46 for seed stitch).

1 Knit 1, purl 1. You now have 2 stitches on the right needle.

2 Insert the left needle into the front of the first stitch (the knit stitch) on the right needle.

3 Pull the first stitch over the second stitch (the purl stitch) and off the right needle.

You have now bound off 1 stitch in pattern, and you have 1 purl stitch on the right needle.

4 Knit the next stitch on the left needle.

5 Insert the left needle into the front of the first stitch (the purl stitch) on the right needle.

6 Pull the first stitch over the second stitch (the knit stitch) and off the right needle.

You have now bound off 2 stitches in pattern, and you have 1 knit stitch on the right needle.

7 Continue working the seed stitch pattern and binding off as you go.

FAQ

Whenever I bind off in pattern with cables, I get an uneven edge. Is there something I can do?

The uneven edge that results from binding off over a cable can be resolved by adding an edging. If the bound-off edge is the final edge, as for a cabled scarf or neckband, you can make the edge neater by decreasing stitches across the cable. For example, if your cable is a 6-stitch cable, you would bind off the first 2 stitches in pattern, then knit the next 2 together, then continue the bind-off in pattern.

Crochet Bind-Off

Most knitting patterns do not specify a crochet bind-off, but this method is useful when you want a flexible bound-off edge, particularly when working with less elastic yarns, such as cotton, linen, silk, and mohair. Choose a crochet hook that is the same size as your knitting needles, and try it out on one of your practice swatches.

1

1 Holding the needle with stitches on it in your left hand, insert the crochet hook as if to knit into the first stitch on the needle.

2 Wrap the working yarn over the hook from back to front, and pull the loop from back to front through the stitch on the needle, allowing the first stitch on the needle to fall off.

2

3

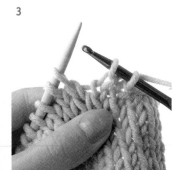

3 Repeat steps 1 and 2 in the next stitch on the needle.

4 Pull the left loop on the hook through the right loop on the hook (a). One stitch left on the hook (b).

5 Repeat steps 3 and 4 across the row.

6 Cut the working yarn, leaving a long enough tail to weave in later, and pull it through the last loop on the crochet hook.

4a

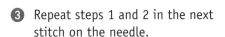

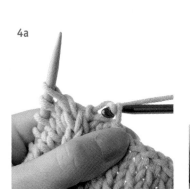

4b

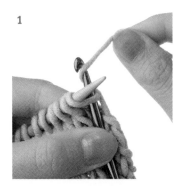

Three-Needle Bind-Off

You can use this method to join a seam by binding off two sets of stitches together. To prepare to join edges with the three-needle bind-off, you need to put each set of stitches onto a knitting needle and have handy a third knitting needle. If one of the sets of stitches has the working yarn still attached, you can use that to knit the seam; otherwise, you can use a piece of the same yarn you used to knit the pieces. The Striped Sweater on page 259 uses this technique to join the shoulder seams.

1 Hold the needles parallel, with the right sides of your knitting facing each other, as shown.

2 Insert a third knitting needle into the first stitch on the front needle as if to knit and then into the first stitch on the back needle as if to knit. Wrap the working yarn around the tip of the third needle as you would to knit.

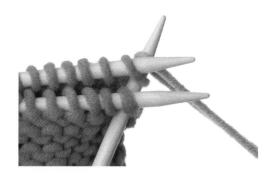

3 Bring the loop through the first stitch on the back needle, just as you would to knit, and then bring the same loop all the way through to the front of the first stitch on the front needle as well.

④ Slip both old stitches off the parallel needles, just as you would to knit them.

You should now have 1 stitch on the third needle.

⑤ Repeat steps 2–4. There should now be 2 stitches on the right needle.

⑥ Pass the first stitch on the right needle (that is, the rightmost stitch) over the second to bind off.

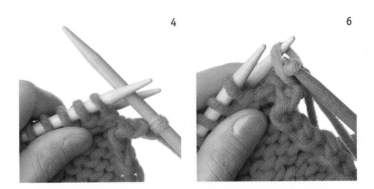

④   6

⑦ Continue knitting together the corresponding stitches from each needle and binding off as you go until only 1 stitch remains on the right needle.

⑧ Cut the yarn, leaving a 6-inch tail, and pull the tail through the last stitch to secure.

NOTE: A contrasting color yarn was used to create the seam here for illustrative purposes. In general, you'll want to work your seams with the same yarn used to knit the pieces.

TIP

Binding Off Loosely

You often see the instruction "Bind off loosely" in knitting patterns. You bind off loosely so your finished edge has elasticity and so the knitting retains its width. An easy way to ensure a loose but even bind-off is to use a needle that is one, two, or even three sizes larger than the needle used for the body of your project. Another method that is good for sweater neckbands, top-down hats, and toe-up socks involves casting on stitches while binding off. This technique is detailed in the Toe-Up Socks pattern on page 274.

CHAPTER 3

Basic Stitch Patterns

Now that you have accomplished knitting and purling, you're ready to move on to learning some basic stitch patterns. You can create myriad patterns using just knit and purl stitches. Very simple stitch repeats can result in highly textured designs. Take some time to experiment.

Here are a few basic stitch patterns that you can try. For some of them, you knit or purl different rows, and for others, you knit and purl in the same row. Many of these patterns are good for allover designs as well as for edgings and borders. Learning new stitch patterns will improve your ability to recognize which stitch is a knit and which stitch is a purl: You can recognize a purl stitch by the bump at the base of the stitch. In contrast, a knit stitch is smooth and has no bump.

Simple Stitch Patterns

GARTER STITCH

Garter stitch is the easiest stitch pattern, and what's great about it is that it always lies perfectly flat. It looks exactly the same on both the front and the back.

1 Row 1: Knit.

2 Repeat row 1 for garter stitch.

   After you knit several rows, you see horizontal ridges appear. Two knit rows form one ridge.

STOCKINETTE STITCH

Stockinette stitch is the pattern most often used for sweaters. It looks like rows of flat V's on the front, called the *right side*, and rows of bumps on the back, called the *wrong side*.

1 Row 1 (right side): Knit.

2 Row 2 (wrong side): Purl.

3 Repeat rows 1 and 2 for stockinette stitch.

REVERSE STOCKINETTE STITCH

Reverse stockinette stitch is the same as regular stockinette, only the bumpy side is considered the right side, and the smooth side is the wrong side.

1. Row 1 (right side): Purl.
2. Row 2 (wrong side): Knit.
3. Repeat rows 1 and 2 for stockinette stitch.

GARTER STITCH STRIPE

This pattern is essentially made up of two rows of stockinette stitch and two rows of garter stitch. It can be worked on any number of stitches. You can also vary the number of rows of stockinette stitch and garter stitch to create your own stripe pattern.

1. Row 1 (right side): Knit.
2. Row 2 (wrong side): Purl.
3. Row 3: Knit.
4. Row 4: Knit.
5. Repeat rows 1–4 for garter stitch stripe.

REVERSE STOCKINETTE STITCH STRIPE

This pattern looks similar to garter stitch stripe, but because the bumpy stripes are done in reverse stockinette stitch, they are fuller and rounder. You can work this pattern on any number of stitches.

1. Row 1 (right side): Knit.
2. Row 2 (wrong side): Purl.
3. Row 3: Knit.
4. Row 4: Purl.
5. Row 5: Purl.
6. Row 6: Knit.
7. Repeat rows 1–6 for reverse stockinette stitch stripe.

SEED STITCH

Seed stitch creates a nice bumpy-textured fabric that lies flat and looks the same on both sides. You knit the purl stitches and purl the knit stitches for seed stitch. You should cast on an even number of stitches.

1 Row 1 (right side): *Knit 1, purl 1; repeat from * to end of row.

2 Row 2 (wrong side): *Purl 1, knit 1; repeat from * to end of row.

3 Repeat rows 1 and 2 for seed stitch.

DOUBLE SEED STITCH

Double seed stitch is a four-row pattern that is similar to seed stitch in appearance but with a larger texture. You work it over an even number of stitches.

1 Row 1 (right side): *Knit 1, purl 1; repeat from * to end of row.

2 Row 2 (wrong side): Repeat row 1.

3 Row 3: *Purl 1, knit 1; repeat from * to end of row.

4 Row 4: Repeat row 3.

5 Repeat rows 1–4 for double seed stitch.

FAQ

I left off in the middle of the row, and now I can't tell the front from the back, or which way to knit. What should I do?

You can tell which side to work from by locating the stitch attached to the working yarn. That's the last stitch you worked, and if you hold that needle in your right hand, your knitting will be properly situated.

SIMPLE SEED STITCH

Simple seed stitch is a good allover pattern for sweaters, vests, and dresses. You work it over a multiple of 4 stitches plus 1 (that is, 5, 9, 13, 17, and so on).

1 Row 1 (right side): Purl 1, *knit 3, purl 1; repeat from * to end.

2 Row 2 (wrong side): Purl.

3 Row 3: Knit.

4 Row 4: Purl.

5 Row 5: Knit 2, purl 1, *knit 3, purl 1; repeat from * to last 2 stitches, knit 2.

6 Row 6: Purl.

7 Row 7: Knit.

8 Row 8: Purl.

9 Repeat rows 1–8 for simple seed stitch.

BOX STITCH

Box stitch looks the same on both sides and lies flat. You work this pattern over a multiple of 4 stitches plus 2 (that is, 6, 10, 14, 18, and so on).

1 Row 1 (right side): Knit 2, *purl 2, knit 2; repeat from * to end of row.

2 Row 2 (wrong side): Purl 2, *knit 2, purl 2; repeat from * to end of row.

3 Row 3: Repeat row 2.

4 Row 4: Repeat row 1.

5 Repeat rows 1–4 for box stitch.

Learn Rib Patterns

Ribbing is used primarily for cuffs and hems because it is very elastic and won't stretch out or lose its shape. But ribbing patterns don't have to exclusively serve this purpose. They work very well as allover patterns on hats, pullovers, scarves, and blankets. You should try to get familiar with which stitches should be knit and which stitches should be purled.

Rib Patterns

1 × 1 RIB

For this 1 × 1 rib, you need to cast on an odd number of stitches. To keep the pattern correct, be sure to knit the stitches that look like V's and purl the stitches that look like bumps. This rib is commonly used on cuffs, and it also works well for scarves.

1. Row 1 (right side): Knit 1, *purl 1, knit 1; repeat from * to end of row.

2. Row 2 (wrong side): Purl 1, *knit 1, purl 1; repeat from * to end of row.

3. Repeat rows 1 and 2 to create 1 × 1 rib.

2 × 2 RIB

You need a multiple of 4 stitches plus 2 (that is, 6, 10, 14, 18, and so on) for this rib.

1. Row 1 (right side): Knit 2, *purl 2, knit 2; repeat from * to end of row.

2. Row 2 (wrong side): Purl 2, *knit 2, purl 2; repeat from * to end of row.

3. Repeat rows 1 and 2 to form 2 × 2 rib.

BROKEN RIB STITCH

This is an easy two-row pattern that looks very different on the front and on the back but is attractive on both sides. You work it on an odd number of stitches.

1. Row 1 (right side): Knit.

2. Row 2 (wrong side): Purl 1, *knit 1, purl 1; repeat from * to end of row.

3. Repeat rows 1 and 2 for broken rib stitch.

RIB-AND-RIDGE STITCH

This rib is not elastic, so it works best as an allover design. The right side looks like a rippled 1 × 1 rib, and the wrong side looks like an interrupted rib. You work this stitch pattern on a multiple of 2 stitches plus 1 (that is, 3, 5, 7, 9, and so on).

1. Row 1 (wrong side): Purl.

2. Row 2 (right side): Knit.

3. Row 3: Knit 1, *purl 1, knit 1; repeat from * to end of row.

4. Row 4: Purl 1, *knit 1, purl 1; repeat from * to end of row.

5. Repeat rows 1–4 for rib-and-ridge stitch.

GARTER RIB

This one-row stitch pattern does not look like most other ribbing but does look the same on both sides. It's very easy to do. You work it on a multiple of 4 stitches plus 2 (that is, 6, 10, 14, 18, and so on).

1. Row 1: Knit 2, *purl 2, knit 2; repeat from * to end.

2. Repeat row 1 for garter rib.

SEEDED RIB

Seeded rib pattern is very attractive, and it results in a highly textured fabric. You work it over a multiple of 4 stitches plus 1 (that is, 5, 9, 13, 17, and so on).

1 Row 1 (right side): Purl 1, *knit 3, purl 1; repeat from * to end.

2 Row 2 (wrong side): Knit 2, purl 1, *knit 3, purl 1; repeat from * to last 2 stitches, knit 2.

3 Repeat rows 1 and 2 for seeded rib.

TWISTED RIB

For twisted rib, you knit stitches through the back loops on right-side rows. You work it over an odd number of stitches.

1 Row 1 (right side): Knit 1 through back of loop, *purl 1, knit 1 through back of loop; repeat from * to end.

2 Row 2 (wrong side): Purl 1, *knit 1, purl 1; repeat from * to end.

3 Repeat rows 1 and 2 for twisted rib.

TWIN RIB

Twin rib pattern looks the same on both sides, even though the two rows that make up the pattern are different. It is good for just about anything—from jackets, sweaters, and dresses to scarves and bags. You work it on a multiple of 6 stitches.

1 Row 1 (right side): *Knit 3, purl 3; repeat from * to end.

2 Row 2 (wrong side): *Knit 1, purl 1; repeat from * to end.

3 Repeat rows 1 and 2 for twin rib.

DIAGONAL RIB

Diagonal rib is a pattern that can be used not only as a decorative border but also as an allover pattern. You work it over a multiple of 4 stitches.

1 Row 1 (right side): *Knit 2, purl 2; repeat from * to end.

2 Row 2 (wrong side): Repeat row 1.

3 Row 3: Knit 1, *purl 2, knit 2; repeat from * to last 3 stitches, purl 2, knit 1.

4 Row 4: Purl 1, *knit 2, purl 2; repeat from * to last 3 stitches, knit 2, purl 1.

5 Row 5: *Purl 2, knit 2; repeat from * to end.

6 Row 6: Repeat row 5.

7 Row 7: Repeat row 4.

8 Row 8: Repeat row 3.

9 Repeat rows 1–8 for diagonal rib.

FAQ

I keep losing track of what row I'm on in the stitch pattern. What can I do to keep track?

Even experienced knitters can lose track of what row they're on in a stitch pattern. The simplest solution is to attach a handy row counter to the needle. If you don't have a row counter, you can jot down the last row worked on a sticky note adhered to your instructions.

You have already worked with some simple knit and purl combinations. Are you ready to try your hand at a few more? You can create some very intricate-looking patterns by following these simple instructions.

More Complicated Knit and Purl Stitch Patterns

ANDALUSIAN STITCH

This stitch, which creates a nice grid pattern, is easy to do. You work it on a multiple of 2 stitches plus 1 (that is, 3, 5, 7, 9, and so on).

1. Row 1 (right side): Knit.

2. Row 2 (wrong side): Purl.

3. Row 3: *Knit 1, purl 1; repeat from * to last stitch, knit 1.

4. Row 4: Purl.

5. Repeat rows 1–4 for Andalusian stitch.

RICE STITCH

This is an easy allover pattern that lies flat and looks like ribbing on the wrong side. You work it over a multiple of 2 stitches plus 1 (that is, 3, 5, 7, 9, and so on).

1. Row 1 (right side): Purl 1, *knit 1 through back of loop, purl 1; repeat from * to end.

2. Row 2 (wrong side): Knit.

3. Repeat rows 1 and 2 for rice stitch.

BASKETWEAVE

There are many forms of basketweave. This one is a small weave that you work on a multiple of 5 stitches plus 3 (that is, 8, 13, 18, 23, and so on).

① Row 1 (right side): Knit.

② Row 2 (wrong side): *Knit 3, purl 2; repeat from * to last 3 stitches, knit 3.

③ Row 3: Knit.

④ Row 4: Repeat row 2.

⑤ Row 5: Knit.

⑥ Row 6: Knit 1, *purl 2, knit 3; repeat from * to last 2 stitches, purl 2.

⑦ Row 7: Knit.

⑧ Row 8: Repeat row 6.

⑨ Repeat rows 1–8 for basketweave.

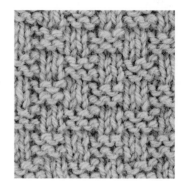

CHECKERBOARD PATTERN

This pattern looks the same on both sides. You work this particular checkerboard on a multiple of 8 stitches plus 4 (that is, 12, 20, 28, 36, and so on).

① Row 1 (right side): Knit 4, *purl 4, knit 4; repeat from * to end.

② Row 2 (wrong side): Purl 4, *knit 4, purl 4; repeat from * to end.

③ Row 3: Repeat row 1.

④ Row 4: Repeat row 2.

⑤ Row 5: Repeat row 2.

⑥ Row 6: Repeat row 1.

⑦ Row 7: Repeat row 2.

⑧ Row 8: Repeat row 1.

⑨ Repeat rows 1–8 for checkerboard pattern.

DIAGONAL CHECK PATTERN

This pattern, worked over a multiple of 5 stitches, looks the same on both sides.

① Row 1 (right side): *Purl 1, knit 4; repeat from * to end.

② Row 2 (wrong side): *Purl 3, knit 2; repeat from * to end.

③ Row 3: Repeat row 2.

④ Row 4: Repeat row 1.

⑤ Row 5: *Knit 1, purl 4; repeat from * to end.

⑥ Row 6: *Knit 3, purl 2; repeat from * to end.

⑦ Row 7: Repeat row 6.

⑧ Row 8: Repeat row 5.

⑨ Repeat rows 1–8 for diagonal check pattern.

DIAMOND BROCADE PATTERN

This is an elegant allover pattern. You work it on a multiple of 8 stitches plus 1 (that is, 9, 17, 25, 33, and so on).

1. Row 1 (right side): Knit 4, *purl 1, knit 7; repeat from * to last 5 stitches, purl 1, knit 4.

2. Row 2 (wrong side): Purl 3, *knit 1, purl 1, knit 1, purl 5; repeat from * to last 6 stitches, knit 1, purl 1, knit 1, purl 3.

3. Row 3: Knit 2, *purl 1, knit 3; repeat from * to last 3 stitches, purl 1, knit 2.

4. Row 4: Purl 1, *knit 1, purl 5, knit 1, purl 1; repeat from * to end.

5. Row 5: *Purl 1, knit 7; repeat from * to last stitch, purl 1.

6. Row 6: Repeat row 4.

7. Row 7: Repeat row 3.

8. Row 8: Repeat row 2.

9. Repeat rows 1–8 for diamond brocade pattern.

DIAMONDS IN COLUMNS

You can repeat any motif in a series of panels. This one works well on sweaters, vests, and pillows. You work this pattern on a multiple of 8 stitches plus 1 (that is, 9, 17, 25, 33, and so on).

1. Row 1 (right side): Knit.

2. Row 2 (wrong side): Knit 1, *purl 7, knit 1; repeat from * to end.

3. Row 3: Knit 4, *purl 1, knit 7; repeat from * to last 5 stitches, purl 1, knit 4.

4. Row 4: Knit 1, *purl 2, knit 1, purl 1, knit 1, purl 2, knit 1; repeat from * to end.

5. Row 5: Knit 2, *[purl 1, knit 1] twice, purl 1, knit 3; repeat from * to last 7 stitches, [purl 1, knit 1] twice, purl 1, knit 2.

6. Row 6: Repeat row 4.

7. Row 7: Repeat row 3.

8. Row 8: Repeat row 2.

9. Repeat rows 1–8 for diamonds in columns pattern.

LINEN STITCH

This stitch pattern has a woven look on one side and a grid of bumps on the other. It lies flat and is wonderful for sweaters, blankets, bags, and scarves. You work it over an even number of stitches.

1 Row 1 (right side): *Knit 1, slip 1 purlwise with yarn at front of work, bring yarn to back of work between needles; repeat from * to last 2 stitches, knit 2.

2 Row 2 (wrong side): *Purl 1, slip 1 purlwise with yarn at back of work, bring yarn to front of work between needles; repeat from * to last 2 stitches, purl 2.

3 Repeat rows 1 and 2 for linen stitch.

VERTICAL DASH STITCH

Vertical dash stitch works well as an allover pattern for sweaters, skirts, and dresses. You work it on a multiple of 6 stitches plus 1 (that is, 7, 13, 19, 25, and so on).

1 Row 1 (right side): Purl 3, knit 1, *purl 5, knit 1; repeat from * to last 3 stitches, purl 3.

2 Row 2 (wrong side): Knit 3, purl 1, *knit 5, purl 1; repeat from * to last 3 stitches, knit 3.

3 Row 3: Repeat row 1.

4 Row 4: Repeat row 2.

5 Row 5: Knit 1, *purl 5, knit 1; repeat from * to end.

6 Row 6: Purl 1, *knit 5, purl 1; repeat from * to end.

7 Row 7: Repeat row 5.

8 Row 8: Repeat row 6.

9 Repeat rows 1–8 for vertical dash stitch.

SINGLE CHEVRON STITCH

Single chevron stitch is a playful pattern that works well on pullovers, cardigans, and vests. You work it over a multiple of 8 stitches.

1 Row 1 (right side): *Purl 1, knit 3; repeat from * to end.

2 Row 2 (wrong side): *Knit 1, purl 5, knit 1, purl 1; repeat from * to end.

3 Row 3: *Knit 2, purl 1, knit 3, purl 1, knit 1; repeat from * to end.

4 Row 4: *Purl 2, knit 1, purl 1, knit 1, purl 3; repeat from * to end.

5 Repeat rows 1–4 for single chevron stitch.

CHAPTER 4

Shaping

Now that you have learned some basic techniques, such as combining knit and purl stitches to create interesting patterns, you're ready to learn about increasing and decreasing to shape your knitting beyond just a rectangle. It's not hard, and once you master a few increase and decrease methods, you'll be able to make a sweater. Take some time to experiment.

Increase 1 Stitch

To make your knitting wider, you need to *increase*—or add—a stitch or stitches. There are many types of increases, each with a different appearance or purpose.

Keeping track of when to increase is easier when you do it on the same side (usually the front side) every time, and you can better see how it will look when finished. It is also a good idea to perform increases 1 or 2 stitches in from the beginning or end of a row so as not to create an uneven edge.

BAR INCREASE

The *bar increase*—also called KFB, because you *k*nit into the *f*ront and the *b*ack of the same stitch—creates a horizontal bar of yarn. You should knit 1 or 2 stitches at the beginning of the row before making a bar increase.

1a    **1b**

① Insert the right needle into the next stitch and knit it, but don't bring the old stitch off the left needle (a); insert the right needle into the back of the same stitch and knit it again (b).

② Bring the stitch you knit into twice off the left needle.

You should have 2 new stitches on the right needle: one made from knitting into the front, and one made from knitting into the back of the same stitch.

Yarn Over

Yarn over, abbreviated yo, is an increase that is often used for decorative increases and lacy patterns because it makes a hole.

YARN OVER WITH KNIT STITCH

1 To do a yarn over before a knit stitch, bring the working yarn between the needles to the front of the work and lay it over the right needle from front to back.

2 Knit the next stitch.

Laying the yarn over the right needle creates another stitch. On the next row, just knit it or purl the new stitch as usual.

YARN OVER WITH PURL STITCH

1 To do a yarn over before a purl stitch, bring the working yarn between the needles to the front of the work, wrap it over and under the right needle, and back to the front to be ready to purl.

2 Purl the next stitch.

Laying the yarn over the right needle creates another stitch. On the next row, just knit or purl the new stitch as usual.

FINISHED YARN OVER INCREASE

After you work a couple of rows, you will see the hole that the yarn over created.

NOTE: If a pattern says to yarn over twice, three times, or more, simply continue wrapping the yarn around the right needle as many times as directed.

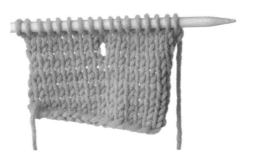

Make One: Right Slanting

The *make one* increase involves lifting the horizontal strand between 2 stitches onto the left needle and then knitting it. This version slants to the right, but is barely visible.

RIGHT-SLANTING MAKE ONE WITH KNIT STITCH (m1r)

1 Before a knit stitch, use the left needle to pick up the horizontal strand *from back to front* between the last stitch worked on the right needle and the next stitch to be worked on the left needle.

2 Insert the right needle into the front of the strand and knit it.

RIGHT-SLANTING MAKE ONE WITH PURL STITCH (m1p)

1 Before a purl stitch, use the left needle to pick up the horizontal strand *from back to front* between the last stitch worked on the right needle and the next stitch to be worked on the left needle.

2 Insert the right needle into the front of the strand and purl it.

FINISHED RIGHT-SLANTING MAKE ONE INCREASE

After you work a few rows, you can see how this make one increase slants to the right.

Horizontal strand

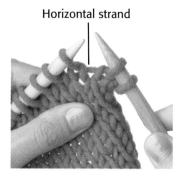

m1r

Horizontal strand

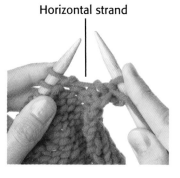

m1p

Right-slanting make one

Make One: Left Slanting

A left-slanting make one is just like a right-slanting make one, except the horizontal strand is picked up from front to back.

LEFT-SLANTING MAKE ONE WITH KNIT STITCH (m1l)

1 Before a knit stitch, pick up the horizontal strand with the left needle *from front to back* between the last stitch worked on the right needle and the next stitch to be worked on the left needle.

2 Insert the right needle into the back of the loop and knit it.

m1l

LEFT-SLANTING MAKE ONE WITH PURL STITCH (m1lp)

1 Before a purl stitch, pick up the horizontal strand with the left needle, *from front to back*.

2 Insert the right needle into the back of the loop *from back to front* and purl it.

m1lp

FINISHED LEFT-SLANTING MAKE ONE INCREASE

After you work a few rows, you can see how this make one increase slants to the left.

Left-slanting make one

Lifted Increases

The lifted increase is a good all-around increase that works well for shaping just about any knitted item. It can be worked on either the knit side or the purl side.

LIFTED INCREASE: KNIT SIDE (li)

1 Insert the right needle from front to back into the back loop of the stitch below the next stitch on the left needle.

NOTE: Access the back of the stitch below the next stitch on the left needle, rotating the left needle toward you so that the backs of the knit stitches are visible.

2 Wrap the working yarn around the tip of the needle as you would to knit a stitch and pull the loop through.

3 Knit the next stitch.

LIFTED INCREASE: PURL SIDE (li)

1 Insert the right needle purlwise into the loop of the stitch below the next stitch on the left needle.

2 Wrap the working yarn around the tip of the needle as you would to purl a stitch and pull the loop through.

3 Purl the next stitch.

Increase Multiple Stitches

Sometimes you need to increase more than 1 or 2 stitches across a row, or you need to increase 2 stitches at a time to shape your knitting in a symmetrical way.

How to Increase Multiple Stitches

DOUBLE BAR INCREASE

This increase is called a double bar increase because you use the bar increase method twice in one row to shape symmetrically. It is usually done over an odd number of stitches, on the front side of a piece of knitting, and in the center of a row. For a refresher on bar increases, see page 58.

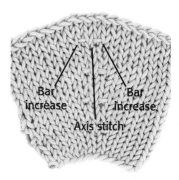

① Knit across to the stitch *before* the center stitch (known as the *axis stitch*) and then work a bar increase.

② Work a second bar increase into the axis stitch. Knit to the end of the row.

Even though the second increase is worked on the axis stitch, the bar appears after it.

DOUBLE MAKE ONE INCREASE

This increase is similar to the double bar increase in that you increase 1 stitch on either side of an axis stitch, but it is less visible. It is also worked on the front side of a piece of knitting, over an odd number of stitches. For a refresher on make one increases, see pages 60–61.

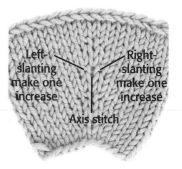

① Knit across to the axis stitch. Perform a right-slanting make one increase, using the horizontal strand between the last stitch worked and the axis stitch.

② Knit the axis stitch.

③ Perform a left-slanting make one increase using the horizontal strand between the axis stitch and the next stitch to be worked on the left needle. Knit to the end of the row.

DOUBLE YARN OVER INCREASE

The double yarn over increase is similar to the two previous double increases in that you work increases on either side of an axis stitch. For a refresher on basic yarn overs, see page 59.

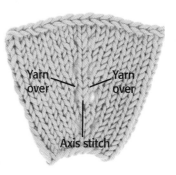

① Knit across to the axis stitch. Perform a yarn over.

② Knit the axis stitch.

③ Perform another yarn over. Knit to the end of the row.

INCREASING MULTIPLE STITCHES EVENLY ACROSS A ROW

Some patterns ask you to increase a certain number of stitches evenly across a row. This is called for when the knitting needs to become substantially wider quickly rather than gradually. Use whichever increase method is best suited to your stitch pattern.

① To figure out how to increase a certain number of stitches evenly across a row, start by adding 1 to the number of stitches that need to be added.

② Divide the number obtained in step 1 into the number of stitches on your needles. The result of this division is the number of stitches you should work between increases across the row. (For example, if you have 30 stitches on your needle and you are asked to increase 5 stitches evenly across, then you knit 5 stitches, increase 1, knit 5, and so on.)

③ If the result of your equation is not exact, approximate and work fewer or more stitches between some of the increases. The most important thing is to spread the correct number of increases across the row as evenly as possible.

CAST-ON INCREASE

For some garments you need to increase multiple stitches at one or both ends of a piece of knitting. In this case, you cast on the number of increases called for, using the backward loop cast-on method (see page 15).

① Before knitting the row, cast on the number of stitches required in front of the stitches already on the needle.

② Work the row as directed, beginning with the newly cast-on stitches.

NOTE: If the instructions call for increasing stitches at both ends of a row, you cast on that number of stitches at the beginning of the next two rows because you can't cast on at the end of a row.

Whenyou need to make your knitting narrower, you *decrease* stitches. There are several methods for decreasing, each with different effects. Take some time to practice the different methods so you can see how they transform your knitting.

Knit 2 Together/Purl 2 Together

These are two of the most commonly used decreases. The knit 2 together is performed with knit stitches, and the purl 2 together with purl stitches. They both slant somewhat to the right on the front side of a piece of knitting and can be used at any point in a row.

KNIT 2 TOGETHER (k2tog)

1. Insert the right needle into the front of the next 2 stitches on the left needle as if to knit.

2. Wrap the yarn around the right needle and knit the 2 stitches as 1 stitch.

PURL 2 TOGETHER (p2tog)

1. Insert the right needle into the front of the next 2 stitches on the left needle as if to purl.

2. Wrap the yarn around the right needle and purl the 2 stitches as 1 stitch.

Knit or Purl 2 Together Through Back of Loop

These are similar to the regular knit 2 together and purl 2 together decreases, only in this case, the 2 stitches are worked together through the *back* of the loops, abbreviated tbl, instead of through the front. Both result in a left-slanting decrease on the front side of a piece of knitting.

KNIT 2 TOGETHER THROUGH BACK OF LOOP

❶ Insert the right needle from front to back into the back of the next 2 stitches on the left needle.

❷ Knit the 2 stitches together as 1 stitch.

PURL 2 TOGETHER THROUGH BACK OF LOOP

❶ Insert the right needle from back to front into the back of the next 2 stitches on the left needle.

❷ Purl the 2 stitches together as 1 stitch.

FINISHED DECREASE

A knit 2 together or a purl 2 together decrease results in shaping that slants to the right (a) on the front side of a piece of knitting. A knit 2 together through back of loop or a purl 2 together through back of loop decrease results in shaping that slants to the left (b) on the front side of a piece of knitting.

a

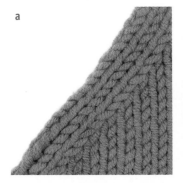

b

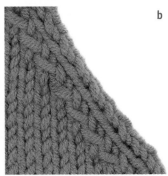

Slip, Slip, Knit

Practically invisible, this decrease, abbreviated ssk, is worked on the front side and slants to the left. If you want to shape your knitting on both sides symmetrically, you can begin a row with a slip, slip, knit and end the row with a knit 2 together.

① Insert the right needle from front to back (knitwise) into the front of the next stitch on the left needle and slip it onto the right needle.

② Repeat step 1.

You have slipped 2 stitches from the left needle to the right needle.

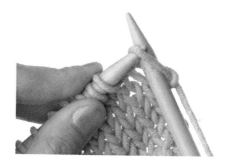

③ Insert the left needle from left to right into the fronts of both slipped stitches and then knit them as 1 stitch.

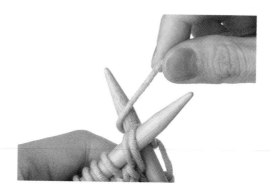

You can see that the slip, slip, knit decrease slants subtly to the left.

Finished decrease

Slip 1, Knit 1, Pass Slipped Stitch Over

This decrease, worked on the front side of a piece of knitting, slants quite visibly to the left. It is also sometimes referred to as slip, knit, pass and abbreviated skp.

1 Insert the right needle from front to back (knitwise) into the front of the next stitch on the left needle and slip it onto the right needle.

2 Knit the next stitch from the left needle.

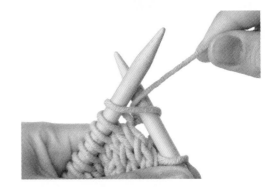

3 Insert the left needle into the front of the slipped stitch and bring the slipped stitch over the knit stitch and off the needle.

You can see that the slip 1, knit 1, pass slipped stitch over decrease slants markedly to the left.

Finished decrease

Slip 1, Purl 1, Pass Slipped Stitch Over

This decrease, worked on the purl side, slants quite visibly to the right on the knit side.

① Insert the right needle from back to front (purlwise) into the front of the next stitch on the left needle and slip it onto the right needle.

② Purl the next stitch from the left needle.

③ Insert the left needle into the front of the slipped stitch and bring the slipped stitch over the purl stitch and off the needle.

You can see how this decrease looks on the knit side.

Decrease Multiple Stitches

You may want to decrease more than 1 stitch at a time over one row. Your instructions might call for decreasing many stitches across a row, which results in a gathered look; or you may need to decrease 2 stitches in tandem over a series of rows, for more gradual shaping.

How to Decrease Multiple Stitches

DECREASING MULTIPLE STITCHES ACROSS ONE ROW

Some instructions may direct you to decrease a certain number of stitches evenly across a row.

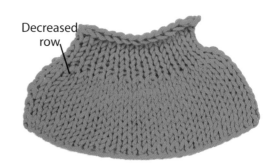

Decreased row

① To figure out how to decrease a certain number of stitches evenly across a row, divide the number of stitches you have on your needles by the number you need to decrease.

② Subtract 2 from the result, and that is the number of stitches you need to work between decreases. (For example, if you have 30 stitches on your needles and you are asked to decrease 10 stitches evenly across, you will knit 1 stitch, work the decrease over the next 2 stitches, knit 1 stitch, and so on.)

This example illustrates what decreasing the number of stitches by half looks like.

KNIT OR PURL 3 TOGETHER

Knit 3 together and purl 3 together, abbreviated k3tog and p3tog, are the easiest double decreases and are good for decreasing more stitches quickly. The resulting stitch is chunky looking and slants visibly to the right.

① To knit 3 together, insert the right needle into the front of the next 3 stitches (knitwise) on the left needle.

② Wrap the yarn around the right needle and knit the 3 stitches as 1 stitch.

You have just decreased 2 stitches.

NOTE: Work the purl 3 together double decrease in the same manner as the purl 2 together, only purl 3 stitches together.

DOUBLE VERTICAL DECREASE

This double decrease results in symmetrical shaping with a raised vertical stitch in the center. It is worked on the right side and is sometimes called slip 2, knit 1, pass 2 slipped stitches over, and abbreviated s2kp.

1 Insert the right needle into the next 2 stitches on the left needle as if to knit them together and then slip them off the left needle and onto the right needle.

2 Knit the next stitch from the left needle.

3 Use the left needle to pick up both slipped stitches at the same time and pass them over the knit stitch and off the right needle.

You have now decreased 2 stitches.

You can see here how the double vertical decrease looks when performed over a progression of rows. The purl rows are worked without decreasing.

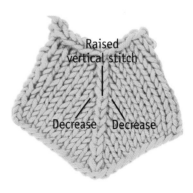

Left-Slanting Double Decrease

This double decrease, also called slip 1, knit 2 together, pass slipped stitch over and abbreviated sk2p, is good for symmetrical shaping. It looks a bit neater than the knit 3 together decrease, but it does slant visibly to the left on the knit side. You work it on the knit side.

1 Insert the right needle from front to back (knitwise) into the front of the next stitch on the left needle and slip it onto the right needle.

2 Knit the next 2 stitches on the left needle together.

3 Insert the left needle tip into the slipped stitch and left it up and over the knit 2 together stitch and off the right needle.

You now have decreased 2 stitches.

TIP

Decorative "Decreases"

Paired yarn overs can add decorative eyelet accents to many of these symmetrical double decreases. The double vertical decrease in particular works well for this purpose. However, because you're decreasing two stitches and increasing two stitches at the same time, you end with the same stitch count and no shaping actually occurs. What does result is a raised axis (created by the double decrease) framed by an eyelet on each side. Simply perform a yarn over before and after the double decrease to create this lovely touch.

Right-Slanting Double Decrease

This double decrease slants to the right and is good for symmetrical shaping. What is unusual about it is that a stitch is passed over on the left needle. You work it on the knit side.

1 Insert the right needle from front to back (knitwise) into the front of the next stitch on the left needle and slip it onto the right needle.

2 Knit the next stitch and then pass the slipped stitch over the knit stitch and off the right needle.

You have now decreased 1 stitch.

3 Slip the decreased knit stitch from the right needle back to the left needle.

4 Insert the right needle into the front of the second stitch on the left needle (as if to purl), and pass it over the decreased knit stitch and off the left needle.

5 Slip the decreased knit stitch from the left needle back to the right needle.

You have now decreased 2 stitches.

3

4

The Best Needle for the Job

Many of these decreases call for slipping stitches and passing stitches over. You have probably noticed that there are different needle tip shapes: tapered, round, and concave. Round-tipped needles are good for knitting bulky single-ply yarns because they are less likely to split the strand, but they're not the best choice for slipping stitches and passing stitches over. For the decreases and increases presented in this chapter, concave tips that can really get under a stitch and hold onto it are best. But if you don't have concave tipped needles, tapered are the next best choice.

Tapered point

Rounded point

Concave point

Shape with Short Rows

Often used to shape sock heels, bonnets, and stuffed toys, *short row shaping* involves working a series of partial rows—instead of decreasing or increasing stitches—to create curved or slanted edges.

How to Shape with Short Rows: Knit Side

Short rows eliminate the uneven stair steps that occur when binding off a series of stitches over a few rows, so they are an excellent choice for shaped shoulders and necklines.

1 Work across the row to the point where your instructions tell you the work should be turned. Keeping the working yarn at the back of the work, slip the next stitch from the left needle—as you would to purl—to the right needle.

2 Bring the working yarn between the needles to the front of the work.

3 Slip the same stitch you slipped in step 1 back to the left needle.

4 Bring the working yarn to the back of the work, thereby wrapping the slipped stitch.

5 Turn your work so that you're ready to work the wrong side.

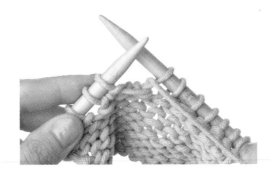

Preventing Holes When Shaping with Short Rows

Short rows involve working partway across a row, turning the work to the other side, working back partway, and repeating this process until you have achieved the desired shaping. To prevent holes from appearing at the turning points, you slip and wrap the turning stitches as shown here.

How to Shape with Short Rows: Purl Side

1 Work across the row to the point where the work should be turned. Keeping the working yarn at the front of the work, slip the next stitch from the left needle—as you would to purl—to the right needle.

2 Bring the working yarn between the needles to the back of the work.

3 Slip the same stitch you slipped in step 1 back to the left needle.

4 Bring the working yarn to the front of the work, thereby wrapping the slipped stitch.

How to Hide Short-Row Wraps

After you complete a short row, hide your wraps so that
your work looks tidy.

HIDING SHORT-ROW WRAPS ON THE KNIT SIDE

1 On the knit side, work to the point where the
wrap is.

2 Insert the right needle knitwise under both the wrap
and the wrapped stitch.

3 Knit the wrap and the wrapped stitch as 1 stitch.

HIDING SHORT-ROW WRAPS ON THE PURL SIDE

1 On the purl side, work to the point where the
wrap is.

2 Insert the right needle from back to front through
the back loop of the wrap. Lift the wrap and place
it onto the left needle with the wrapped stitch.

3 Purl the wrap and the wrapped stitch as 1 stitch.

After you complete your short-row shaping, you can
bind off or continue your pattern as established.

NOTE: Shoulders that have been shaped with short rows
can be sewn together invisibly (see page 166). If the
stitches have *not* been bound off, the shoulders can be
grafted together for a seamless look (see page 40).

CHAPTER 5

Correcting Mistakes

Has a mysterious hole appeared in your knitting? Or do you have fewer stitches on your needle than you should? Dropped stitches, twisted stitches, incomplete stitches—these are all common errors beginners (and even experts!) make. You can fix them easily, using the methods described in this chapter.

 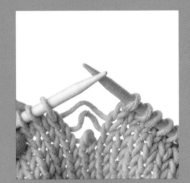 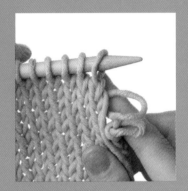

Avoid Accidental Increases

This often happens with beginner knitters: You're knitting your first 20-stitch swatch, and you notice after a several rows that you now have 25 stitches on your needle. How does this happen?

How to Avoid Accidental Increases

How you hold the working yarn when you begin a new row can result in accidental increases. If you're pulling the working yarn *over* the top of the needle so that it's hanging down *behind* the needle, you're causing the first stitch to pull up onto the needle so that it looks like 2 stitches, as shown here. By knitting into each strand of the 1 stitch, you're adding a new stitch at the beginning of the row.

When you begin a new row, make sure the working yarn is at the front of the needle, hanging down straight, as shown here. When you pull it back to knit the first stitch or to the front to purl the first stitch, bring it under the left needle, not over it. Check that the first stitch is really just 1 true stitch.

Sometimes stitches become twisted, resulting in an uneven finish to the knitted fabric. To recognize the problem, you need to familiarize yourself with how stitches should sit on the needle. When you look at the stitches on your needle, the right side of each loop should rest on the front of the needle, and the left side of each loop should rest against the back of the needle. If you see a stitch that has the left side of the loop in front, you have a twisted stitch.

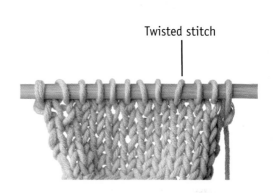

Twisted stitch

How to Correct Twisted Stitches

❶ Work across the stitches from the left needle until you get to the twisted stitch.

❷ Use the right needle to pick up the twisted stitch from the left needle.

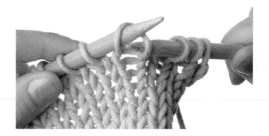

❸ Turn the twisted stitch around and place it back on the left needle so that the right side of the loop is in front.

Correct Incomplete Stitches

A stitch is **incomplete** when the working yarn does not get pulled through the loop. The stitch gets transferred but is not knit or purled, and the working yarn is wrapped over the needle, crossing over the mistakenly slipped stitch.

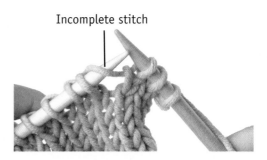

Incomplete stitch

How to Correct Incomplete Stitches

① Work across the stitches from the left needle until you get to the incomplete stitch.

② Insert the right needle as if to purl (from back to front) into the incomplete stitch.

③ Pull the incomplete stitch over the unworked strand and off the needle.

Pick Up Dropped Stitches

A **dropped stitch** is one that has slipped off your needles. Accidentally dropped stitches can unravel vertically through many rows, so it's important to learn how to fix them.

How to Pick Up a Dropped Knit Stitch One Row Below

When you realize that you have dropped a stitch on the row before the row you're currently working, you can fix it with your knitting needle.

1 Work across the stitches from the left needle until you get to the dropped stitch.

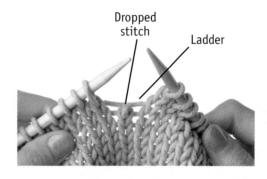

Dropped stitch

Ladder

2 Insert the right needle into the dropped stitch and under the horizontal strand (the "ladder") behind the dropped stitch.

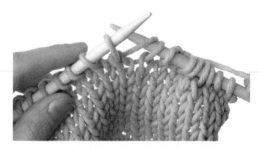

3 Insert the left needle from back to front into the dropped stitch on the right needle and pull it over the ladder and off the right needle.

4 Use the right needle to transfer the repaired stitch back to the left needle.

The repaired stitch is ready to be worked as usual.

How to Pick Up a Dropped Purl Stitch One Row Below

1 Work across the stitches on the left needle until you get to the dropped stitch.

2 Insert the right needle into the dropped stitch, as if to purl, and under the horizontal strand (the "ladder") in front of the dropped stitch.

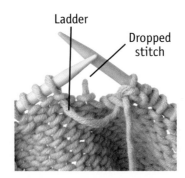

Ladder

Dropped stitch

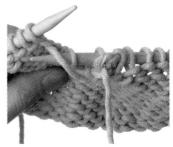

3 Use the left needle to lift the dropped stitch on the right needle up over the ladder and off the right needle.

4 Insert the left needle into the back of the repaired stitch to transfer it back to the left needle.

The repaired stitch is ready to be worked as usual.

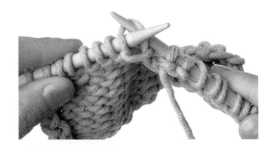

How to Pick Up a Dropped Stitch Several Rows Below

A dropped stitch that has unraveled several rows is called a *run*. To repair a run, you can use a crochet hook the same size or one size smaller than your needles. If you're working on the purl side when you discover the run, you just turn your work to the knit side to correct it.

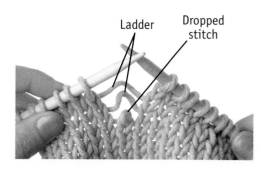

Ladder   Dropped stitch

1 Work across the stitches from the left needle until you get to where the dropped stitch should be.

2 Insert the crochet hook from front to back into the dropped stitch. Pull the lowest horizontal rung of the ladder, from back to front, through the dropped stitch.

3 Repeat step 2 until you have no more rungs left on your ladder.

4 Place the repaired stitch onto the left needle, being sure not to twist it.

The repaired stitch is ready to be worked as usual.

How to Pick Up a Dropped Edge Stitch Several Rows Below

An edge stitch that has been dropped and let run for several rows has a different appearance from a run down the interior of a piece of knitting. Instead of seeing a row of horizontal ladders, you see two loops at the edge: the dropped stitch and a large loop of yarn at the edge. For this repair, you use a crochet hook the same size as or one size smaller than your needles.

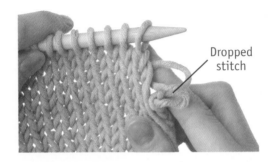

Dropped stitch

① Insert the crochet hook from front to back through the dropped stitch. Pull the big loop through it to the front.

② Repeat step 1 until you get to the top.

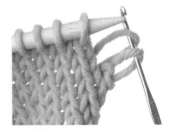 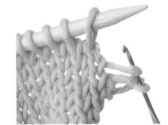

③ Use the crochet hook to pull the working yarn through the last stitch created.

④ Use the crochet hook to place the repaired stitch back onto the left needle.

The repaired stitch is ready to be worked as usual.

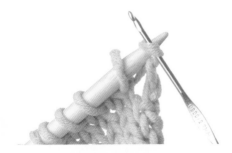

If you make an error that can't be fixed by using any of the previous methods, you probably need to unravel some of your work. For example, if you are working a particular stitch pattern and make a mistake in your pattern that is visibly wrong, you can unravel back to that point and correct it. If you make an error that is on the same row that you're working on, you can unravel stitch by stitch.

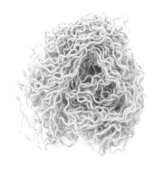

How to Unravel Stitch by Stitch

When you get good at unraveling stitch by stitch, it will feel like you're knitting backward, or "un-knitting."

UNRAVELING STITCH BY STITCH ON THE KNIT SIDE

1 On the knit side, hold the working yarn in back and insert the left needle from front to back into the stitch in the row below the next stitch on the right needle.

2 Drop the stitch above off the right needle and pull the working yarn to un-knit it.

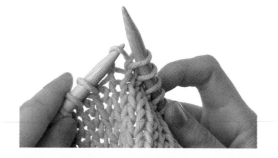

UNRAVELING STITCH BY STITCH ON THE PURL SIDE

1 On the purl side, hold the working yarn in front and insert the left needle from front to back into the stitch in the row below the next stitch on the right needle.

2 Drop the stitch above off the right needle and pull the working yarn to un-purl it.

How to Unravel Row by Row

If you make an error that is more than one row down from where you are currently working, you need to unravel row by row.

① Slide the stitches off the needle and pull the working yarn until you have unraveled the desired number of rows.

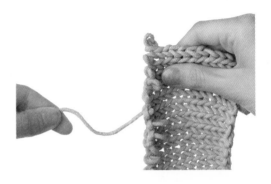

② Using a needle that is smaller in diameter than the working needle, carefully slide the stitches back onto that needle. Take care not to twist the stitches when you put them back onto the needle.

You can now resume knitting with the working needles.

A Safer Way to Unravel

To avoid dropping stitches as you unravel, you can use another method:

① Weave a needle that is smaller in diameter than the working needles in and out of the stitches in the row below the point to which you would like to unravel.

Be sure the needle goes under the right side of each stitch and over the left side of each stitch.

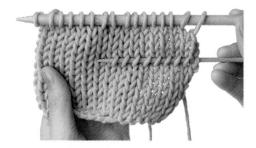

② When the entire row is on the needle, pull the working yarn to unravel the rows above the needle.

③ Resume knitting with the working needles.

CHAPTER 6

Learning to Read Written Instructions

By now you've probably looked at some knitting patterns and thought, "Is this in English?" Knitting instructions use a lot of unfamiliar terms and abbreviations that can be intimidating at first. This chapter will help you learn to understand what you are reading the next time you look at a knitting pattern.

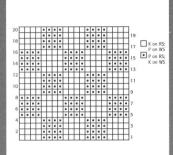

Getting to Know Gauge

Gauge (referred to as **tension** in the UK) is the number of stitches and rows per inch—using stockinette stitch, unless the pattern notes otherwise. Different yarns knit to different gauges, the same yarn knits to a different gauge on different sizes of needles, and different knitters knit the same yarn on the same needles at different gauges.

Understanding Gauge

A good knitting pattern will specify the gauge required to create the desired size or fit of the garment. For example, it will read something like "Gauge: 20 stitches and 30 rows to 4 inches over stockinette stitch on size 7 (4.5 mm) needles." To create a sweater or hat with the same measurements that the pattern specifies—so that it fits properly—you need to be sure that you are knitting to that gauge. Though your yarn label should indicate what size needle to use with the yarn and what the desired gauge is, you should use that recommendation only as a guide, as tension varies from knitter to knitter.

These three swatches were all made using 20 stitches and 30 rows, but with different yarns and different needle sizes. You can see how varied the sizes of the final results are. That's why making sure you're getting the same gauge the pattern calls for—with the yarn you have chosen for the project—is so important. Even a slight discrepancy can have a tremendous effect. A 1-stitch-per-inch difference in gauge, over a large number of stitches, can result in a final size that is several inches smaller or larger than desired.

Understanding Gauge Differences with Stitch Patterns

Sometimes a knitting pattern will cite the gauge for a particular stitch pattern, if that's what is primarily used for the garment. Like needle size and yarn type, stitch pattern can also affect gauge. For example, the same yarn, worked in stockinette stitch on size 7 needles, knits to a different gauge in a ribbed pattern on the same size needles.

These three swatches are all made from the same yarn and using the same needles, over 20 stitches and 30 rows, but with different stitch patterns. You can see how varied the sizes of the final results are.

Cables

2 x 2
ribbing

Seed
stitch

Make and Measure a Gauge Swatch

Before starting a project, always make a gauge swatch to ensure that you are knitting to the gauge the pattern calls for. A *gauge swatch* is a small square of knitting used to measure how many stitches and rows per inch you are getting with a particular yarn on a certain size needle. It takes only a few minutes to make one, and you will definitely not regret it. Many new knitters skip this step and spend hours on a sweater that ends up too big or too small.

How to Make a Gauge Swatch

To make a gauge swatch, use the yarn and needle size that the pattern calls for. It's not a bad idea to have handy three pairs of needles: the size called for, the next size smaller, and the next size larger. (If you don't use them for this project, you will need them someday for another project.)

1 Cast on the same number of stitches that the pattern says is equal to 4 inches.

2 Work in stockinette stitch (knit on the right side and purl on the wrong side) until the swatch is 4 inches long (measuring from the cast-on edge to the needle).

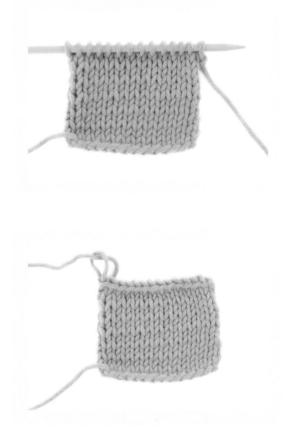

3 Bind off your stitches somewhat loosely, cut the working yarn, leaving about a 6-inch tail, and pull the tail through the last stitch.

NOTE: If you think you may be short on yarn for your project, don't cut the yarn after finishing the swatch. Simply measure your gauge (as instructed on the next page) and then unravel the swatch so you can use the yarn for your project.

How to Measure a Gauge Swatch

Remember the stitch and needle gauge tool from Chapter 1? Now is the time to use it. If you don't have one, you can use a ruler or tape measure. Before measuring, block your swatch: Take a warm steam iron to the swatch, pressing only lightly. Let it cool and dry before measuring. Blocking your gauge swatch is particularly important to accurately measure gauge for certain stitch patterns, like cables, which cinch in, and lace, which spreads out.

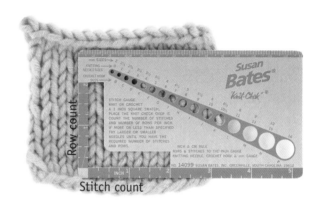

Row count

Stitch count

① Lay your swatch on a flat surface. Place your stitch and needle gauge (or other measuring device) so that the opening is centered both horizontally and vertically on the swatch.

② Count the stitches in the horizontal 2-inch space and the rows in the vertical 2-inch space.

③ Divide these numbers by 2. That is the number of stitches and rows you are getting *per inch*.

④ If your pattern lists gauge as a certain number of stitches and rows over 4 inches, multiply the stitch and row counts you got for the 2-inch square.

What should I do if my gauge is different from the gauge listed in the pattern?

If you are getting more stitches per 4 inches than the pattern calls for, try switching to a needle that is one size larger. If you are getting fewer stitches per 4 inches than the pattern calls for, try switching to a needle that is one size smaller. Make a new gauge swatch and measure again. If necessary, go up or down another needle size, create a new swatch, and re-measure.

It's difficult to match both stitch and row gauge, but matching the stitch gauge is more important. If the row gauge is slightly off, remember that when you're working vertically, you may have to go more by the garment's measurements than by the row counts.

Knitting Terms

Learning to read knitting instructions is like learning a new language. Familiar words pair together to form unfamiliar phrases. The following is a list of common knitting terms and phrases and their translations. For a list of knitting abbreviations that you'll find in most pattern instructions, refer to the inside cover.

A

as established   Work in a particular pattern, as previously set.

as foll   Work as the instructions direct below.

as if to knit   Knitwise; insert the needle into the stitch the same way you would if you were knitting it.

as if to purl   Purlwise; insert the needle into the stitch the same way you would if you were purling it.

at the same time   Work more than one set of instructions simultaneously.

B

bind off in patt   Work stitch pattern while binding off.

bind off loosely   Bind off without pulling the working yarn too tight, so that the finished edge is elastic.

block   Lay knitted pieces out flat and dampen or steam them to form them to the proper shape and measurements.

C

change needles   Use the larger (or smaller) needles specified in the pattern, starting with the next row.

continue in patt   Continue to work the stitch pattern as previously established.

E

ending with a RS row   Work a right side row as the last row you work.

ending with a WS row   Work a wrong side row as the last row you work.

every other row   Work as instructed on alternate rows only.

F

from beg   From the cast-on edge; usually used to direct where to start measuring a knitted piece.

G

gauge   The number of stitches and rows per inch, usually presented in knitting instructions as the number of stitches and rows per 4 inches.

I

increase stitches evenly across row (around)   Position the number of increased stitches at regular intervals across the row or round.

J

join round   When knitting in the round, work the first stitch of the round so that the last stitch and the first stitch join, forming a circle.

K

knitwise   As if to knit; insert the needle into the stitch the same way you would if you were knitting it.

M

marker   Something used to mark a point in a stitch pattern or in your knitting, be it a plastic ring stitch marker, safety pin, or tied piece of yarn.

N

next row   The row following the current row, usually followed by specific instructions pertaining to that row.

O

on following alternate (alt) rows   Every other row, after the current row.

P

pick up and knit   A method of picking up stitches, as for a collar or button band, where the knitting needle is inserted into the work, yarn is wrapped around the needle as if to knit, and the new loop is pulled through.

place marker   Slip a stitch marker onto the knitting needle to indicate special instructions regarding the stitch following; or place some other sort of marker, such as a safety pin, to indicate where buttons will be.

preparation row   A setup row that occurs prior to beginning the stitch pattern repeat.

purlwise   As if to purl; insert the needle into the stitch the same way you would if you were purling it.

R

rep from * to * or between *s   Rep the set of instructions that appear between the two asterisks the number of times indicated or to the end of the row or round.

rep from * to end (or until a particular number of stitches rem)   Rep the set of instructions that begin after the asterisk until the end of the row or round (or until the number of stitches indicated remains before the end of the row or round).

reverse shaping   When working something like a cardigan, where the fronts are mirror images of each other, instructions for shaping are given for one front; you need to reverse those instructions for shaping the other front.

right side (RS)   The side of the knitting that will show.

S

selvage   An extra stitch (or stitches) that will be used for the seam.

slip marker   Slip the stitch marker from the left needle to the right needle.

slip stitches to holder   Put the stitches onto a stitch holder, usually to be worked later.

T

turn   Turn work from right side to wrong side, or vice versa, to begin a new row or to begin working part of a row, as in short row shaping.

turning ridge   A row of stitches, usually purled on the right side of stockinette stitch, where a hem will be folded under.

W

weave in ends   When finishing a project, sew loose ends in and out of the backs of stitches or into seams to prevent them from unraveling.

with RS facing   Work with the right side facing you; usually used when instructions are telling you to pick up stitches for a button band or collar.

with WS facing   Work with the wrong side facing you.

work even   Work without increasing or decreasing.

work to end   Finish the row.

working needle   The needle that is being used to knit or purl stitches.

working yarn   The yarn that is being used to knit or purl stitches.

wrong side (WS)   The side of the knitting that will not show.

How to Read a Knitting Pattern

A knitting pattern contains all the information you need to make a certain design. In addition to the instructions, a pattern should list what sizes the design can be knit for, the tools and materials required, and any particular stitch patterns used. Some patterns also contain diagrams of the finished pieces, called **schematics**, which show the shape of the pieces and their measurements.

READING THE PATTERN FIRST

There are so many knitting patterns and books to choose from these days that you may be overwhelmed. When you find something that you would like to knit, read over the pattern first to see if the instructions are clear and make sense to you. Choose a pattern within your skill level. Many patterns are rated, ranging from very easy to expert. If the pattern isn't rated, reading it over will let you know if it's something you can handle. Trying to knit something that is too difficult may turn you off to knitting forever, and you certainly don't want that. Also, make certain that the instructions are written for a size that you would like to knit.

What Size to Knit?					
Actual Body Measurement	**Finished Measurements**				
Chest	**Tight Fit**	**Tailored Fit**	**Normal Fit**	**Loose Fit**	**Oversized Fit**
31"–32"	30"	32"	34"	36"	37"–38"
33"–34"	32"	34"	36"	38"	39"–40"
35"–36"	34"	36"	38"	40"	41"–42"
37"–38"	36"	38"	40"	42"	43"–44"
39"–40"	38"	40"	42"	44"	45"–46"

READING INSTRUCTIONS FOR SIZE

Most knitting patterns are written for more than one size. The smallest size is listed first, with the remaining sizes listed in parentheses—for example, S (M, L). Throughout the pattern, the instructions contain information pertaining to the various sizes, such as stitch counts and numbers of decreases or increases, using a parallel format. For example, a pattern written for S (M, L) may instruct you to cast on 50 (60, 70) stitches. That means if you're knitting the medium size, you need to cast on 60 stitches. Some knitters avoid confusion by highlighting or underlining the part of the instructions that pertain to the size they are knitting.

CHOOSING A SIZE

Knitting patterns list the measurements for the sizes included in the instructions. These measurements usually indicate the finished sizes of the knitted garment. Different designers use unique templates based on their idea of what fits a certain age or size range. So the best way to figure out what size to knit for yourself or for someone else is, if possible, to take body measurements. Then you can decide whether you want the garment to have a loose, comfortable fit, or a more snug, tailored fit. You then check your measurements against the pattern's finished measurements and make your choice.

TAKING BODY MEASUREMENTS

To take body measurements, you need a tape measure. Measure the bust or chest by placing the tape measure around the fullest part of the chest, at the underarm. For the waist, measure around the smallest part of the torso. For the hip, measure around the fullest part of the lower torso. Measure for the sleeve length by placing the tape measure at the edge of the shoulder and extending down (with arm held straight at side) to the wrist. Also measure from the underarm to the wrist to obtain a measurement for where to begin the sleeve cap shaping. The measurements of some parts of a knitted garment should be a few inches larger than the actual body measurements, or the garment will be too tight. If the garment is very tailored, you may want to also measure the circumference of the upper arms, wrists, and neck.

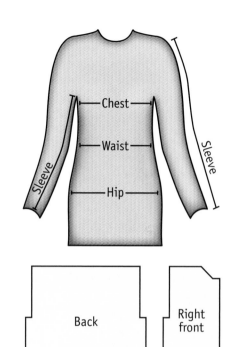

READING SCHEMATICS

Schematics are diagrams of the finished knitted pieces for a project. They indicate the measurements for each piece before everything has been sewn together. Schematics are a handy reference: You can measure your knitting as you go along and compare it to the schematic to make sure your knitting is the right size. Or if your row gauge is slightly off, you can follow the schematic instead of the row counts in the instructions to make certain your pieces will be the correct length. However, it's important to remember that the measurements listed on schematics do not include embellishments such as collars, button bands, or decorative edgings that are added later.

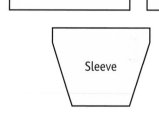

GATHERING MATERIALS AND TOOLS

A knitting pattern lists the materials and tools needed to complete the project. Some knitting patterns specify a number of balls of a particular brand of yarn. If you plan to substitute, be sure to purchase the same number of *yards* of a yarn that knits to the same gauge—not just the same total weight of yarn. Some patterns simply specify a number of yards of a particular weight yarn. Either way, it's not a bad idea to buy an extra ball, just in case. A pattern usually also lists needle types and sizes, as well as special tools you need. It's a good idea to gather these materials before starting. However, you can wait until you have sewn your sweater together before purchasing buttons or other fasteners.

How to Read a Knitting Chart

At some point, you will come across a stitch chart or color chart on a knitting pattern, particularly if the design employs color work, textured stitches, or cables. Don't be intimidated by all the symbols and hieroglyphics; most patterns provide a key to the symbols used in each chart.

READING A CHART IN THE RIGHT DIRECTION

Each square on a knitting chart represents a stitch; a horizontal row of squares represents a row. You read a chart as you work the knitting: from bottom to top and starting at the lower-right corner. The first horizontal row of squares represents a right side row (unless otherwise specified) and is read from right to left. The second horizontal row, a wrong side row, is read from left to right. (For circular knitting, all chart rows are read from right to left.) Most charts represent only a partial section of the knitting that is repeated to create the overall pattern. So, after you work the last stitch in a chart row, you return to the beginning of the same chart row and repeat. Working row-wise is the same: After you work the last row of the chart, you repeat the chart from the bottom.

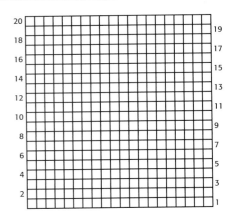

READING A COLOR CHART

When a chart is used to represent a color pattern, each square is filled with a particular color or a symbol that corresponds with the color of yarn in which that stitch and/or row should be worked. You read this type of chart as described above: from bottom to top and back and forth, starting with the lower-right corner.

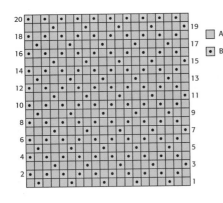

□ A
⊡ B

READING A STITCH PATTERN CHART

When a chart is used to represent a textured stitch pattern, each square is either empty or contains a symbol. Symbols vary from pattern to pattern. For simple knit and purl patterns, an empty square means "knit on the right side rows and purl on the wrong side rows." A square that contains a dot means "purl on the right side rows and knit on the wrong side rows." More complex stitch patterns, such as cable patterns, for example, contain many symbols representing different techniques.

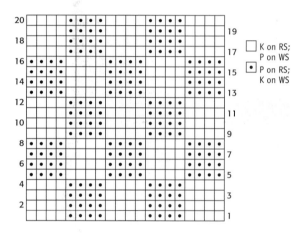

COMMON SYMBOLS USED IN KNITTING CHARTS

Symbol charts employ a language of symbols to convey instructions relating to a particular stitch or group of stitches. Unfortunately, these symbols vary from one designer to another—particularly symbols for cable stitches—so it's important to use the key that is provided with a chart. All good patterns include clear written instructions along with the chart, so don't feel you have to learn symbols by heart. The following table shows a number of knitting chart symbols you might encounter.

Common Knitting Chart Symbols	
Symbol	**Meaning**
	K on RS; P on WS
●	P on RS; K on WS
O	Yarn over (yo)
V	Slip st as if to knit, with yarn in back on RS; slip stitch as if to knit, with yarn in front on WS
⊻	Slip st as if to purl, with yarn in back on RS; slip stitch as if to purl, with yarn in front on WS
⋉	Perform make one (M1) increase
⋀	Knit 2 stitches together (k2tog)
⟋⟍	Purl 2 stitches together (p2tog)

CHAPTER 7

Knitting in the Round

Knitting in the round, or *circular knitting,* is what you do when you want to knit a tube. Hats, socks, mittens, gloves, and skirts are frequently knit in the round. When you knit in the round, you knit around and around on the right side only. So if you're working in stockinette stitch, knitting in the round eliminates the need to purl. It also reduces the necessity of sewing seams.

Cast On with Circular Needles

Circular needles are basically needle tips connected with a plastic or nylon cord. Used mainly for knitting tubular items, they come in a variety of materials and lengths. Whether you use wood, metal, or plastic is up to you. The circumference of what you are going to knit determines what length needle you can use, and your pattern will specify the length. The key to casting on to a circular needle is ensuring that the stitches do not get twisted when you join the round.

How to Cast On with Circular Needles

If the cord on your circular needle is very curly and hard to manage, immerse it in hot water for a minute or two and then straighten it. It will be much easier to work with.

1 Cast on stitches in the same manner you would with straight needles, using the method of your choice.

2 When you have cast on the correct number of stitches, make sure that your row of stitches is not twisted around the needle.

NOTE: To avoid twisted stitches, make sure the cast-on edge is going around the inside of the needle.

Knit Using Circular Needles

When you knit on circular needles, you knit in *rounds*, not rows. Every round is a right side row, so if you're working in stockinette stitch, you do not have to purl.

Take care not to let the stitches get twisted around the needle before joining your round. If they are twisted and you knit a few rounds, the entire piece of knitting will be twisted. The only way to correct this is to unravel all the way back to the cast-on row. The good news is that once you've done it properly when you join to knit the first round, you don't have to worry about it anymore!

How to Knit on Circular Needles

1 Hold the end of the needle that the working yarn is attached to in your right hand. Attach a ring marker after the last stitch that was cast on to mark the end of the round.

2 Use the needle in your right hand to knit the first cast-on stitch from the needle in your left hand, giving the yarn a firm tug (on this first stitch only) so that the join is snug.

Knitting the first stitch joins the round.

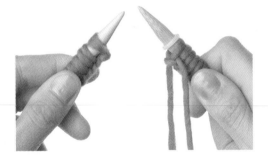

3 Knit all the way around until you reach the stitch marker. To begin the second round, slip the marker from the left to right needle, after the last stitch of the round, and knit the first stitch as in step 2.

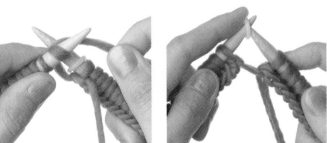

Cast On with Double-Pointed Needles

Before circular needles were invented, all circular knitting was done on double-pointed needles. Today, double-pointed needles are used mainly for smaller items, like hats and socks. They are sold in sets of four or five. You need four for this lesson.

Casting on with double-pointed needles is similar to casting on with circular needles in that you must avoid twisting the stitches. The difference is that you spread the cast-on stitches over three needles.

How to Cast On with Double-Pointed Needles

❶ Cast on all the stitches called for onto one double-pointed needle. Then slip approximately one-third of the stitches onto a second needle and one-third onto a third needle.

NOTE: If all stitches won't fit onto a double-pointed needle, cast on all the stitches onto a long straight or circular needle and then transfer them to the three double-pointed needles.

❷ Arrange the three needles so that they form a triangle: The needle with the working yarn attached should be the right side of the triangle (a), the center needle should be the base of the triangle (b), and the needle with the first cast-on stitch should be the left side of the triangle (c).

NOTE: Make sure the cast-on edge is running around the center of the triangle, not twisted around the needles.

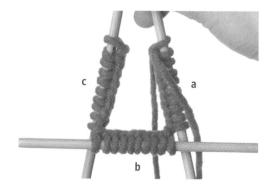

Knit Using Double-Pointed Needles

Knitting on double-pointed needles can feel awkward at first, but once you work a few rounds, it will all come together. It is really the best way to knit socks and gloves, so it's worth giving this type of knitting a try.

How to Knit on Double-Pointed Needles

1 Hold the needle with the working yarn attached to it in your right hand. Attach a ring marker after the last stitch that was cast on to mark the end of the round. Hold the needle with the first cast-on stitch on it in your left hand.

2 Using your fourth needle, join the round by knitting the first cast-on stitch from the left needle, giving the yarn a firm tug (on this first stitch only) so that the join is snug.

Knitting the first stitch joins the round.

3 Knit all the way around all three needles until you reach the stitch marker. To begin the second round, slip the marker from the left to right needle, after the last stitch of the round, and knit the first stitch as in step 2.

Knit in the Round on Two Needles

If you don't like knitting on double-pointed needles, there is good news: You can knit small-circumference items like hats, socks, and mittens on two circular needles. To practice knitting in the round on two needles, you need a ball of yarn, a split-ring stitch marker, and two circular needles in the diameter recommended for your yarn. The needles don't have to be the same length. This technique may feel awkward at first, but that won't last past the fifth or sixth round.

How to Knit in the Round on Two Needles

① Cast on at least 30 stitches to one of the circular needles.

② Slip half of the stitches onto the second circular needle.

③ Slide each set of stitches to the end of its circular needle, as shown. Arrange the needles so that the working yarn is coming from the needle in your right hand.

NOTE: Take care not to twist the point where the cast-on stitches split onto the two needles.

④ Slide the stitches on the needle with the working yarn attached so that they are positioned on the flexible cable section of the needle. Drop that needle and hold the empty end of the needle holding the first half of the stitches in your right hand, ready to knit.

5 Use the needle end in your right hand to knit the first stitch on the left needle, giving the working yarn a firm tug to close the round.

Knitting this first stitch joins the round.

NOTE: Watching for the tail left over from casting on is one way to mark the end of the round, but if you prefer, attach a split-ring marker to the last cast-on stitch.

6 Knit the rest of the first half of the stitches from the left needle and slide these worked stitches to the flexible cable section of the needle. Drop that needle.

7 Slide the unworked stitches to the tip of their needle so that the cast-on tail is at the bottom and the next stitch of the round is ready to be worked.

8 Use the empty end of the needle holding the unworked stitches to knit the rest of the stitches to complete the round.

9 Repeat steps 4–8 for each new round.

TIP

Using two different looking needles or marking the shafts of one needle pair with a dab of nail polish can help you remember which needle tips should be used together.

Knit Small Circumferences on One Circular Needle

Here's another technique for knitters who dislike double-pointed needles. You use a very long circular needle to knit small-circumference items like hats and socks by pulling part of the cable between the stitches, forming a loop. This method is also known as the "magic loop." To practice, you'll need a ball of yarn and a circular needle at least 30 inches long.

How to Knit in the Round on One Circular Needle

1 Cast on 30 stitches to the circular needle.

2 Slide the cast-on stitches to the center of the cable section of the needle.

3 Fold the needle in half, forming a loop with the cable. Divide the stitches in half and gently pull the loop of cable out from the center, between the two sets of stitches.

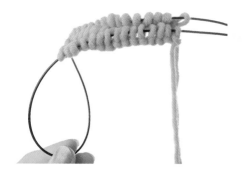

4 Holding the needle with the cast-on tail and working yarn attached in your right hand and holding the needle with the first half of the cast-on stitches in your left, slide the 15 stitches on the left side of the needle toward the needle tip so that they're ready to be knit. Leave the 15 stitches on the right side of the needle resting on the cable.

The first half of the cast-on stitches are now on the left needle tip, and the last half are on the flexible cable. Check that the stitches are not twisted.

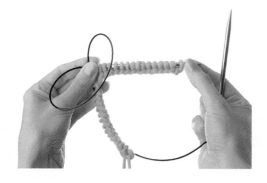

⑤ Use the right needle to knit the first stitch from the left needle, giving the working yarn an extra tug to join the round.

Reaching the right needle to knit the first stitch on the left needle forms a second loop of cable.

NOTE: You may have to shorten or lengthen the loop you pulled from the center of the stitches to be able to comfortably reach the first stitch on the left needle with the right needle.

⑥ Knit the 14 stitches remaining on left needle.

⑦ Slide the stitches from the cable section to the left needle tip, ready to be knit. Slide the stitches you just knit on the right needle to the cable section of the needle, leaving the loop dividing the stitches and making enough of a second loop to use the right needle tip to knit.

⑧ Knit the 15 stitches from the left needle.

You have now knit one complete round.

⑨ Slide the stitches from the cable section to the left needle tip, ready to be knit. Slide the stitches you just knit on the right needle to the cable section of the needle, leaving the loop dividing the stitches and making enough of a second loop to use the right needle tip to knit.

⑩ Repeat steps 5–9.

7

9

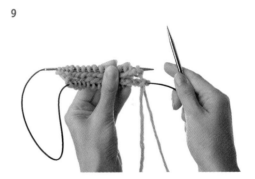

111

CHAPTER 8

Bobbles, Cables, and Textured Stitches

This chapter covers stitch treatments you need to know to make a highly textured sweater: bobbles, knots, and cables. Most cable work involves holding a stitch or stitches on a cable needle, working the next stitch or few, and then working the stitches from the cable needle. Simple cables are easy to do and can add a sculptural accent to your knitting. Included here are a variety of bobble stitches, knot stitches, and cables. Experiment with some of the combinations here and then see if you can create your own.

Make Bobbles

obbles add an exciting three-dimensional accent to your knitting. Bobbles can be used for effect in many ways: as a single row along a border, repeated in an allover pattern, or placed inside cables. Different designers make bobbles in different ways; experiment to find the way that suits you best.

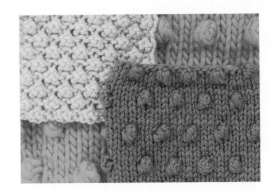

HOW TO MAKE AN EASY BOBBLE

This is the easiest bobble because you don't have to turn your work to make it. The abbreviation for make a bobble is mb.

1. Work to the point where you want the bobble. Knit into the front, back, front, back, and front (that's five times) of the next stitch.

2. Without turning your work, use the left needle to pick up the fourth stitch and pass it over the fifth and off the needle; pass the third stitch over the fifth and off the needle; pass the second stitch over the fifth and off the needle; and finally, pass the first stitch over the fifth and off the needle.

Knitting five times into 1 stitch and then passing the 4 extra stitches, one at a time, over the last stitch forms this bobble.

HOW TO MAKE A BIGGER BOBBLE

This bobble is made by knitting five times into 1 stitch, as for an easy bobble, but then you work a few rows on the 5 stitches before decreasing back to 1 stitch.

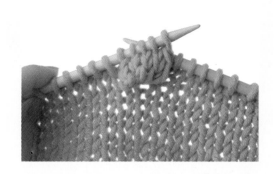

1 Work to the point where you want the bobble. Knit into the front, back, front, back, and front (that's five times) of the next stitch.

2 Turn your work, so that the wrong side is facing, and purl the 5 bobble stitches.

3 Turn again, so that the right side is facing, and knit the 5 bobble stitches.

4 Repeat step 2.

5 Repeat step 3.

6 Do not turn work. Still on the right side, use the left needle to pick up the fourth stitch and pass it over the fifth and off the needle; pass the third stitch over the fifth and off the needle; pass the second stitch over the fifth and off the needle; and finally, pass the first stitch over the fifth and off the needle.

Knitting five times into 1 stitch, then working on the 5 stitches alone for a few rows before passing the 4 extra stitches, one at a time, over the last stitch forms this bobble.

Make Simple Cables

Cables look more complicated than they actually are. If you can knit, purl, put stitches on a holder, and count, you can make a simple cable.

You make simple cables by holding one or more stitches on a cable needle to the front or the back of your work, knitting or purling the next one or more stitches from the left needle, and then knitting or purling the stitches from the cable needle. Whether you hold the stitches to the back or front determines which direction the cable crosses.

Simple Back Cross Cable

To practice making a cable, you need needles, yarn, a row counter, and a cable needle. Cast on 16 stitches and then work rows 1 and 2 shown below to set up for the cables. This cable, which slants to the right, is worked on the 6 stitches at the center, with 5 stitches of reverse stockinette stitch on either side. Remember to click your row counter ahead each time you complete a row.

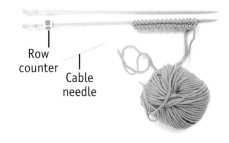

Row counter

Cable needle

1 Row 1 (RS): P5, k6, p5.

2 Row 2 (WS): K5, p6, k5.

3 Row 3 (cable row): P5, slip the next 3 sts purlwise to a cable needle (cn) and hold at back of work (a). K the next 3 sts from the left needle. K the 3 sts from the cn, starting with the first st that was slipped (b), p5.

4 Row 4: Rep row 2.

5 Rep rows 1–4 for back cross, or right, cable.

NOTE: You can slip the held stitches to the left needle before knitting them.

3a

3b

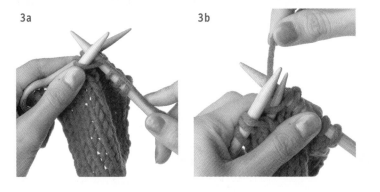

116

Simple Front Cross Cable

Making a front cross cable will be easy now that you have made a back cross cable. The only difference is that for this cable, you hold the stitches on the cable needle to the front of your work, so the cable slants to the left. You need to cast on 16 stitches, as before.

① Row 1 (RS): P5, k6, p5.

② Row 2 (WS): K5, p6, k5.

3a

③ Row 3 (cable row): P5, slip the next 3 sts to a cable needle as if to purl and hold at front of work (a). Knit the next 3 sts from the left needle. Now use the right needle to knit the 3 sts from the cable needle, starting with the first st that was slipped onto the needle (b), p5.

④ Row 4: Rep row 2.

⑤ Rep rows 1–4 for front cross, or left, cable.

3b

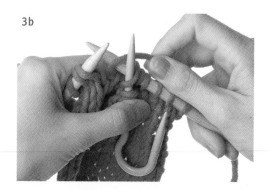

FAQ

There are different sizes and types of cable needles. Which one should I chose?

Always use a cable needle that is slightly smaller in diameter than your working knitting needle. If you use one that is too thick, you will stretch out your stitches. The type you choose depends entirely on your preference. Many knitters choose one that looks like a tiny double-pointed needle because it's easier to knit directly from it. Others prefer a hook-shaped cable needle because the stitches don't fall off easily, and it hangs down out of the way when you're knitting the other stitches. Experiment with the various types to find the style that suits you best.

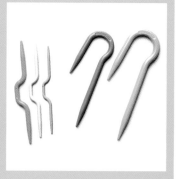

Knit 1 in the Row Below

Many textured stitch patterns include the instruction to "knit 1 in the row below." It's an easy stitch maneuver that causes the knitted fabric to pucker slightly, giving it more dimension.

How to Knit 1 in the Row Below

① Holding the working yarn at the back, insert the right needle from front to back into the stitch directly below the next stitch on the left needle.

NOTE: Be sure to insert the needle all the way through to the back before knitting, so that the stitch above becomes caught up by the new stitch.

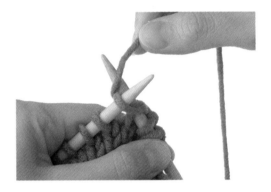

② Wrap the working yarn around the tip of the right needle and knit as usual, sliding the stitch above off the left needle at the same time.

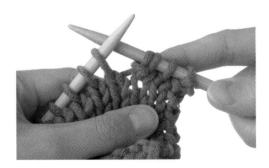

A common direction in knitting patterns is "k1 tbl" or "knit 1 through back of loop." Likewise, you often see "p1 tbl" or "purl 1 through back of loop." Knitting or purling through the back loop twists the stitch, and so it is a frequently-used maneuver in textured, twist-stitch patterns. It is also used in the bar increase, where you knit into the front and back of the same stitch. You also find "tbl" in the decreases k2tog tbl and p2tog tbl.

How to Knit Through Back of Loop

① Holding the working yarn at the back, insert the right needle knitwise, from front to back, into the back loop of the next knit stitch on the left needle.

② Wrap the working yarn around the tip of the right needle and knit as usual.

How to Purl Through Back of Loop

① Holding the working yarn at the front, insert the right needle purlwise, from back to front, into the back loop of the next purl stitch on the left needle.

② Wrap the working yarn around the tip of the right needle and purl as usual.

Knit with Bobbles and Knots

You learned how to make a single bobble a few pages ago. Now you can create stitch patterns that incorporate many bobbles or knots. Knots are textural stitches similar to bobbles, but they're smaller and usually formed by simultaneously increasing and decreasing.

Bobble and Knot Stitches

BOBBLE STITCH

Here's a pattern where on right side rows you work a bobble (as described in How to Make an Easy Bobble, on page 114) every 4th stitch on every 6th row. You work this pattern on a multiple of 4 stitches plus 3.

① Row 1 (RS—bobble row): *K3, make bobble (mb); rep from * to last 3 sts, k3.

② Rows 2, 4, and 6 (WS): Purl.

③ Rows 3 and 5: Knit.

④ Row 7 (bobble row): K1, mb, *k3, mb; rep from * to last st, k1.

⑤ Rows 8, 10, and 12: Purl.

⑥ Rows 9 and 11: Knit.

⑦ Rep rows 1–12 for bobble stitch.

TRINITY STITCH

Trinity stitch, which is also referred to as *bramble stitch,* works very well alongside cable panels. You work it on a multiple of 4 stitches plus 2.

① Row 1 (RS): Purl.

② Row 2 (WS): K1, *[k1, p1, k1] into the next st, p3tog; rep from * to last st, k1.

③ Row 3: Purl.

④ Row 4: K1, *p3tog, [k1, p1, k1] into the next st; rep from * to last st, k1.

⑤ Rep rows 1–4 for trinity stitch.

KNOT STITCH

This is a textured stitch pattern that works well for sweaters, jackets, and bags. You work it over a multiple of 2 stitches plus 1.

1 Rows 1 and 3 (RS): Knit.

2 Row 2 (WS): K1, *p2tog without slipping sts off the needle, bring yarn to back and knit the same 2 sts together and slide them off the needle; rep from * to end of row.

3 Row 4: *P2tog without slipping sts off the needle, bring yarn to back and knit the same 2 sts together and slide them off the needle; rep from * to last sts, k1.

4 Rep rows 1–4 for knot stitch.

PILLARED KNOT STITCH

This interesting pattern resembles a rib, and it does pull in like a rib but without a lot of elasticity. You work it over a multiple of 4 stitches plus 1.

1 Row 1 (RS): K1, *p3tog without slipping sts from the left needle, bring yarn to back and knit the same 3 sts together without slipping sts from the left needle, bring yarn back to the front and purl the 3 sts together (this time slipping the sts off the left needle to complete the knot), k1; rep from * to end of row.

2 Row 2 (WS): Purl.

3 Rep rows 1 and 2 for pillared knot stitch.

STAR STITCH

In this easy stitch, the little knots resemble stars. It is worked on a multiple of 4 stitches plus 1. This pattern uses the following abbreviation:

ms (make star): P3tog, leaving sts on the left needle, then wrap yarn around right needle and purl the same 3 sts together again (this time slipping the sts off the needle to complete the knot).

1 Rows 1 and 3 (RS): Knit.

2 Row 2 (WS): P1, *ms, p1; rep from * to end of row.

3 Row 4: P3, ms, *p1, ms; rep from * to last 3 sts, p3.

4 Rep rows 1–4 for star stitch.

Learn More Cable Patterns

Now that you have seen how you can move stitches and cross them in your knitting, you are ready to try some other cable patterns.

Most instructions for cable knit garments break down the various stitch patterns and cable elements into panels so that they're easier to follow. The following cable panels include 2 stitches in reverse stockinette stitch on each side of the cable.

More Cable Patterns

BRAIDED CABLE (12-STITCH PANEL)

This cable is easier to make than it looks.

1 Row 1 (RS—cable row): P2, *slip the next 2 sts to a cable needle and hold at back, knit the next 2 sts from the left needle, knit the 2 sts from the cable needle; rep from * to last 2 sts, p2.

2 Rows 2 and 4 (WS): K2, p8, k2.

3 Row 3 (cable row): P2, k2, slip the next 2 sts to a cable needle and hold at front, knit the next 2 sts from the left needle, k2 sts from the cable needle, k2, p2.

4 Rep rows 1–4 for braided cable.

Is it possible to work a cable without a cable needle?

You can work small, simple cables without a cable needle. This is not recommended for cables that require moving more than 3 stitches or those that require moving more than one set of stitches. Here's how to work a simple 4-stitch cable:

4

1. Work up to the 4 cable stitches and slip them purlwise from the left needle to the right needle.

2. Insert the left needle tip from left to right into the front of the first 2 stitches slipped.

3. Carefully slide the right needle out of all 4 cable stitches, leaving the first 2 stitches originally slipped on the left needle and leaving the third and fourth stitches loose at the back of your work.

4. Carefully re-insert the right needle into the third and fourth stitches.

5. Slip the third and fourth stitches onto the left needle tip. The first 2 stitches are now crossed over in front of the third and fourth stitches.

6. Knit across the 4 cable stitches and then across the rest of the row.

WAVE CABLE (10-STITCH PANEL)

This cable is similar to the simple cables you made earlier, except that you perform both the front cross and back cross in the same cable.

1. Row 1 (RS): P2, k6, p2.

2. Row 2 (WS): K2, p6, k2.

3. Row 3 (cable row): P2, slip the next 3 sts to a cable needle and hold at back, knit the next 3 sts from the left needle, knit the 3 sts from the cable needle, p2.

4. Row 4: Rep row 2.

5. Rows 5–8: Rep rows 1 and 2 twice.

6. Row 9 (cable row): P2, slip the next 3 sts to a cable needle and hold at front, knit the next 3 sts from the left needle, knit the 3 sts from the cable needle, p2.

7. Rows 10 and 12: Rep row 2.

8. Row 11: Rep row 1.

9. Rep rows 1–12 for wave cable.

DOUBLE CABLE (12-STITCH PANEL)

You can make this cable so that it looks like it's pointing upward (shown on the left) or downward (shown on the right). Here's how to make a downward-pointing cable:

1. Row 1 (RS): P2, k8, p2.

2. Row 2 (WS): K2, p8, k2.

3. Row 3 (cable row): P2, slip the next 2 sts to a cable needle and hold at front, knit the next 2 sts from the left needle, knit the 2 sts from the cable needle; slip the next 2 sts to a cable needle and hold at back, knit the next 2 sts from the left needle, k2 sts from the cable needle; p2.

4. Row 4: Rep row 2.

5. Rows 5–8: Rep rows 1 and 2 twice.

6. Rep rows 1–8 for double cable.

NOTE: To make the cable point upward, work all rows the same way, except on row 3 reverse the order of the front and back crosses.

Upward cable   Downward cable

HONEYCOMB CABLE (20-STITCH PANEL)

You can widen this interesting cable by adding multiples of 8 stitches.

1 Row 1 (RS—cable row): P2, *slip the next 2 sts to a cable needle and hold at back, knit the next 2 sts from the left needle, knit the 2 sts from the cable needle; slip the next 2 sts to a cable needle and hold at front, knit the next 2 sts from the left needle, knit the 2 sts from the cable needle; rep from * to last 2 sts, p2.

2 Rows 2, 4, 6, and 8 (WS): K2, p16, k2.

3 Rows 3 and 7: P2, k16, p2.

4 Row 5 (cable row): P2, *slip the next 2 sts to a cable needle and hold at front, knit the next 2 sts from the left needle, knit the 2 sts from the cable needle; slip the next 2 sts to a cable needle and hold at back, knit the next 2 sts from the left needle, knit the 2 sts from the cable needle; rep from * to last 2 sts, p2.

5 Rep rows 1–8 for honeycomb cable.

GARTER AND STOCKINETTE STITCH CABLE (14-STITCH PANEL)

Here's a pretty cable that you don't see very often.

1 Row 1 (RS): P2, k10, p2.

2 Row 2 (WS): K2, p5, k7.

3 Rows 3–6: Rep rows 1 and 2 twice.

4 Row 7 (cable row): P2, slip the next 5 sts to a cable needle and hold at back, knit the next 5 sts from the left needle, knit sts from the cable needle, p2.

5 Row 8: K7, p5, k2.

6 Row 9: Rep row 1.

7 Rows 10–16: Rep rows 8 and 9 three more times; then rep row 8 once more.

8 Row 17 (cable row): Rep row 7.

9 Rows 18–20: Rep row 2 once; then rep rows 1 and 2 once more.

10 Rep rows 1–20 for garter and stockinette stitch cable.

H ere are a few cables that integrate bobbles, knots, or textured stitches into their structure. Most of these combinations take on an embossed, or sculptural, quality, which is what is so fascinating about knitting with cables.

Fancy Cable Stitches

KNOTTED CABLE (10-STITCH PANEL)

This cable involves moving the cable needle from front to back and working the held stitches in stages.

1. Rows 1, 5, 7, and 9 (RS): P2, k2, p2, k2, p2.

2. Rows 2, 4, 6, and 8, and 10 (WS): P4, k2, p4.

3. Row 3 (cable row): P2, slip the next 4 sts to a cable needle and hold at the front, knit the next 2 sts from the left needle; then slip 2 sts from the cable needle back to the left needle. Bring the cable needle (with the remaining 2 sts on it) to the back, purl the 2 sts that were moved back to the left needle; knit the 2 sts from the cable needle, p2.

4. Rep rows 1–10 for knotted cable.

BOBBLE CABLE (13-STITCH PANEL)

This cable uses the following techniques:

mb (make bobble): For a refresher on how to make a bobble, see page 114.

3-st right purl cable: Slip the next st to a cable needle and hold at back, k2 from the left needle, p1 from the cable needle.

3-st left purl cable: Slip the next 2 sts to a cable needle and hold at front, p1 from the left needle, k2 from the cable needle.

1 Row 1 (RS—cable row): P3, 3-st right purl cable, p1, 3-st left purl cable, p3.

2 Rows 2 and 8 (WS): K3, p2, k3, p2, k3.

3 Row 3 (cable row): P2, 3-st right purl cable, p3, 3-st left purl cable, p2.

4 Rows 4 and 6: K2, p2, k5, p2, k2.

5 Row 5 (bobble row): P2, k2, p2, mb, p2, k2, p2.

6 Row 7 (cable row): P2, 3-st left purl cable, p3, 3-st right purl cable, p2.

7 Row 9 (cable row): P3, 3-st left purl cable, p1, 3-st right purl cable, p3.

8 Rows 10 and 12: K4, p5, k4.

9 Row 11 (cable row): P4, slip the next 3 sts to a cable needle and hold at back, knit the next 2 sts from the left needle, then p1, k2 from the cable needle, p4.

10 Rep rows 1–12 for bobble cable.

RIBBED CABLE (15-STITCH PANEL)

This interesting cable is worked in k1, p1 ribbing.

1 Row 1 (RS): P2, k1, *p1, k1; rep from * four times to last 2 sts, p2.

2 Row 2 (WS): K2, purl into back of next st, *k1, purl into back of next st; rep from * four times to last 2 sts, k2.

3 Row 3 (cable row): P2, slip the next 6 sts to a cable needle and hold at back, k1, [p1, k1] twice from the left needle, then [p1, k1] three times from the cable needle; p2.

4 Row 4: Rep row 2.

5 Rows 5–14: Rep rows 1 and 2 five times.

6 Rep rows 1–14 for ribbed cable.

WISHBONE AND SEED STITCH CABLE (12-STITCH PANEL)
This delicate cable looks complicated but is easy to do.

1. Row 1 (RS—cable row): P2, slip the next 3 sts to a cable needle and hold at back, k1, [p1, k1, p1] from the cable needle; slip the next st to a cable needle and hold at front, [k1, p1, k1], k1 from the cable needle; p2.

2. Rows 2, 4, and 6 (WS): K2, *p1, k1; rep from * twice, p2, k2.

3. Rows 3 and 5: P2, *k1, p1; rep from * twice, k2, p2.

4. Row 7: P2, k1, p1, k3, p1, k2, p2.

5. Row 8: K2, p1, k1, p3, k1, p2, k2.

6. Rep rows 1–8 for wishbone and seed stitch cable.

HOLLOW OAK CABLE (15-STITCH PANEL)
This beautiful cable uses the following techniques:

mb (make bobble): For a refresher on how to make a bobble, see page 114.

3-st right purl cable: Slip the next st to a cable needle and hold at back, k2 from the left needle, p1 from the cable needle.

3-st left purl cable: Slip the next 2 sts to a cable needle and hold at front, p1 from the left needle, k2 from the cable needle.

1. Rows 1 and 5 (RS—bobble row): P5, k2, mb, k2, p5.

2. Rows 2, 4, 6, and 20 (WS): K5, p5, k5.

3. Row 3 (bobble row): P5, mb, k3, mb, p5.

4. Row 7 (cable row): P4, 3-st right purl cable, p1, 3-st left purl cable, p4.

5. Row 8: K4, p2, k1, p1, k1, p2, k4.

6. Row 9 (cable row): P3, 3-st right purl cable, k1, p1, k1, 3-st left purl cable, p3.

7. Row 10: K3, p3, k1, p1, k1, p3, k3.

8. Row 11 (cable row): P2, 3-st right purl cable, [p1, k1] twice, p1, 3-st left purl cable, p2.

9. Row 12: K2, p2, [k1, p1] three times, k1, p2, k2.

10. Row 13: P2, k3, [p1, k1] twice, p1, k3, p2.

11. Rows 14, 16, and 18: Rep rows 12, 10, and 8, respectively.

12. Row 15 (cable row): P2, 3-st left purl cable, [p1, k1] twice, p1, 3-st right purl cable, p2.

13. Row 17 (cable row): P3, 3-st left purl cable, k1, p1, k1, 3-st right purl cable, p3.

14. Row 19 (cable row): P4, 3-st left purl cable, p1, 3-st right purl cable, p4.

15. Rep rows 1–20 for hollow oak cable.

CHAPTER 9

Openwork

Remember the yarn over stitch from Chapter 4? That simple act of bringing the yarn over the needle to create a new stitch—and at the same time a hole—can create beautiful and elaborate lace and openwork patterns in your knitting.

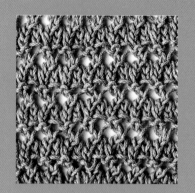

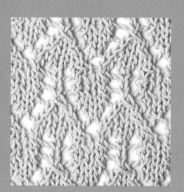

Learn Drop Stitch and Yarn Over Patterns

Most drop stitch patterns involve performing a yarn over two or more times in the same place across a row. When you work the next row, you knit across, dropping the yarn overs from the needle; this results in a band of meshlike vertical strands between regular rows. Yarn over patterns employ yarn overs in conjunction with decreases in various configurations, resulting in a broad range of openwork fabrics.

Drop Stitch Patterns

DROP STITCH GARTER PATTERN

This easy drop stitch pattern makes wonderful scarves, throws, and shawls. You can work it on any number of stitches.

1 Row 1 (RS): Knit.

2 Row 2 (WS): Knit.

3 Row 3: K1, *yo twice, k1; rep from * to end of row.

4 Row 4: Knit across, dropping the yo loops as you go.

5 Rep rows 1–4 for drop stitch garter pattern.

SEAFOAM PATTERN

This charming drop stitch pattern is great for scarves, wraps, shawls, and baby blankets. You work it on a multiple of 10 stitches plus 6.

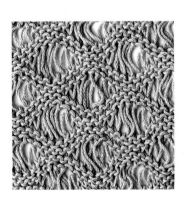

1 Row 1 (RS): Knit.

2 Row 2 (WS): Knit.

3 Row 3: K6, *yo twice, k1, yo three times, k1, yo four times, k1, yo three times, k1, yo twice, k6; rep from * to end of row.

4 Rows 4 and 8: Knit across, dropping the yo loops as you go.

5 Rows 5 and 6: Knit.

6 Row 7: K1, *yo twice, k1, yo three times, k1, yo four times, k1, yo three times, k1, yo twice, k6; rep from * across, but end last rep with k1.

7 Rep rows 1–8 for seafoam pattern.

Yarn Over Patterns

YARN OVER STRIPE PATTERN

This easy openwork pattern repeats as a horizontal stripe. You work it on an even number of stitches. Your stitch count will increase on row 1 and decrease on row 3.

1. Row 1 (RS): K1, *yo, k1; rep from * to last st, k1.

2. Row 2 (WS): K1, purl across to last st, k1.

3. Row 3: K1, *k2tog; rep from * to last st, k1.

4. Rows 4 and 5: K1, *yo, k2tog; rep from * to last st, k1.

5. Row 6: Knit.

6. Rep rows 1–6 for yarn over stripe pattern.

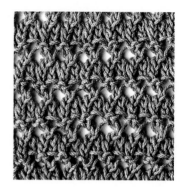

MESH PATTERN

This easy and versatile pattern combines a yarn over with an skp (slip 1, knit 1, pass slipped stitch over). (For a refresher on skp, see page 68.) It looks great in both fine and bulky yarns. You work it on an even number of stitches.

1. Row 1 (RS): K1, *yo, skp; rep from * to last st, k1.

2. Row 2 (WS): Rep row 1.

3. Rep rows 1 and 2 for mesh pattern.

BRIOCHE HONEYCOMB PATTERN

Brioche patterns combine yarn overs with slipped stitches and knit (or purl) 2 togethers. The result is usually a loose but 3-dimensional fabric. Going up a needle size gives this pattern a nice, soft drape. You work it on an even number of stitches.

1. Row 1 (WS): *Yo, slip 1 with yarn at back, k1; rep from * to end of row.

2. Row 2 (RS): *K1, k2tog (these will be the slipped st and the yo from row 1); rep from * to end of row.

3. Row 3: K1, *yo, slip 1 with yarn at back, k1; rep from * to last st, k1.

4. Row 4: K2, *k2tog, k1; rep from * to end of row.

5. Rep rows 1–4 for brioche honeycomb pattern.

Experiment with Eyelet Patterns

*E*yelets are the little holes that you create by combining a yarn over with a decrease. Eyelet patterns usually have more knitted fabric between the holes than lace patterns, and they are therefore less open. Eyelet patterns generally add a delicate touch, suitable for baby clothes, elegant spring sweaters, or little girls' dresses.

Eyelet Patterns

CELL STITCH

This is an easy and very open eyelet pattern. It makes great scarves and throws. Note that the first row is a wrong-side row. You work this pattern on a multiple of 3 stitches.

1 Rows 1 and 3 (WS): Purl.

2 Row 2 (RS): K2, *k2tog, yo, k1; rep from * to last st, k1.

3 Row 4: K2, *yo, k1, k2tog; rep from * to last st, k1.

4 Rep rows 1–4 for cell stitch.

EYELET CHEVRONS

This pattern uses an skp (slip 1, knit 1, pass slipped stitch over). You work it on a multiple of 9 stitches.

1 Row 1 (RS): *K4, yo, skp, k3; rep from * to end of row.

2 Rows 2, 4, 6, and 8 (WS): Purl.

3 Row 3: *K2, k2tog, yo, k1, yo, skp, k2; rep from * to end of row.

4 Row 5: *K1, k2tog, yo, k3, yo, skp, k1; rep from * to end of row.

5 Row 7: *K2tog, yo, k5, yo, skp; rep from * to end of row.

6 Rep rows 1–8 for eyelet chevrons.

FALLING RAIN PATTERN

This eyelet pattern is worked on a background of reverse stockinette stitch. You work it on a multiple of 6 stitches.

1. Row 1 (RS): *P4, yo, p2tog; rep from * to end of row.

2. Rows 2, 4, and 6 (WS): K1, *p1, k5; rep from * to last 5 sts, p1, k4.

3. Rows 3 and 5: P4, *k1, p5; rep from * to last 2 sts, k1, p1.

4. Row 7: P1, *yo, p2tog, p4; rep from * to last 5 sts, yo, p2tog, p3.

5. Rows 8, 10, and 12: K4, *p1, k5; rep from * to last 2 sts, p1, k1.

6. Rows 9 and 11: P1, *k1, p5; rep from * to last 5 sts, k1, p4.

7. Rep rows 1–12 for falling rain pattern.

KNOTTED EYELETS

This pattern is easy to work, and the result is a fancy textured stitch that looks great for babies', girls', and women's knits. You work this pattern on a multiple of 3 stitches.

1. Row 1 (RS): K2, *yo, k3, pass the first of these 3 knit sts over last 2 sts just worked; rep from * to last st, k1.

2. Rows 2 and 4 (WS): Purl.

3. Row 3: K1, *k3 pass the first of these 3 knit sts over last 2 sts just worked, yo; rep from * to last 2 sts, k2.

4. Rep rows 1–4 for knotted eyelets.

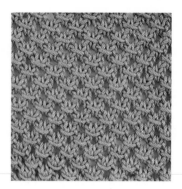

SNOWFLAKE BAND

This works well as a decorative border along a hem or cuff, or it can be repeated as an allover pattern. It uses a double vertical decrease, s2kp (see page 71). You work this pattern on a multiple of 8 sts, plus 5.

1. Row 1 (WS): Knit.

2. Rows 2 and 10 (RS): Knit.

3. Rows 3, 5, 7, and 9: Purl.

4. Rows 4 and 8: K4, *k2tog, yo, k1, yo, k2tog, k3; rep from * to last st, k1.

5. Row 6: K5, *yo, s2kp, yo, k5; rep from * to end of row.

6. Rep rows 1–10 for snowflake band.

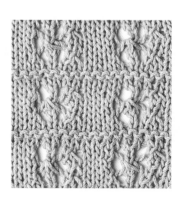

Work with Lace Patterns

Lace patterns, like eyelet patterns, are generally somewhat dainty and elegant. Lace appears in all kinds of designs—fancy sweaters, shawls, throws, tablecloths, and as decorative borders. It's a wonder to watch your pattern develop row by row.

Lace Patterns

LACE RIB

This pattern uses the ssk decrease (slip, slip, knit). (For a refresher on ssk, see page 67.) Also called *faggoting*, this lace is worked on a multiple of 3 stitches plus 1.

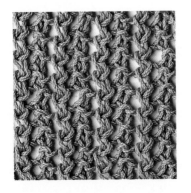

1. Row 1 (RS): K1, *yo, ssk, k1; rep from * to end of row.

2. Row 2 (WS): K1, *yo, p2tog, k1; rep from * to end of row.

3. Rep rows 1 and 2 for lace rib.

LACE LEAF PANEL

This lovely panel works well as an accent. Try it on throws or centered on sleeves. It begins and ends with 9 sts, but your stitch count will vary in between.

1. Row 1 (RS): P3, [k1, yo] twice, k1, p3.

2. Rows 2 and 8 (WS): K3, p5, k3.

3. Row 3: P3, k2, yo, k1, yo, k2, p3.

4. Rows 4 and 6: K3, p7, k3.

5. Row 5: P3, ssk, k1, [yo, k1] twice, k2tog, p3.

6. Row 7: P3, ssk, k3, k2tog, p3.

7. Row 9: P3, ssk, k1, k2tog, p3.

8. Rows 10 and 12: K3, p3, k3.

9. Row 11: P3, yo, slip 2 tog knitwise, k1, pass the 2 slipped sts tog over, yo, p3.

10. Rep rows 1–12 for lace leaf panel.

DIAGONAL LACE

This simple lace is lovely for baby clothes and summer cardigans. This pattern uses the ssk decrease (slip, slip, knit). You work this pattern on a multiple of 6 stitches.

1. Row 1 (RS): *K1, yo, ssk; rep from * to end of row.

2. Rows 2, 4, and 6 (WS): Purl.

3. Row 3: *K2, yo, ssk, k2; rep from * to end of row.

4. Row 5: *K3, yo, ssk, k1; rep from * to end of row.

5. Rep rows 1–6 for diagonal lace.

ARROWHEAD LACE

This lace pattern is easy to follow and works well in a shawl or throw. You work it on a multiple of 6 stitches plus 1.

1. Row 1 and all other odd-numbered rows (WS): Purl.

2. Row 2 (RS): K3, *yo, ssk, k4; rep from * to last 4 sts, yo, ssk, k2.

3. Row 4: K1, *k2tog, yo, k1, yo, ssk, k1; rep from * to end of row.

4. Row 6: K2tog, yo, *k3, yo, slip 1, k2tog, psso, yo; rep from * to last 5 sts, k3, yo, ssk.

5. Rows 8 and 10: K1, *yo, ssk, k1, k2tog, yo, k1; rep from * to end of row.

6. Rep rows 1–10 for arrowhead lace.

TRIANGLE LACE

This very textured lace pattern is great for baby blankets, throws, and scarves. You work it over an odd number of stitches.

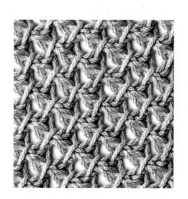

1. Row 1 (RS): K1, *yo, slip 1, k1, yo, pass the slipped st over the k st and the yo over; rep from * to end of row.

2. Row 2 (WS): *P2, drop the yo from the previous row; rep from * to last st, p1.

3. Row 3: K2, *yo, slip 1, k1, yo, pass the slipped st over the k st and the yo; rep from * to last st, k1.

4. Row 4: P3, *drop the yo from the previous row, p2; rep from * to end of row.

5. Rep rows 1–4 for triangle lace.

CHAPTER 10

Color Knitting

So far you have learned a lot about how to use knit and purl stitches to create patterns. Now it's time to think about using color to create beautiful, vibrant designs. There are several methods of using color in knitting: simple horizontal striping; Fair Isle knitting, which involves the stranding of two colors in one row; and intarsia knitting, which involves the use of bobbins to create isolated blocks of color, to name a few.

A Look at Color

One of the many joys of knitting is choosing colors. It's easy to choose one color of yarn; but choosing colors that work well together can be challenging. Remember that you'll be spending many hours knitting in the scheme you choose, so you want to use colors that complement each other and colors that you like—whether they be different shades of green or high-contrast opposites. Here are a few color concepts to assist you in making these choices.

Choosing Colors That Work Well Together

Sometimes it's hard to choose colors that go well together. You may find yourself drawn to the same color combinations over and over again and decide you need a nudge in a new direction; or perhaps the color combination you would choose is not available in a particular yarn. You can use a color wheel like this one to help you in your choice. To use it, you simply choose a starting color. Then you aim one of the arrows or points of the triangles or rectangles to the starting color and see what colors the color selector recommends. A color wheel might help you find a color combination you never would have thought of on your own.

CHOOSING A MONOCHROMATIC COLOR SCHEME
One easy way to select colors that work well together—and you don't need a color wheel for this—is to choose monochromatic colors. A monochromatic scheme uses variations of the same color, like the swatch here, which is a soothing, quiet combination of blue colors.

CHOOSING AN ANALOGOUS COLOR SCHEME

Another easy color option is an analogous color scheme—that is, a scheme made up of three to five colors that are adjacent on the color wheel. The result of this type of combination is generally harmonious and peaceful, as in the swatch shown here. Say, for example, you have one color of yarn you know you want to use, and you would like to choose some colors to go with it. You can match your yarn to its corresponding color on the wheel and then choose yarns that match the adjacent colors on either side.

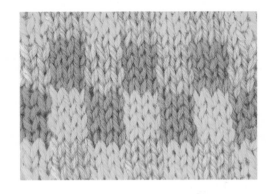

CHOOSING A COMPLEMENTARY COLOR SCHEME

A complementary color scheme is made up of two colors that are opposites on the color wheel. This high-contrast combination is bold and appealing; however, sometimes bright opposites placed together vibrate so much that they're hard to look at. The swatch here is knit in the complements violet and yellow; blue and orange are also complements, as are red and green.

CHOOSING A TRIADIC COLOR SCHEME

The color wheel is made up of 12 color segments. When you choose 3 colors that are equidistant from one another on the wheel, you have selected a triadic color scheme. There are four triadic color schemes: the primary triad, made up of red, yellow, and blue; the secondary triad, made up of orange, green, and violet; and two tertiary triads, one made up of red-orange, yellow-green, and blue-violet and the other made up of red-violet, yellow-orange, and blue-green. The primary triadic color scheme conveys a childlike simplicity and can be a little sterile, while secondary and tertiary triadic schemes are rich, subtle, and complex. The swatch shown here is made up of red, yellow, and blue.

CHOOSING A SPLIT COMPLEMENTARY COLOR SCHEME

This swatch is an example of a split complementary color scheme. This type of color scheme is made up of three colors: a starting color and the two colors on either side of its complement. For example, if you had violet yarn and wanted to try a split complementary color combination, you would choose a ball of yellowish green and a ball of orange to go with it because those are the two colors on either side of yellow—violet's complement.

CHOOSING A TETRADIC COLOR SCHEME

Things begin to get complicated when you work with a tetradic color scheme. Usually a daring color statement, a tetradic color scheme is made up of two sets of complementary colors. For example, a tetradic color scheme might be made up of red, green, orange, and blue because red and green are complements, as are orange and blue. Experiment with various amounts of each of these colors, as four competing opposites can be difficult to look at all at once. Note how the swatch here is made up of more orange-red than the other colors.

EXPERIMENTING WITH COLOR

After you've pored over the color wheel, you can knit up test swatches in different color combinations to see how they actually work. This swatch uses the same stitch pattern in three assorted combinations. It's remarkable how dissimilar the same design can look in different color combinations.

Make Horizontal Stripes

Working horizontal stripes is the easiest way to combine more than one color in your knitting. If you know how to knit, purl, and change to a new ball of yarn, then you can knit horizontal stripes. Stripe patterns are easiest to knit if you use an even number of rows for each stripe. This way, changing colors always occurs at the same edge, enabling you to carry the yarn up the side of your work, and ultimately saving you the trouble of weaving in a lot of ends later.

How to Make Horizontal Stripes in Stockinette

① To make a stripe in a contrast color, work as many rows as you want the first stripe to be. At the beginning of the next row, drop the old yarn and knit or purl across the row in the new yarn, depending on which side you are on.

② Carry the yarns up the side by twisting the first yarn around the second yarn at the edge of every other row. (If the stripes are only two rows each, this isn't necessary.)

How to Make Horizontal Stripes in Ribbing

1 Using the desired ribbing pattern, work as many rows as you want the first stripe to be, ending with a wrong side row.

2 At the beginning of the next row, drop the old yarn and knit all stitches in the new color.

If you work the color change row in the ribbing pattern, the color break will not look tidy. This striped ribbing illustrates the result of working the color change row in the rib pattern. Little nubs of the old color appear along the color break, producing an uneven line.

One-Row Stripes in Two Colors

You can work one-row stockinette stitch stripes without having to cut yarn at the end of every row. You use a circular needle, but you work flat.

1. Using your first color, cast on the sts and knit the row.

2. Push the sts back to the end of the needle where you began and join the second color, ready to begin another right side (knit) row. Knit the row in the second color.

3. Now both yarns are at the same end, ready to turn and work a wrong side (purl) row. Purl the row in the first color.

4. Push the sts back to the end of the needle where you began the wrong side row and purl the row in the second color. You now have four single stripes in two colors.

5. Repeat the last four rows for the single-row stripes.

Work Seamless Stripes in the Round

Stripes with flat knitting is a snap, but have you tried knitting stripes in the round? Because circular knitting is actually knitting a spiral, lining up stripes at the beginning and end of each new round can be tricky. You end up with a little stair step where the old round ends and the new round begins.

Some knitters accept the stair step as a matter of course. However, if you find this little imperfection undesirable, you can try the following to diminish the stair step.

How to Work Seamless Stripes in the Round

1 After you finish the first color stripe, change to the new color at the beginning of the round and knit one round.

2 Before knitting the first stitch of the next round (the second round of the new color), lift the stitch below the first stitch (in the old color) and put it onto the left needle ahead of the first stitch of the next round.

3 Knit the 2 stitches together and complete the round as usual.

4 Repeat steps 1–3.

You can work ribbing in two colors using vertical stripes, called *corrugated ribbing*. You see corrugated ribbing on the cuffs and hems of Scandinavian sweaters. It's a lively accent that creates a firm edging that looks like ribbing but isn't as stretchy.

The corrugated ribbing demonstrated here is a 2 × 2 rib.

How to Work Corrugated Ribbing

To begin, you need two colors of the same yarn, which will be called color A and color B, and needles in the appropriate size for the yarn. To practice, use color A to cast on a number of stitches that is divisible by 4—20 stitches is a good number. Join color B so that you're ready to use both colors for the first rib row.

1 Row 1 (RS): *K2 in color B, bring color A under color B to the front and p2, bring color A to the back; rep from * to end, always bringing the new color under the old color before working it.

2 Row 2 (WS): *Bring color A to the back and k2 in color A, return color A to the front of work, bring color B over the top of color A and with color B in front, p2; rep from * to end.

3 Repeat rows 1 and 2 for corrugated ribbing.

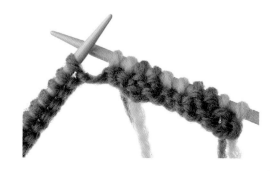

Learn Fair Isle Knitting

air Isle knitting is a method of knitting that probably originated in Fair Isle, one of the smallest of the Shetland Islands, off northern Scotland. It involves working with two colors across a row, carrying both yarns across the back. The challenge in Fair Isle knitting is maintaining tension: If the yarns stranded along the back are too tight, your knitting will pucker and have no elasticity; if they are too loose, your stitches will look uneven.

One-Handed Stranding

When color knitting, if there are no more than 4 stitches between color changes, you can do *one-handed stranding*—knitting your usual way but changing colors based on the pattern.

KNIT SIDE

To avoid puckering, you need to keep the stitches on the right needle spread apart so you can strand a sufficient length of the non-working yarn across the back.

1 Work to the point in the row where you need to change colors. Let go of yarn A, pick up yarn B and bring it above and over yarn A, and knit the correct number of stitches in yarn B.

2 Work to the point in the row where you need to change colors again. Let go of yarn B, pick up yarn A and bring it underneath yarn B, and knit until the next color shift.

3 Repeat steps 1 and 2, taking care to keep yarn A underneath yarn B when changing colors.

NOTE: Always carry both yarns to the end of the row because the color pattern may call for the other color to begin the next row.

PURL SIDE

1 Work to the point in the row where you need to change colors. Let go of yarn A, pick up yarn B and bring it above and over yarn A, and purl the correct number of stitches in yarn B.

2 When you reach the point in the row where you need to change colors again, let go of yarn B, pick up yarn A and bring it underneath yarn B, and purl until the next color shift.

3 Repeat steps 1 and 2, taking care to keep yarn A underneath yarn B when changing colors.

NOTE: Always carry both yarns to the end of the row because the color pattern may call for the other color to begin the next row.

FAQ

How can I keep yarns from tangling when color knitting?

Always keep the same yarn above and the same yarn below when changing colors. Also, don't twist yarns when you switch sides. You can keep each yarn in its own container to keep them from getting tangled. If the yarns do get snarled, just move the containers around to correct the problem.

Two-Handed Stranding

Two-handed stranding is more efficient than one-handed stranding and results in an effortlessly neater back. It requires you to hold one color in each hand, working the English method and the Continental method at the same time to alternate colors without stopping. When you work more than 4 stitches of one color successively, you have to weave or twist the color not in use in and out of the backs of those stitches.

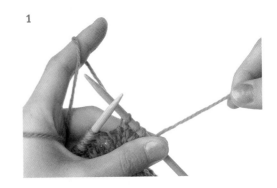

KNIT SIDE

Two-handed stranding is an excellent way to work Fair Isle knitting. To practice knitting with both hands at the same time, try a very easy two-color pattern first so you can focus on technique.

1. Hold yarn A in your right hand, English style (see page 22), and yarn B in your left hand, Continental style (see page 23).

2. Knit with yarn A in your right hand, holding it above yarn B, to the point in the row where you need to change colors.

3. Knit with your left hand using yarn B, which should automatically come from underneath yarn A.

4. Repeat steps 1–3 across the row.

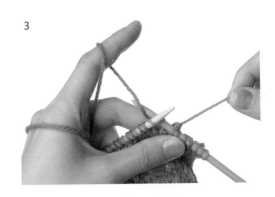

NOTE: Always carry both yarns to the end of the row because the color pattern may call for the other color to begin the next row.

PURL SIDE

❶ Hold yarn A in your right hand, English style, and yarn B in your left hand, Continental style.

❷ Purl with yarn A in your right hand, holding it above yarn B, to the point in the row where you need to change colors.

❸ Purl with your left hand using yarn B, which should automatically come from underneath yarn A.

❹ Repeat steps 1–3 across the row.

NOTE: Always carry both yarns to the end of the row because the color pattern may call for the other color to begin the next row.

FAQ

When I knit Fair Isle patterns, my knitting doesn't pucker, but I don't get the same gauge as I do with stockinette stitch using the same yarn on the same size needles. I want to make a sweater that combines both techniques, but I'm worried that the gauge will not be uniform. Is there something I can do to compensate?

Fair Isle knitting can affect gauge. Usually, the row gauge is closer to or equal to the stitch gauge because Fair Isle stitches have a more square appearance. It is not uncommon for the stitch gauge to be slightly compressed. If you're working on a fabric that combines large blocks of non–Fair Isle with segments of Fair Isle, you might try working the Fair Isle section in needles one size larger. You can try working up a gauge sample that combines the stitches used to see if this works for you.

Weave Yarns in Color Knitting

When you're working with a color pattern in which there are more than 4 stitches between color changes or more than two colors per row, you need to carry the non-working yarn along the back by weaving it in and out of the backs of every few stitches made in the working yarn. How you do this depends on whether you're knitting or purling, as well as on which hand is holding the working yarn and which is holding the weaving yarn.

Weaving In, Knit Side: Working Yarn Right, Weaving Yarn Left

Hold yarn A, the working yarn, in your right hand, English style, and yarn B, the yarn that will be woven in back, in your left hand, Continental style.

① Insert the right needle into the next stitch on the left needle. Move your finger to bring yarn B from back to front and lay it against the tip of the right needle. Wrap yarn A as usual to prepare to knit the stitch.

② Knit the stitch.

③ Move your finger to bring yarn B away from the needles as usual. When you knit the next stitch, yarn B gets caught under the horizontal bar between this new stitch and the last stitch.

Weaving In, Knit Side: Working Yarn Left, Weaving Yarn Right

Hold yarn A, the weaving yarn, in your right hand, English style, and yarn B, the working yarn, in your left hand, Continental style.

1 Insert the right needle into the next stitch on the left needle. Wrap yarn A around the right needle as you would to knit; then wrap yarn B around the right needle as you would to knit.

2 Bring yarn A back off the right needle to where it came from, leaving yarn B wrapped around the right needle, ready to be knit.

3 Knit the stitch.

Weaving In, Purl Side: Working Yarn Right, Weaving Yarn Left

Hold yarn A, the working yarn, in your right hand, English style, and yarn B, the yarn that will be woven in back, in your left hand, Continental style.

1 Insert the right needle into the next stitch as if to purl. Move your finger to bring yarn B from front to back and lay it against the tip of the right needle. Wrap yarn A as usual to prepare to purl the stitch.

2 Purl the stitch.

3 Before purling the next stitch, bring yarn B down and away from the needles as shown (a); wrap yarn A as usual and then purl the stitch (b).

3a

3b

Weaving In, Purl Side: Working Yarn Left, Weaving Yarn Right

Hold yarn A, the weaving yarn, in your right hand, English style, and yarn B, the working yarn, in your left hand, Continental style.

1 Insert the right needle into the next stitch as if to purl. Bring yarn A under the right needle from front to back; then lay yarn B over the tip of the right needle from front to back.

2 Bring yarn A back to the front—to where it came from (it will be hooked around yarn B)—and then draw yarn B through to purl the stitch.

3 Hold yarn A down away from the needles and purl another stitch using yarn B.

Experiment with a Few Simple Color Patterns

Here are a few simple color knitting patterns that you can try. Most of them employ only two colors so that you can get a feel for Fair Isle without getting overwhelmed by too many yarn ends and color symbols. Each pattern is illustrated with a stitch pattern chart and a companion color key. See page 100 for information on reading charts.

Color Patterns

COLOR PATTERN 1: TWO COLORS

This 6-stitch repeat can be used as a border when worked over just four rows, or it can be used as a stripe pattern if repeated every six rows.

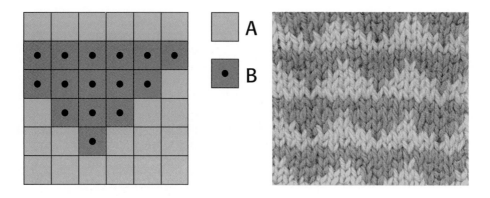

COLOR PATTERN 2: TWO COLORS

This 6-stitch, four-row repeat is an easy allover pattern.

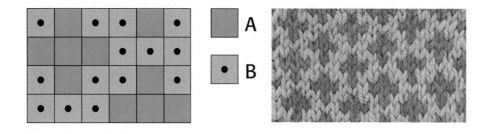

COLOR PATTERN 3: TWO COLORS

This 8-stitch border pattern works well at the hem or cuff of a Fair Isle sweater.

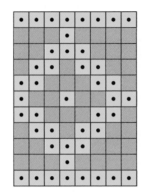

A
• B

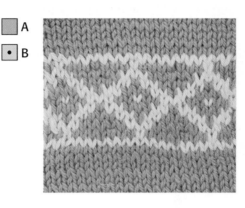

COLOR PATTERN 4: THREE COLORS

This 4-stitch repeat looks great worked over seven rows along a border.

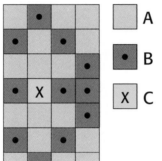

A
• B
X C

COLOR PATTERN 5: TWO COLORS

This 4-stitch, 12-row repeat creates a very modern-looking allover pattern.

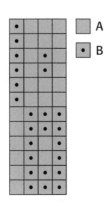

A
• B

Try Intarsia

*I*ntarsia, or *bobbin knitting*, is a form of color knitting. Unlike Fair Isle—where colors are worked and carried across rows in a repetitive pattern—with intarsia you can scatter isolated blocks of color over your knitting or put one large motif on a background of another color. You knit each motif using a separate ball or bobbin of yarn. When changing colors, you twist yarns together on the wrong side to avoid having holes on the right side.

Intarsia with Two Colors

Before beginning an intarsia project, wind your main and contrast colors onto two or three bobbins for each color.

❶ On the right side, knit to the place where the intarsia motif is to begin, drop the main color yarn, and get ready to knit with the contrast color yarn.

NOTE: To help maintain even tension, tie the new yarn to the old yarn before knitting the first stitch of the new color. You can untie it and secure the loose end later. Leave at least a 6-inch tail on the new yarn.

❷ Knit as many stitches in the contrast color as your pattern calls for.

③ Drop the contrast color and begin knitting from a new bobbin of your main color. Work to the end of the right side row.

NOTE: When changing colors on the right side, pick up the new yarn from underneath the old yarn to twist the yarns together on the back. This prevents gaps where the two colors meet.

④ On the wrong side, purl using the main color until you reach the point where the color change should occur.

⑤ Drop the main color, twist the yarns together by bringing the contrast color up from underneath the main color, and purl as many stitches in the contrast color as the pattern requires.

⑥ Drop the contrast color, twist the yarns together by picking up the main color from underneath the contrast color, and purl the next stitch. Continue as the pattern directs.

Work a Few Simple Intarsia Motifs

H ere are a few simple intarsia motifs that you can practice on or incorporate into your knitting. Before you begin, be sure to wind bobbins in the main color as well as the contrast colors for the motif.

Intarsia Motifs

INTARSIA HEART

This is an easy motif that adds a warm, homey touch to a knitted piece.

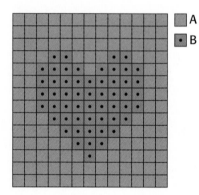

INTARSIA STAR

This star adds a fun accent to a rolled-brim hat or centered on the front of a pullover.

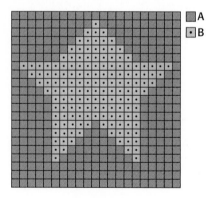

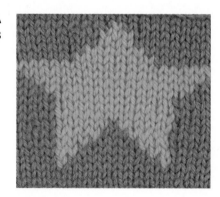

INTARSIA DUCK

This is a perfect motif for baby
sweaters and blankets.

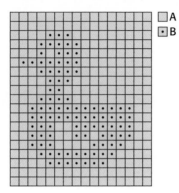

☐ A
⊡ B

INTARSIA BUTTERFLY

This motif can be embellished
with embroidery (see pages
207–208) for added color.

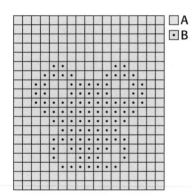

☐ A
⊡ B

INTARSIA FLOWER

This motif uses two contrast
colors. Like the star, it adds a
whimsical accent to a hat or
sweater.

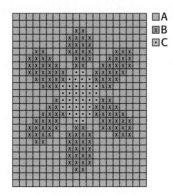

☐ A
☒ B
⊡ C

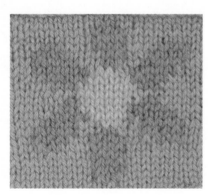

CHAPTER 11

Finishing Techniques

When you complete the knitting stage of a project, it's time to move on to finishing. *Finishing* involves weaving in all the loose ends hanging off your knitting, blocking your pieces to the correct measurements, and putting the project together by sewing seams. Although most knitters prefer knitting to finishing, mastering tidy finishing techniques will ensure that you are happy with your completed projects.

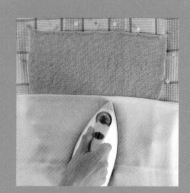

Weave In Ends

W eaving in ends is what you do to get rid of all the loose yarns dangling from your knitting. The instructions so far have said to leave ends no shorter than 6 inches. You need at least that length to weave in an end properly.

To weave in ends, you need a pair of scissors and a tapestry needle that is appropriate for the thickness of yarn you are using. You can weave in ends across the work or vertically up the side of the work.

How to Weave In Ends Up the Side

① With the wrong side facing, thread a tail of yarn through a tapestry needle.

② Bring the tapestry needle in and out from back to front up the side of the knitting.

③ After you have woven in the end 2 to 3 inches, cut it close to the work, taking great care not to cut your knitting.

How to Weave In Ends Across the Back

1 With the wrong side facing, thread the tail of yarn through the tapestry needle.

2 Weave the tapestry needle in and out of the backs of the stitches in a straight diagonal line for 2 to 3 inches.

3 Weave the tapestry needle in and out of the backs of the stitches in the opposite direction, right next to the first diagonal line, for about 1 inch.

4 Cut the yarn end close to the work, taking great care not to cut your knitting.

NOTE: You can lightly stretch your knitting to pull the yarn end farther into the work to conceal it.

Block Your Knitting

Blocking is a wonderful fixer of imperfections. It involves moistening knitted pieces, shaping them to the correct measurements, and allowing them to dry so that they hold the proper shape.

To block a project, you need a padded surface that is big enough to lay your largest piece of knitting flat, a set of long, rustproof pins, and a measuring tape. For wet blocking, you need a clean spray bottle; for steam blocking, you need a steam iron or hand steamer.

Wet Blocking

Wet blocking involves wetting your knitted pieces thoroughly. You can wet the pieces by immersing them in a basin of water or you can pin them to their proper measurements first and then wet them with a spray bottle. Before wet blocking, read your ball band to ensure that washing in water is safe for your yarn. Wet blocking is best for wool blends, some synthetics, and hairy yarns like angora and mohair. It works wonders on textured and cable knits.

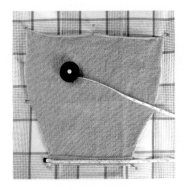

① Lay a knitted piece flat on a padded surface. Pin only at enough points to hold the piece straight for the time being.

② Measure the knitted piece to ensure that it has the dimensions that the pattern specifies. Adjust the pins to match the measurements.

NOTE: Do not stretch and pin ribbing at cuffs and hems unless the pattern indicates to do so. After ribbing is stretched and blocked, it is no longer elastic.

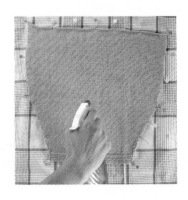

③ When the measurements are correct, pin the piece all around.

④ Wet the piece thoroughly with a spray bottle.

⑤ Allow the piece to dry; remove the pins.

⑥ Repeat steps 1–5 for all pieces of your project. Sew seams when all pieces are completely dry.

Steam Blocking

Steam blocking involves using a steam iron or hand steamer. You can get fast results with steam blocking because the drying time is shorter than with wet blocking. Again, you need to check your ball band's care instructions to ensure that it is safe to apply steam to your yarn and at what temperature. Steam blocking is best for wool, cotton, cashmere, and alpaca. The key to steam blocking is not to press the knitting with the iron but to run the iron lightly above the knitting to steam it. Lay a light cloth, such as a pillowcase, over the piece to be blocked; this will protect your work from the high heat and any potential staining.

1 Lay a knitted piece flat on a padded surface. Pin only at enough points to hold the piece straight for the time being. (See middle on the previous page.)

2 Measure the knitted piece to ensure that it has the dimensions that the pattern specifies. Adjust the pins as necessary to match the measurements and to make the piece even.

NOTE: Do not stretch and pin ribbing at cuffs and hems unless the pattern indicates to do so. After ribbing is stretched and blocked, it is no longer elastic.

3 When the measurements are correct, pin the piece all around.

4 Cover the piece with a light cloth. (You can dampen the cloth with a spray bottle, if desired.) Slowly and gently, run the iron over the entire piece, excluding ribbing, taking care not to press or distort the knitting.

5 Allow the piece to dry and then remove the pins.

6 Repeat steps 1–5 for all pieces of your project. Be sure that all the pieces are completely dry before sewing the seams.

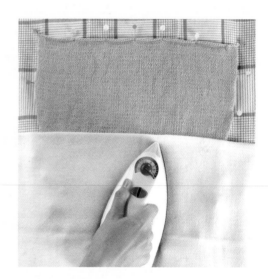

TIP

Pressing and Blocking Synthetic Yarns

Most synthetic yarns require cool pressing temperatures, so be sure to read the yarn label before choosing the iron setting.

Many novelty yarns—such as fuzzy, hairy, bumpy multi-colored yarns—are made of synthetic fibers. In general, you do not block these yarns; just knit and wear.

Sew Seams

There are numerous ways to sew seams. Some seams are best for shoulders, while others are preferable for vertical seams or certain stitch patterns. Taking time and care when sewing blocked pieces together is well worth the effort.

You sew seams with a tapestry needle and with the main color yarn used to knit the project. When knitting with novelty yarns, sew seams with a matching plied yarn that calls for the same care instructions as the main yarn.

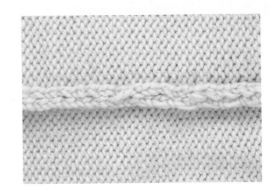

Invisible Horizontal Seam

This seam joins horizontal edges invisibly.

1. Thread a tapestry needle with enough yarn to sew the seam.

2. Line up the right sides of the bound-off edges. Insert the needle from the back through the middle of the first stitch of the lower piece, leaving a 6-inch tail.

3. Use the needle to pick up the two loops (the V) of the corresponding stitch on the upper piece. Pull the yarn through.

4. Bring the needle across the seam to the next stitch on the lower piece and use it to pick up the loops (the upside-down V), threading it through all the way.

5. Rep steps 3 and 4 across the seam, pulling the yarn lightly every couple stitches to neaten it.

6. Weave in the loose ends.

NOTE: A contrast color yarn was used for illustrative purposes. Be sure to sew your seams with the same yarn used to knit the pieces.

Backstitch Seam

You can use this firm seam almost anywhere in constructing a project. You work it with the right sides of the pieces facing each other, so that they are inside out. Work it about 1 stitch in from the edge.

1 Thread a tapestry needle with a long enough strand of yarn to sew the seam and leave a 6-inch tail.

2 Place the pieces together, with the right sides facing each other and the seam edge lined up. Secure the edge stitches by bringing the needle through both thicknesses from back to front at the right edge, 1 stitch down from the bound-off stitches. Do this twice and pull the yarn through.

3 Insert the needle through both thicknesses, from back to front, about 2 stitches to the left, and bring the yarn through.

4 Insert the needle from front to back, about 1 stitch in to the right, and pull the yarn through.

2–3

4

5 Bring the needle ahead 2 stitches to the left and insert it from back to front.

6 Repeat steps 4 and 5 across the seam until you reach the end, taking care to insert the needle at the same depth each time.

7 Weave in the loose ends.

NOTE: A contrast color yarn was used to sew the seam for illustrative purposes. Be sure to sew your seams with the same yarn used to knit the pieces.

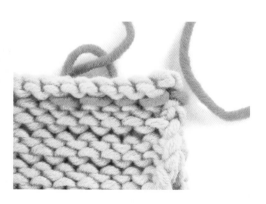

Invisible Vertical Seam

This seam works beautifully for sweater sides and under-arm seams. It lays flat and is invisible.

2

① Thread a tapestry needle with a long enough strand of yarn to sew your seam and leave a 6-inch tail.

② With the right sides up, line up the vertical edges exactly. Sew 1 stitch at the base of the seam to join the pieces: Insert the needle from back to front through the space between the first and second stitches on the lower-right corner of the left piece, pulling yarn through until only about 6 inches remains; insert the needle from front to back between the first and second stitches in the lower-left corner of the right piece; bring the needle back through the same spot on the left piece again. Pull the yarn through snugly.

③ Find the horizontal bar of yarn between the first and second stitches. Insert the needle under this horizontal bar, 1 stitch up from the joining stitch, on the right piece. Pull the yarn through.

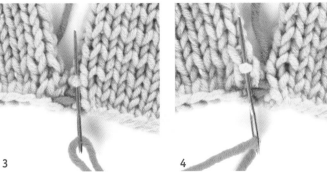

3

4

④ Insert the needle under the horizontal bar between the first and second stitches, 1 stitch up from the joining stitch, on the left piece. Pull the yarn through.

⑤ Insert the needle under the next horizontal bar up on the right side and then under the corresponding bar on the left side. Continue in this manner, alternating from side to side, to the end of the seam.

⑥ Weave in the loose ends.

NOTE: A contrast color yarn was used to sew the seam for illustrative purposes. Be sure to sew your seams with the same yarn used to knit the pieces.

5

Invisible Vertical-to-Horizontal Seam

This seam is excellent for joining a bound-off edge to a side edge, as in joining a sleeve cap to an armhole.

1. Thread a tapestry needle with a long enough strand of yarn to sew your seam and leave a 6-inch tail.

2. With the right sides facing, line up the bound-off edge and the side edge.

3. Insert the needle from back to front through the V of the first stitch on the right side of the lower piece, below the bound-off edge, and pull the yarn through until about 6 inches remain.

4. Insert the needle on the other side of the join—directly across from the same point on the vertical piece—under one of the bars between the first and second stitches on the horizontal piece. Pull the yarn through.

NOTE: Because you are matching rows to stitches in this join, and because there are usually more rows per inch than stitches, you need to pick up two of the bars on the horizontal piece every other stitch or so to keep the seam even.

5. Bring the yarn across the join and pick up the loops that make the point of the upside-down V of the next stitch on the vertical piece, pulling the yarn through, trying to imitate the size of each stitch in the knitted piece.

6. Continue alternating back and forth between the upper and lower pieces until you finish the seam.

7. Weave in the loose ends.

NOTE: A contrast color yarn was used to sew the seam for illustrative purposes.

Graft Seams

Kitchener Stitch, good for joining unshaped shoulders and toes of socks, involves grafting open stitches to another open row of stitches. The result looks like a row of stockinette stitch.

Kitchener Stitch

To prepare to join edges with Kitchener stitch, put each set of stitches onto a knitting needle.

1. Using yarn that matches your knitting, thread a tapestry needle with a strand that is roughly twice the length of the seam.

2. Lay both pieces of knitting on a table, with the wrong sides down and the needles running parallel to each other, with the tips facing to the right.

3. Insert the tapestry needle into the first stitch on the lower needle as if to purl; pull the yarn through until a tail about 6 inches remains. Leave the stitch on the needle.

4. Insert the tapestry needle into the first stitch on the upper needle as if to knit and pull the yarn through snugly, leaving the stitch on the needle.

5. Insert the tapestry needle into the first stitch on the lower needle again, this time as if to knit (a); then slip this stitch off the needle (b).

NOTE: A contrast color yarn was used for illustrative purposes. Be sure to sew your seams with the same yarn used to knit the pieces.

5a

5b

6 Insert the tapestry needle into the next stitch on the lower needle as if to purl. Leave the stitch on the needle.

7 Insert the tapestry needle into the first stitch on the upper needle again, this time as if to purl (a); then slip this stitch off the needle (b).

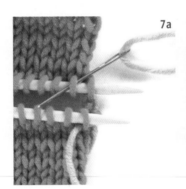

7a

7b

8 Insert the tapestry needle into the next stitch on the upper needle as if to knit. Leave the stitch on the needle.

9 Repeat steps 5–8 until all the stitches have been completed.

Remember: On the lower needle, the first insertion is as if to purl, the second is as if to knit, and then the stitch comes off; on the upper needle, the first insertion is as if to knit, the second is as if to purl, and then the stitch comes off.

NOTE: Another grafting method is the three-needle bind-off, which is described on page 40 in Chapter 2.

Assemble a Sweater

Now that you are familiar with several different ways to attach knitted pieces to each other, you can assemble a simple sweater. How a sweater is made—whether it is knit in the round or on straight needles, how the sleeves are created, whether it is a cardigan or a pullover—determines not only how it is put together but also the order in which the pieces are assembled.

ORDER OF ASSEMBLY

Generally, sweaters that are knit flat in pieces are joined in this order:

1. Join the front(s) to the back at the shoulders.

2. Attach the sleeves.

3. Sew the side and underarm seams.

Use long straight pins to pin pieces together before seaming. You can neaten up seams by lightly steaming with an iron.

WHICH SEAM TECHNIQUE FOR WHICH PART?

Sometimes knitting instructions specify the best seaming technique for a given join. If no specific technique is indicated, you can always safely use the backstitch seam for the shoulders, whether they are shaped or not. If the shoulders are not shaped, you can try using the invisible horizontal seam or the three-needle bind-off. The invisible vertical seam is an excellent choice for side and underarm seams. The table below provides some guidance on which seams work best for joining different parts of a project.

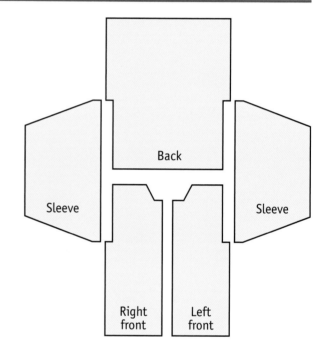

Type of Seam	Use It to Join	Examples
Invisible horizontal seam	Two horizontal edges	Bound-off shoulder seams
Backstitch seam	All edges	Shaped shoulders, side seams, add-on collars
Invisible vertical seam	Two vertical edges	Sweater sides and underarm seams
Invisible vertical-to-horizontal seam	A bound-off edge and a side edge	Sleeve cap joined to an armhole
Grafted seam	Two horizontal edges	Unshaped shoulders, toes of socks, mitten tips

ATTACHING SLEEVES

There are many different ways to shape armholes and sleeve caps. The type of armhole shaping always determines the sleeve cap shaping. After blocking all pieces, working the edging on the neck, and joining and pressing the shoulder seams, you can attach the sleeves. Find the center of the sleeve cap by folding the sleeve in half lengthwise and then mark the center with a pin. After pinning the center of the sleeve cap to the shoulder seam, with the right sides facing each other, you can pin the rest of the sleeve cap to the armhole, lining up the sleeve cap shaping with the corresponding armhole shaping. Then you can sew the sleeve in place.

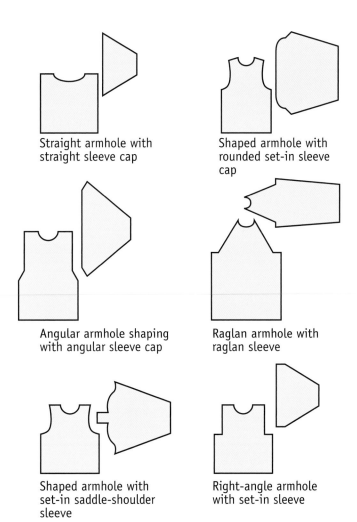

Straight armhole with straight sleeve cap

Shaped armhole with rounded set-in sleeve cap

Angular armhole shaping with angular sleeve cap

Raglan armhole with raglan sleeve

Shaped armhole with set-in saddle-shoulder sleeve

Right-angle armhole with set-in sleeve

Felting

The felting process involves exposing a piece of knitting to moisture, heat, and friction in order to shrink it and transform it into a dense, firm, and very strong fabric. Felting requires a carefree attitude because the outcome is not always predictable.

HOW FELTING WORKS

You may have accidentally felted a sweater by washing it in the machine in hot water. When you expose something knit in wool or another animal fiber to wet heat and agitate it, it is likely to shrink and become matted. The fibers open up and become interlocked, creating the dense fabric of felt.

Felting is not an exact science; it's more like a science experiment. Many variables can affect the outcome: water temperature, water hardness, how much agitation occurs, how the fibers were treated before felting, what the fiber blend is, how long the fibers are exposed to heat and moisture, and the amounts of soap and water used. Be prepared for any outcome and be willing to experiment.

THE BEST YARNS FOR FELTING

The best yarns for felting are 100% wool or other animal fibers, such as alpaca, angora, mohair, and llama. You can also try using blends of these fibers. (Superwash wools have been treated so that they will not shrink, so don't use them.) Synthetics are not good felters, but you can try to felt a wool/synthetic blend, as long as it isn't more than 10% to 15% synthetic.

Fibers that have been bleached, such as bright whites, and bright colors that have been treated with bleach to take the dye are also not always the best for felting. It is not recommended to use different yarn types in the same felted piece because they will felt differently. And you need to be careful when felting together multiple colors as they can bleed. No matter what yarn you choose, you should felt a knitted swatch first to get a sense of whether and how it will work.

EQUIPMENT NEEDED FOR FELTING

Felting is easiest and fastest when done in a washing machine. If you don't have a washing machine, you can felt in a bucket or in a bathtub or sink. Don't use a front-loading machine, though, as you must open the machine to check on your item every few minutes.

A zippered mesh laundry bag or pillowcase will protect your washer from the wads of fuzz that come off in the felting process. You also need bleach-free laundry soap, or mild dish soap if you're felting by hand. A tablespoon is plenty. Because agitation and friction are key factors in felting, a pair of jeans, a canvas sneaker, or a couple of old tennis balls to throw in the machine with your item can speed the process, too.

HOW TO KNIT FOR FELTING

You need to knit the item you want to felt larger than you want it to be—to account for shrinkage—and to knit it at a loose gauge, using needles that are 2 mm larger than the size specified for the yarn. For example, if your yarn calls for a size 6 (4 mm) needle, you'd knit your item with a size 10 (6 mm) needle. A tightly knit fabric can end up too rigid, but only experimentation with swatches will tell.

EXPERIMENT WITH SWATCHES FIRST

Felting is unpredictable. However, you can get at least some sense of the outcome beforehand by swatching. So before you spend the time knitting something that is twice the size you want it to be, test felt a swatch in the same yarn first. Be sure to measure the swatch before and after to get a sense of how much shrinkage occurs when you felt it. If you follow a pattern written for felting and use the same materials suggested, you'll likely be delighted with the bit of magic you've performed.

TIP

Fun with Felted Swatches

Before you venture into a large felting project, experiment with swatches knit in different animal fibers and varied stitch patterns. You can use the swatches later as coasters. Cut them into interesting shapes or embellish them with embroidery after felting for a more finished look.

If a swatch is large enough, you can whipstitch it onto the outside of a felted bag as a pocket. To make a great baby toy, sew six same-size swatches together to form a cube and stuff it with cotton balls or polyester filling.

How to Felt Using a Washing Machine

After you have loosely knit your item to size based on your felted test swatch, weave in the ends and sew all the seams.

1 Place the knitted item into a zippered pillowcase or lingerie bag and close.

NOTE: You'll keep the knitted item in the zippered bag through the whole process, except to check it during the cycle.

2 Set the washer to the warm or hot wash/cold rinse cycle (small load), start filling the washer, and add approximately 1 tablespoon mild dish soap.

3 When the washer is almost done filling, add a canvas sneaker or a couple old tennis balls and the zippered bag containing your knitted item.

4 After the machine begins the wash cycle, stop it and check your item every so often to see how it's doing. (At the very beginning, don't worry if it looks as though it's grown.)

5 Stop when the item looks felted or when the wash part of the cycle is through, whichever comes first. The knitted item should have a dense feel, and the stitches should be barely visible, if visible at all. If the project is felted enough at this point, go to step 7.

6 If the item is not felted enough after one wash cycle (not including rinse and spin), put it through the wash cycle again, as many times as needed, until it is.

7 Put the newly felted item back into the washer and let it rinse and spin. The cool water locks the fibers and rinses the soap. Spinning removes excess water.

8 Take the item out of the washer and form it to the desired shape while it is still wet. Stuff the item with plastic bags to help shape it, if appropriate, and set it on a towel to air dry.

How to Felt by Hand

Although felting is easiest and fastest when done using a washing machine, you can also felt in a bucket or in a bathtub or sink. This method is not recommended for large knitted items.

After you have loosely knit your item to size based on your felted test swatch, weave in the ends and sew all the seams.

1. Fill a bucket, sink, or bathtub partway with hot or very warm water and add 1 tablespoon mild dish soap.

2. Add your knitted item to the water and agitate it with your hands or a wooden spoon.

NOTE: When felting by hand, there is no need to put your knitted item into a zippered pillowcase or lingerie bag.

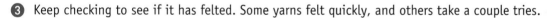

3. Keep checking to see if it has felted. Some yarns felt quickly, and others take a couple tries.

4. Stop when the item looks felted. It should have a dense feel, and the stitches should be barely visible, if visible at all. If the item is felted enough at this point, go to step 6.

5. If the item is not felted enough and the water is cooling, gently squeeze the excess water from (do not twist or wring) the item and refill the sink or tub with hot water and soap. Agitate the item in the water again. Do this as many times as needed until the item is felted enough.

6. Rinse the item in cool water. Gently squeeze out the excess water and roll the item in a towel to get even more water out.

7. Form your item to the desired shape while it is still wet. Stuff it with plastic bags to help shape it, if appropriate, and set it on a towel to air dry.

CHAPTER 12

Finishing Details

Sometimes the finishing phase of a hand-knit sweater can take almost as long as the knitting phase. Besides blocking and seaming pieces together, there are many finishing details that may be called for, such as button bands, collars, hems, and pockets.

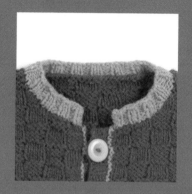

Pick Up Stitches

Pick up stitches to add button bands, neckbands, collars, or decorative borders to the finished edges of your knitting. After picking up stitches along an edge, you use them to knit the part you want to add—without having to sew the piece on. You can also pick up stitches at an armhole edge and knit a sleeve from the top down. You can pick up stitches along straight edges (button bands) or curved edges (collars).

(Note: A contrast color yarn is used for instructional purposes.)

How to Pick Up Stitches Along a Bound-off Edge

Using a needle a size or two smaller than your working needles, pick up stitches starting at the top-right corner.

1 With the right side facing, insert the needle into the center of the V of the first stitch, just below the bound-off row.

2 Wrap the working yarn around the needle as you would to knit, holding a 6-inch tail, as shown.

3 Bring the loop of the working yarn to the front, as you would to knit.

You have now picked up your first stitch.

4 Repeat steps 1–3 across the edge, working from right to left, for each stitch.

NOTE: When you are done picking up stitches and are ready to begin knitting, be sure to switch back to your working needles.

How to Pick Up Stitches Along a Vertical Edge

Picking up stitches along a vertical edge is very similar to picking them up along a bound-off edge, except that instead of inserting the needle into the center of each stitch along the horizontal row, you insert the needle into the spaces between the stitches all along the vertical row.

1 Turn your work so that the vertical rows run horizontally and the right side is facing. Start at the right corner of the pick-up edge.

2 Insert the right needle from front to back into the space between the first and second stitches, as shown.

3 Wrap the working yarn around the right needle as you would to knit, holding a 6-inch tail, as shown.

4 Bring the loop of working yarn to the front, as you would to knit.

You have now picked up your first stitch.

5 Repeat steps 2–4 across the edge, working from right to left, skipping a row every few stitches.

NOTE: Because there are more rows per inch than stitches, you do not need to pick up a stitch between every pair of stitches along a vertical edge. If you do, your edge will look stretched out; skipping a row every few pick-up stitches makes up for the difference. Picking up 3 stitches every 4 rows works well most of the time.

How to Pick Up Stitches Along a Curved Edge

Picking up stitches along a curved edge, as with neck shaping, requires you to combine what you know about picking up stitches along horizontal and bound-off edges.

1 Starting at the top-right corner, with the right side facing, insert the needle into the center of the V of the first stitch, just below the bound-off edge of the shaping.

2 Wrap the working yarn around the needle, as you would to knit, holding a 6-inch tail, as shown.

3 Pick up all the stitches on the horizontal section of the shaping until you get to the vertical section.

4 Pick up stitches as you would for a vertical edge, skipping a row every few stitches, if necessary.

NOTE: Be sure not to insert the needle into any large holes caused by the shaping, as doing so will result in a hole in your picked-up edge.

How to Pick Up Stitches Evenly

Knit-on edgings require picking up stitches evenly along an edge. If you don't pick up stitches evenly, your final result will look decidedly off: It will cinch in or look stretched. To pick up stitches evenly, place markers at regular intervals along the edge, and then pick up the same number of stitches between each pair of markers.

1 Place pins, spaced evenly, along the edge where stitches are to be picked up.

2 Calculate how many stitches should be picked up between markers by dividing the total number of stitches to be picked up by the number of spaces between pins.

3 Pick up the appropriate number of stitches between each pair of markers.

TIP

Picking Up Large Numbers of Stitches

Use a circular needle to pick up and work stitches on long stretches, but work back and forth with the circular needle, as you would with straight needles. Measure the length of the pick-up edge, and use the closest length of circular needle available.

Button Bands, Neckbands, and Collars

Some sweater patterns call for bands and collars that are knit as separate pieces and sewn on at the end. Others indicate that you knit the band or collar directly onto the garment by picking up stitches. Either way, it's a good idea to acquaint yourself with the various parts of a sweater.

BUTTON BANDS

Some cardigans are finished with strips of knitting along the vertical edge called *button bands*; one button band has buttonholes on it, and the other has buttons sewn to it. Button bands are commonly worked in ribbing, seed stitch, or garter stitch, so they lie flat. They are frequently worked using needles that are one or two sizes smaller than the needles used for the garment, to give a neat appearance. When working button bands, you should knit the band that holds the buttons first: you mark the placement of the buttons on the band by using stitch markers; then when you knit the buttonhole band, you work the buttonholes to correlate with your markings. You place buttons on the left band for women and on the right band for men.

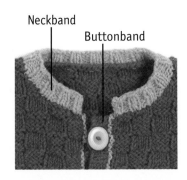

Neckband

Buttonband

NECKBANDS

Like button bands, neckbands are frequently worked on smaller needles in ribbing, seed stitch, or garter stitch. Neck shaping by itself often has an unfinished or uneven look to it, so it is generally desirable to attach or knit on a neckband. There are many varieties of neckbands—crewneck, V-neck, and square neck, to name a few.

COLLARS

You work some collars by picking up the stitches around the neck and knitting on the collar directly; you work others as separate pieces that you sew on to the neck later.

When knitting a collar directly onto a sweater, be sure to pick up stitches from the wrong side if the collar is going to fold down. One way to create a collar for a pullover is to pick up stitches and work the collar in the round after joining the shoulders. Another method is to work back and forth with one shoulder still open and then sew a seam later.

D ifferent styles of sweaters call for different
types of buttonholes. The size and type of
button you're using also influence your choice of
buttonhole. However, the eyelet buttonhole, the
one-row horizontal buttonhole, and the two-row
horizontal buttonhole should get you through most
situations.

Before making buttonholes on your finished pieces,
practice the various techniques a few times to make
sure you come up with a nice, neat buttonhole.

How to Make a 1-Stitch Eyelet Buttonhole

This is the easiest buttonhole to make. It works very well
for children's and babies' clothes, as well as for small
buttons. It is worked by combining a yarn over with a
knit 2 together: The yarn over makes the hole, and the
knit 2 together decreases to maintain the original stitch
count.

① Work to the point where you want the buttonhole
to be and then k2tog, yo; continue the row as
established.

② On the next row, work the yo as you would a regular
stitch.

You have made a 1-stitch eyelet buttonhole.

NOTE: You can make a larger eyelet buttonhole by k2tog,
yo twice, ssk on the first row. On the second row, purl
into the first yo, then purl into the back of the second yo.

How to Make a One-Row Horizontal Buttonhole

There are several methods for making horizontal button-holes over two rows, but this one-row buttonhole looks much neater and does not need to be reinforced later.

1 On the right side, work to the point where you want the buttonhole to be placed. Bring the yarn to the front, slip the next stitch from the left needle as if to purl, and bring the yarn to the back. *Slip the next stitch from the left needle to the right and pass the first slipped stitch over it and off the needle. Repeat from * three times, keeping the yarn at the back the whole time.

You have bound off 4 stitches.

2 Slip the last bound-off stitch back to the left needle.

3 Turn your work so that the wrong side is facing and bring the yarn to the back.

4 Insert the right needle between the first and second stitches on the left needle and wrap the yarn around the right needle as if to knit.

⑤ Bring the loop through to the front as if to knit, but instead of slipping the old stitch off the left needle, use the right needle to place the new loop onto the left needle.

You have used the cable cast-on method to cast on 1 stitch.

⑥ Repeat steps 4 and 5 four more times and then turn the work back so that the RS is facing.

You have cast on 5 stitches.

⑦ Bring the yarn to the back and slip the first stitch from the left needle to the right needle; pass the additional cast-on stitch over the slipped stitch to close the buttonhole. Work to the end of the row as usual.

You have made a one-row horizontal buttonhole.

How to Make a Two-Row Horizontal Buttonhole

For this buttonhole, bind off stitches on one row, then cast on stitches on the next.

1 On the RS, work to where you want the buttonhole to be, then k2.

2 Bind off the first stitch of the pair just knit.

3 K1 and bind off the stitch before it.

4 Rep step 3 twice. You have bound off 4 buttonhole stitches.

5 Work to the end of the row as usual.

6 On the WS, work up to the bound-off stitches.

7 Make a loop with the working yarn as shown; insert the right needle into the loop and pull to tighten.

You have used the backward-loop method to cast on 1 stitch.

8 Repeat step 7 three more times.

You have cast on 4 stitches.

9 Work to the end of the row as usual.

You have completed a two-row horizontal buttonhole.

2

4

7

Sewing a button onto your knitting is somewhat different from sewing a button onto a shirt because the knitted fabric is a much looser weave. If your button's holes are large enough, you can use your knitting yarn to sew it in. Sometimes it's easier to separate your yarn into a few plies and use a thinner strand to sew the button.

How to Sew On a Button

① Thread a tapestry needle as you would to sew your knitting, leaving a 6-inch tail coming out one side of the eye.

② Insert the needle from back to front through the knitting and through one of the holes in the button. Pull the yarn through until you have about 6 inches of yarn left coming out the back of your knitting.

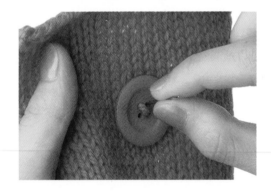

③ Insert the needle from front to back through another hole in your button and pull the yarn through all the way.

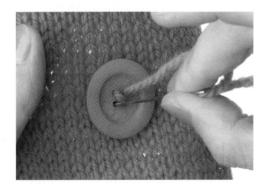

4️⃣ Continue until you have several stitches holding the
button in place. With the yarn pulled through to the
front of the fabric, but not through the button, wrap
the yarn around the button stitches—between the
back of the button and the front of the knitting—a
few times. Then insert the needle back through the
knitting to the wrong side.

5️⃣ Tie the two yarn ends in a knot and weave the ends
into your knitting.

**My yarn is too thick to use to sew on my button. I would like
to use thread, but the knot at the end keeps coming through
the knitting. Is there something I can do to prevent this?**

Yes. First, tie a knot in the end of your thread. Then insert the
needle under the V where you want the button to be sewn and
reinsert the needle between the strands near the knot. Pull it
tight to secure the thread. Be sure to move the thread ends near
the knot to the wrong side of your work and cut them short so
they look tidy.

Knot

Sew In Zippers

You can sew a zipper into the front of a cardigan instead of using buttons. A thin but firm edging like garter stitch or single crochet will help it look neat. The following instructions are for sewing a zipper into a sweater, but you can use the same technique to attach a zipper to a knitted bag.

How to Attach a Zipper

Be sure that the edge that the zipper is sewn to is the same length as the zipper, or your garment will be distorted.

1 With the zipper closed and the RS of your garment facing, pin the zipper along and under the front edges so that the edges are almost touching each other and so that they cover the teeth of the zipper.

2 Still working on the RS, use a contrast color thread to baste the zipper to the sweater edges to temporarily hold it in place. Make sure your stitches are close to the zipper teeth for a firm hold.

3 Working on the wrong side, use thread in a matching color to neatly and evenly whipstitch the outside edges of the zipper to the fronts of the sweater.

4 Turn back to the right side and neatly sew the edges of the sweater to the zipper, right next to the teeth, but not so close as to interfere with the zipper's functioning.

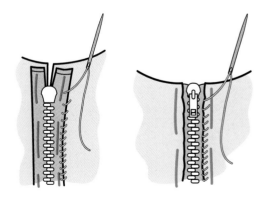

Make Pockets

You can add a pocket to almost anything you knit—a sweater, a coat, a vest, or even a scarf. Patch pockets (like the one shown here) are the easiest to make. You just knit a square or rectangle the size you want and sew it onto your knitting. Or you can pick up stitches from your knitting and knit a patch pocket directly on. Inset pockets are a little more challenging, but if you know how to bind off, you can make those, too.

How to Attach a Patch Pocket

To attach a patch pocket, first you need to knit and steam block (see page 165) the pocket you want to sew on. (The sample here is a 4-inch square.) You also need a tapestry needle, straight pins, and yarn to sew the pocket.

1. Pin the pocket in place exactly where you want it to be. Thread a tapestry needle as you would to sew your knitting together, leaving a 6-inch tail coming out one side of the eye.

2. Insert the tapestry needle from back to front through both the knitting and the upper-right corner of the pocket. Loop the yarn around from front to back to front once more to reinforce the corner.

3. Sew on the pocket, using the whipstitch (see page 207), ending at the upper-left corner. Reinforce the corner as in step 2, ending with the needle on the wrong side.

4. Weave in the loose ends.

How to Pick Up a Patch Pocket

To pick up a patch pocket, you need straight pins, a tapestry needle, and yarn and needles to knit the pocket. You also need a knitting needle one or two sizes smaller than the one used to knit the garment so you can pick up the pocket stitches.

1 Using straight pins, mark the outline of where you want the patch pocket on your garment.

2 Weave the smaller knitting needle under and over horizontally along the stitches where the base of the pocket will be.

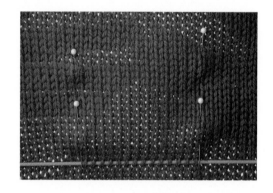

3 Using the yarn you intend to knit the pocket with and the working knitting needle, purl across the picked-up stitches. (This first row is a wrong-side row.)

4 Work from here in stockinette stitch (that is, knit across on the right side, purl across on the wrong side) until the pocket is the length you want it to be.

5 Bind off loosely.

6 Pin the pocket sides as shown.

7 Stitch the pockets sides in place, using the whipstitch (see page 207).

NOTE: This stockinette stitch pocket has a rolled edge at the top. If you prefer a flat edge, try working the last ½ inch or so in ribbing, seed stitch, or garter stitch. You may also want to steam the pocket flap to neaten it up before sewing it in place.

How to Make an Inset Pocket

Inset pockets have a less noticeable appearance than patch pockets, as the front of the pocket is actually your knitted garment. You knit the back of the pocket, or the lining, ahead of time and put it on a stitch holder; then you incorporate it when knitting the face of the garment that contains the pocket. Follow your pattern's instructions for size and placement of an inset pocket. The following steps illustrate how to create an inset pocket.

① Knit the pocket lining(s) to the size indicated in your pattern's instructions. Instead of binding off the stitches, put them on a stitch holder. Steam the lining to block it (see page 165).

NOTE: Pocket linings are usually knit in stockinette stitch so that they lie flat. You can knit a pocket lining in the same color as the overall piece, or, if you prefer, you can knit the lining in an accent color or even a pattern.

② On the piece of the garment that will hold the pocket, work across the row on the right side to where the pocket will be placed. Bind off the same number of stitches as used to knit your pocket lining and work to the end of the row.

③ On the following row (wrong side), work across to the bound-off stitches. Hold your pocket lining so that the wrong side is facing you. (The right side of the lining should face the wrong side of the main garment piece.) Work across the lining stitches from the holder.

NOTE: You may have to slip your lining stitches from the holder to a needle if the stitch holder feels awkward or is not facing the right direction for you to work from it.

4 On the next row (right side), work across as usual.

5 Continue working this piece of the garment as established.

6 At the finishing stage of your garment, pin the bottom and sides of the pocket lining in place.

7 Stitch to attach, using the whipstitch (see page 207), being careful to keep your stitches from showing on the right side.

8 Steam the sewn-in lining to flatten it, taking care not to press, which would bring the outline of the lining to the front of your work.

NOTE: You can also make an inset pocket by putting the stitches where the pocket is to be placed onto a holder after working across them on the right side. Then you continue across the row to the end and place the lining as illustrated here. At the finishing stage, you can then work from the held stitches to create an edging, such as ribbing, seed stitch, or garter stitch.

Turned Hems

A *turned hem* creates a neat edge and can be used instead of ribbing at a hemline, a neck, on a cuff, or along the button band on a cardigan.

HEM WITH PURLED TURNING ROW

To knit a hem with a purled turning row, knit the facing in stockinette stitch, on smaller needles than used for the project, to the desired length, and then purl the turning row on the right side. You work the garment from there in the pattern, using the standard needle size being used for the project. When it is time to finish the garment, fold over the hem at the purled row and then pin and stitch it in place. A turning row is worked at the fold line to make a neat edge that folds easily.

NOTE: The stockinette stitch is used here because is lays flat.

HEM WITH PICOT TURNING ROW

This is a pretty hem that looks like a row of tiny scallops. It works well on dresses and baby clothes. You begin a hem with a picot turning row similarly to how you begin a hem with a purled turning row, only you form the picot turning row on an even number of stitches on the right side by working a knit 2 together, yarn over eyelet pattern across, ending with a single knit stitch. When you finish the garment, fold the hem along the eyelet row and pin and stitch it in place.

PICOT TURNED BUTTON BAND

When using a picot hem to make a buttonhole band, work the buttonholes symmetrically on either side of the turning row. Finish the band in the same manner as you would a hem, only reinforce the buttonholes using the whipstitch (see page 207) through the two thicknesses.

If you're the type of knitter who enjoys minimal finishing, this hem is for you. It is created in a similar fashion to the hems shown on the opposite page, except that instead of sewing it in place at the finishing stage, you attach it by knitting the cast-on edge onto the main part of the garment.

How to Knit In a Hem

1 Work a 1-inch facing in stockinette stitch on a smaller needle than your project requires, as described on the opposite page, ending with a wrong-side row.

2 Purl the next right-side row to create the turning row.

3 Change to the needles used to knit the main part of your garment, and when you have worked 1 inch beyond the turning row, ending with a wrong-side row, you are ready to knit in the hem.

4

4 With the right side facing, use a separate ball of yarn and the smaller needles you used to knit the hem facing to pick up stitches (see pages 180–183) along the cast-on edge, being sure to evenly pick up the same number of stitches that you have on the knitting needle for your garment. Cut the yarn used to pick up stitches, leaving a 6-inch tail.

5 Turn the hem so that the wrong side of the facing and the wrong side of your work are facing each other. Hold the knitting needles parallel to each other in your left hand, with the right side of your garment facing.

6

6 Insert the third needle, your working needle, into the first stitch on the front needle, then into the first stitch on the needle holding the picked-up stitches, and use your main working yarn to knit the 2 stitches as 1; then slip them off the needles.

You should now have 1 stitch on the working needle.

7 Repeat step 6 across until you have knit together all the picked-up stitches and all the main garment stitches. Continue from here as established.

CHAPTER 13

Decorative Details

Personalize your knitting projects with decorative touches. Besides adding pompoms to hats, fringe to scarves, or tassels to blankets and pillows, you can embroider and crochet directly onto your knitting. This chapter covers some basic finishing touches and embellishments that come up frequently in knitting patterns, as well as a few special techniques.

Make Pompoms

Pompoms add a finishing touch to hats, scarves, and other projects. They are easy to make, and you can make them using one color or many.

How to Make a Pompom

The following method creates a loose pompom that can be left with loopy ends. You need a pair of scissors, yarn, and flexible cardboard (shirt cardboard works well).

1 Cut a piece of cardboard into a rectangle the same width as the size you want your pompom to be. (So, for a 3-inch pompom, cut a piece of cardboard that's 3 inches wide.)

2 Wrap the yarn around the cardboard about 50 times.

NOTE: Thin yarn requires more wraps than thick yarn.

3 Carefully remove the cardboard from the wrapped yarn.

4 Wrap a 12-inch strand of yarn tightly around the center of the yarn loops twice, and then tie it in a firm knot.

5 Cut the loops and fluff up the pompom to even it out.

NOTE: You can leave the ends uncut for a loopy pompom.

6 Use the tie ends to sew the pompom to your knitting.

Perfect Pompoms

You can buy a pompom maker from your local yarn shop or craft store. Most come in a set with three or four sizes ranging from small 1-inch pompom makers to large 3- or 4-inch pompom makers like the ones shown here. You won't have to fuss with cut cardboard, and you'll have firm, round, velvety pompoms every time.

TIP

Make Tassels

You can embellish pillows, baby blankets, hats, sashes, and scarves with tassels. They are very easy to make, and, like pompoms, can be made in one color or in two or more colors.

To make a tassel, you need a piece of rigid cardboard, a pair of scissors, a tapestry needle, and yarn.

How to Make a Tassel

① Cut the cardboard into a rectangle that is the same length you want your tassel to be. (So, for a 6-inch-long tassel, cut a piece of cardboard that's 6 inches long.)

② Wrap the yarn around the cardboard to the desired thickness.

NOTE: Thin yarn requires more wraps than thick yarn.

③ Thread a tapestry needle with a 12-inch strand of the same yarn used for the tassel and insert the needle between the cardboard and the wrapped strands. Pull the yarn all the way through.

④ Separate the tapestry needle from the yarn and tie the strand's ends together tightly in a knot at the top edge of the cardboard to secure the tassel.

5 Insert scissors between the wrapped strands and the cardboard at the opposite end from the tied end and cut the tassel free along the bottom edge of the cardboard.

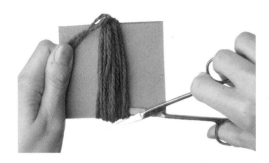

6 Wrap a 10-inch strand of yarn around the tassel a few times, about ½ inch down from the tied end; then tie the ends tightly in a knot.

NOTE: You can use the same color yarn or an accent color for step 6.

7 Conceal the yarn ends from step 6 by threading them through a tapestry needle and inserting the needle back into the tassel near the top. Pull the tapestry needle out at the tassel end.

8 Trim the tassel ends to neaten them.

9 Use the tail coming out of the top of the tassel to sew it onto your knitting project.

Add Fringe

Fringe works well on scarves, throws, sweater hems, wraps, and ponchos. You can make fringe with all kinds of yarn. Combining two or more different colors or types of yarn to make fringe can have a lovely effect, so experiment by holding various yarn odds and ends together to see how they look.

To make fringe, you need yarn, a pair of scissors, and a crochet hook. Fringe can use up a fair amount of yarn, so make sure you have enough before you begin.

How to Add Fringe

Fringe made of thick yarn requires fewer strands of yarn than fringe made with thin yarn. Experiment with different thicknesses to see what works best for your particular project.

1. Determine how long you want your final fringe to be. Then cut yarn to double that length, plus 1 inch extra for the knot.

2. Hold the strands together, with the ends matched up, creating a loop at the top.

3. Hold your knitting with the right side facing you. Insert the crochet hook from front to back into the upper-right corner, just below the cast-on row.

4. Use the crochet hook to take hold of your loop of folded strands.

5 Use the crochet hook to pull the loop of strands through from back to front.

6 Grab the fringe ends with the hook and pull them through the loop and tighten.

7 Repeat steps 2–6 across the edge of your knitting to complete the fringe.

8 When you have finished attaching the fringe, trim it with scissors so that it is even.

Knit a Cord

You can knit tubular cords and put them to all sorts of decorative uses. Knitted cords make excellent bag handles; they can also be looped and configured to make linear appliquéd designs and floral hat toppers. Or, instead of adding fringe to scarf ends, you can attach knitted cords.

Knitting a cord is like knitting in the round on a tiny scale. You need two double-pointed needles suitably sized for your yarn.

How to Knit a Cord

1 Cast on 5 or 6 stitches onto one of your dpns (double-pointed needles).

2 Knit across the stitches but do not turn your work.

3 Push the stitches back to the other end of the dpn, so you're ready to work a right side row again. Insert the second dpn into the first stitch to knit as usual, firmly pull the working yarn from the end of the row, and knit.

NOTE: Beginning the row (round, actually) by pulling the yarn from the opposite end closes the tube.

4 Repeat steps 2 and 3 until the cord is the desired length. Bind off or cut the yarn and pull it through all the stitches to tighten.

Decorate with Embroidery

After you have blocked your knitting, you can decorate it with embroidery stitches. Embroidered edgings add color and a homespun look to casual knits, baby blankets, and scarves. Embroidered motifs look best on flat stitch patterns. You can use yarn or embroidery floss to embroider on your knitting.

Embroidery Stitches

WHIPSTITCH

Whipstitch is one of the easiest and most basic stitches you can use.

1 Thread a tapestry needle. Tie a knot in the yarn end about 6 inches up from the bottom. Bring the threaded needle up through the knitting from back to front, until the knot stops it.

2 Bring the tapestry needle in and out from back to front up the side of the knitting.

3 When you're finished, pull the yarn through to the wrong side, knot it, and weave in the loose ends.

BLANKET STITCH

Blanket stitch adds a rustic feel to sweaters, blankets and edgings.

1 Thread a tapestry needle. Tie a knot in the yarn end about 6 inches up from the bottom. Bring the needle through at the edge of your knitting from back to front, pulling the yarn through until the knot stops it.

2 Moving right to left, insert the needle at the desired depth into the edge and bring it out again to the front, as shown, taking care that the needle tip overlaps the yarn coming out of the starting point.

3 Repeat step 2 along the edge of your knitting to create blanket stitch. When you are done, weave in the loose ends.

DUPLICATE STITCH

This stitch duplicates the knit stitch—the V—right on top of it to create motifs that look knit in.

1 Thread a tapestry needle. Bring the needle through the knitting at the hole just below the V that you want to duplicate. Pull the yarn through, leaving a 6-inch tail.

2 Insert the needle from right to left under both loops of the V above the stitch you want to duplicate; pull the yarn through all the way.

3 Reinsert the needle into the hole below your stitch—the same hole that the needle came through in step 1—and bring it out again below the next stitch to be worked, all in one movement.

4 Repeat steps 2 and 3 to create duplicate stitch. When you are done, weave in the loose ends.

COUCHING STITCH

For the couch stitch, you lay yarn or thread onto your fabric in the shape or design you want and whipstitch it in place with a second, thinner, yarn or thread. It results in colorful, playful outlines.

1 Begin by arranging the thicker thread on your knitting in the shape or line you want it to ultimately be.

2 Whipstitch it in place, using a needle threaded with a thinner yarn.

3 When you are done, weave in the loose ends.

FRENCH KNOT

French knots add a three-dimensional effect.

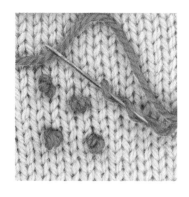

1 Thread a tapestry needle. Tie a knot in the yarn 6 inches up from the end. Bring the needle through the knitting from back to front, pulling through until the knot stops it.

2 Grasp the yarn about 1 inch above the point where it came out and wind the yarn around the tip of the needle three times, moving from the eye of the needle to the tip, as shown.

3 Still grasping the wound yarn, reinsert the needle right next to the point where it came out and pull it through all the way to the back to create the knot.

Crochet Edgings

You don't have be a crochet expert to finish your knitting with simple crochet edgings or chains. A crochet edge neatens and firms up unstable or curling edges; it also adds colorful or eye-catching detail to a plain-looking piece of knitting.

To crochet, you need yarn and a crochet hook that is the correct size for the yarn you're using.

How to Crochet a Chain

Chain stitch in crochet is the equivalent of casting on: It creates the foundation row of stitches from which to work. When you're working crochet directly onto your knitting, you don't necessarily need this foundation row. However, knowing how to work a chain will enable you not only to make decorative cords but also to incorporate button loops and picot trim into your crochet edgings.

Crochet instructions generally indicate working chain stitch with the abbreviation *ch* followed by the number of chain stitches to make (instructions to chain 3 read *ch3*).

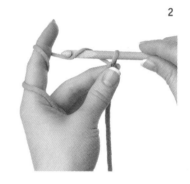

2

① Make a slipknot, leaving a 6-inch tail. Insert a crochet hook of an appropriate size for the yarn into the slipknot.

② Wrap the working yarn around the crochet hook from back to front (creating a yarn over loop) so that the hook catches the yarn.

③ Holding the working yarn in your left hand and the hook in your right, pull the yarn over loop on the hook through the slipknot.

You have made 1 loop in a chain.

④ Repeat steps 2 and 3 until the chain is the desired length. Cut the yarn, leaving a 6-inch tail, and pull it snugly through the last loop to finish the chain.

4

Slip Stitch Edging

You can slip stitch along an edge as a decorative touch, or as a base row underneath a second row of crochet. You work this edging from right to left.

Crochet instructions indicate slip stitch with the abbreviation *sl st* followed by the number of slip stitches to make.

1 Choose a crochet hook that is one or two sizes smaller than the needles used for your knitting. Insert the hook into your knitting at the right corner of the edge.

2 Loop the yarn around the hook (yarn over) and pull the loop through.

3 Insert the crochet hook into the next stitch of the knitting, yarn over again, and pull the loop through both the knitting and the loop on the hook from step 2.

You should now have 1 loop remaining on the hook.

4 Repeat step 3 across the edge. Cut the yarn and pull it snugly through the last loop to finish the edging.

NOTE: If a crochet edge is causing your knitting to flare and stretch, try a smaller hook or try skipping a stitch on the knitting every so often. If the edge is too tight, try a larger hook or try crocheting with a looser touch.

Single Crochet Edging

Single crochet provides a neat, firm edge that is a little more substantial than a slip stitch edge. You work this edging from right to left.

Crochet instructions indicate single crochet with the abbreviation *sc* followed by the number of single crochet stitches you should make.

① Choose a crochet hook that is one or two sizes smaller than the needles used for your knitting. Insert the hook into your knitting at the right corner of the edge.

② Loop the yarn around the hook (yarn over) and pull the loop through.

③ Working from the front, yarn over and pull a new loop through the first loop.

④ Insert the crochet hook into the next stitch to the left on the knitting, yarn over, and pull a new loop through.

You should now have 2 loops on the crochet hook.

⑤ Yarn over the crochet hook again and pull this new loop through both loops already on the hook.

⑥ Repeat steps 4 and 5 across the edge. Cut the yarn and pull it snugly through the last loop to finish the edging.

Picot Edging

Crocheting a picot edging makes a fancy edge that looks great on feminine sweaters and baby knits.

1 Choose a crochet hook that is one or two sizes smaller than the needles used for your knitting. Insert the hook into your knitting at the right corner of the edge.

2 Work 1 single crochet (see steps 2–5 on page 211).

3 Chain 3 (or 4, if desired) (see steps 2 and 3 on page 209).

4 Insert the crochet hook back into the same stitch, yarn over, and bring up a loop.

5 Yarn over again and pull the loop through both loops on the hook.

6 Single crochet 2 (into the next 2 stitches, moving left).

7 Repeat steps 3–6 across the edge to create picot edging. Cut the yarn and pull it snugly through the last loop to finish the edging.

NOTE: To create more space between picots, you can single crochet 3 or 4 times at step 6.

Knit Fancy Borders and Edgings

Sometimes a plain sweater needs to be dressed up a little. You can work a fancy ruffle or border at the edge to add that accent to your knitting. The following ruffles, borders, and edgings are all easy to create. You can work them in the same color as your knitting or in an accent color.

How to Make Ruffles

BASIC RUFFLE

For this ruffle, you need to start with twice the number of stitches as there are in the main part of your knitting. For example, if you are knitting the back of a sweater over 60 stitches, you cast on 120 stitches for this ruffle. You work this basic ruffle over an even number of stitches.

1 CO twice the number of sts that you want to end up with.

2 Work in St st to the desired length of the ruffle, ending with a purl row.

3 K2tog across the entire row. You end up with half the number of sts you cast on.

NOTE: You can work three rows of garter stitch to reinforce the decrease row.

CURLY RUFFLE

This fun ruffle looks great on baby blankets and little girls' sweaters. You need to cast on four times the number of stitches you want to end up with, minus 3. For example, if you want to end up with 60 stitches, you cast on 237 stitches to create a curly ruffle. You work this border on a multiple of 2 stitches plus 1.

1 Row 1 (RS): K1, *k2, pass the first of these 2 sts over the second and off the needle; rep from * to end of row.

2 Row 2 (WS): P1, *p2tog; rep from * to end of row.

NOTE: You can work the ruffle on smaller needles if you want it to be tighter.

How to Make Borders

BOBBLED BORDER

This border creates a nice three-dimensional edge; work it on a multiple of 6 stitches plus 5 using the mb (make bobble) technique (page 114).

1 Row 1 (WS): Knit.

2 Row 2 (RS—bobble row): K2, *mb, k5; rep from * to last 3 sts, mb, k2.

3 Rows 3–5: Knit.

MINI SCALLOPS

This edging adds a delicate touch. You work this border on a multiple of 5 stitches plus 2.

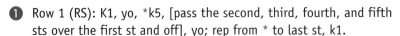

1 Row 1 (RS): K1, yo, *k5, [pass the second, third, fourth, and fifth sts over the first st and off], yo; rep from * to last st, k1.

You now have a multiple of 2 sts plus 3 on your needle.

2 Row 2 (WS): P1, *[p1, yo, k1 tbl] all in next st, p1; rep from * to end of row.

You now have a multiple of 4 sts plus 1 on your needle.

3 Row 3: K2, k1 tbl, *k3, k1 tbl; rep from * to last 2 sts, k2.

4 Rows 4–6: Knit.

EASY POINTED BORDER

This border creates a series of diagonally biased points. You make the border as long as the edge you need to attach it to and then sew it on. To create it, cast on 6 stitches.

1 Row 1 (RS): K3, yo, k3—7 sts.

2 Rows 2, 4, 6, 8, and 10 (WS): Knit.

3 Row 3: K3, yo, k4—8 sts.

4 Row 5: K3, yo, k5—9 sts.

5 Row 7: K3, yo, k6—10 sts.

6 Row 9: K3, yo, k7—11 sts.

7 Row 11: K3, yo, k8—12 sts.

8 Row 12: BO 6 sts, k5—6 sts.

9 Rep rows 1–12 until the edging is the desired length. BO all stitches.

Knitting beads directly into your work is an embellishment that can have varied effects. You can create elegant purses and eveningwear by knitting delicate glass beads with fine yarns, or you can create a more casual look by knitting wooden beads into a thick, sturdy, natural-looking yarn. Since beading has grown in popularity, you can find a wide selection of beads at large craft stores. Be sure that your beads and yarn have compatible care instructions.

How to Knit with Beads

To knit with beads, you must thread all the beads directly onto your ball of working yarn before beginning to knit. You need to make sure that the beads you're using are suited to your yarn visually and in terms of size. The beads should slide along the yarn with ease. This beaded sample is worked on the right side of stockinette stitch.

1. Thread the end of the working yarn into a sewing needle that is small enough to fit through the hole in the bead. Thread all the beads you will need onto the working yarn, sliding them down toward the yarn ball.

2. Cast on stitches and work your knitting pattern's instructions.

3. When you get to the point on a right side row where you're ready to add a bead, bring the working yarn to the front, between your needles.

4. Slide the first bead up the yarn so that it rests snugly against the last knit stitch.

⑤ Use the tip of the right needle to slip the next stitch on the left needle knitwise to the right needle.

⑥ Bring the working yarn to the back, adjust the bead so that it is placed where you want it, and knit the next stitch snugly to hold the bead firmly in place.

You have beaded 1 stitch.

FAQ

I want to use very small beads but am finding it hard to get a threaded needle through the hole. Is there another method I can use to thread the beads onto the yarn?

Yes, as long as your yarn is not so thick that it can't be threaded into the hole of the bead at all. To thread tiny beads onto fine yarn, you can use a beading needle threaded with thin thread to bring your yarn through the hole. Simply loop the thread around a fold in your yarn and then insert both ends of the thread into the eye of the needle. Slide the bead over the needle and then pull the needle, the thread, and the yarn through the bead hole.

A felted flower adds a feminine touch to hats, bags, sweaters, slippers—you name it. You can also attach a pin to the back of the flower and use it to adorn a jacket or sew an elastic hair band onto the back to create a fun hair accessory.

The instructions that follow are for just one type of flower, but you can find instructions for all kinds of knitted flowers and then felt those, too.

How to Make a Felted Flower

To make a felted flower, you need three colors of yarn that is 90%–100% wool, alpaca, or some blend of animal fiber (but not superwash yarn). Thin yarns will make small flowers; thick yarns will make larger flowers. Use needles that are a couple sizes larger than your yarn recommends.

① Using Color A, CO 3 sts.

② Row 1 (RS): Slip 1, knit into the front and back of the next st, knit to end of row—4 sts.

③ Row 2 (WS): Slip 1, purl into the front and back of the next st, purl to end of row—5 sts.

④ Rep rows 1 and 2 three times—11 sts.

⑤ Beg with a knit row, work 4 rows St st.

⑥ Next row (RS): [Ssk] twice, k3, [k2tog] twice—7 sts.

⑦ Next row (WS): P1, p2tog, p1, p2tog, p1—5 sts.

⑧ Cut yarn but leave rem sts on needle, pushing them to the end for later.

⑨ Rep steps 1–8 four more times, until you have a total of five petals side-by-side on the needle—25 sts.

⑩ Rejoin Color A and knit across all sts to join the petals.

⑪ Cut yarn, leaving a 12-inch tail. Thread tail through the sts and pull tight to cinch the center of the flower together. Set aside.

⑫ Using Color B, CO 3 sts.

⑬ Work as for the first set of petals through step 3.

⑭ Rep rows 1 and 2 twice—9 sts.

⑮ Beg with a knit row, work 4 rows St st.

⑯ Next row (RS): [Ssk] twice, k1, [k2tog] twice—5 sts.

⑰ Next row (WS): [P2tog], p1, [p2tog]—3 sts.

⑱ Cut yarn but leave rem sts on needle, pushing them to the end for later.

⑲ Rep steps 12–18 four more times, until you have a total of five smaller petals on the needle—15 sts.

⑳ Rejoin Color B and knit across all sts to join the petals; then rep step 11. Set aside.

㉑ Using Color C, CO 7 sts.

㉒ Knit 2 rows.

㉓ BO 6 sts, leaving 1 st on the right needle.

㉔ Using the backward-loop method (see page 15), CO 6 sts. Switch the needle back to your left hand, ready to knit.

㉕ Rep steps 22–24 four times and then rep step 23 once more, leaving 1 st on the right needle.

㉖ Cut yarn, leaving a 10-inch tail. Thread the tail into a tapestry needle, pull it through the last stitch, and stitch along the bases of each of these smallest petals to form a star. Cinch tight and secure.

㉗ Weave in loose ends.

㉘ Felt all three sets of petals according to the felting instructions on pages 176–177; shape and air dry.

㉙ When the petals are dry, lay them together in order from largest to smallest, as shown. Sew together at the center, using strong matching thread or embroidery floss.

㉚ Embellish the center with a button, bead, or French knot.

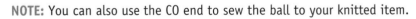

A knitted ball makes a playful accent for hats, scarves, and pillows. You can sew it directly onto your knitting or first sew it to a knitted or twisted cord and then attach it to your project so it dangles. To make a knitted ball, you need a set of double-pointed needles several sizes smaller than your yarn ball recommends and some cotton balls or polyester filling.

1. CO 8 sts and divide among 3 dpns (double-pointed needles), leaving a 6-inch tail.

2. Join rnd and, using a fourth dpn, knit into the front and then the back of every st—16 sts.

3. Knit 3 rnds.

4. Next rnd: K1, m1 *k2, m1; rep from * to last st, k1—24 sts.

5. Knit 5 rnds, or until ball is about the length you want it to be. This will vary according to yarn thickness.

6. Next rnd: *K2tog; rep from * to end of rnd—12 sts.

7. Rep last rnd—6 sts.

8. Cut yarn, leaving a 6-inch tail. Pull the tail through the remaining sts, cinch tight, and secure.

9. Stuff the cotton balls or bits of polyester through the hole at the CO end until the ball is firm.

10. Thread the CO tail through a tapestry needle and weave it in and out along the CO edge. Cinch tight and secure.

NOTE: You can also use the CO end to sew the ball to your knitted item.

11. Weave in the end at the top, pulling it down through the center of the ball and trimming it to neaten up the top.

Line a Knitted Bag

Lining a knitted bag is easy. The lining will protect your knitting and enable the bag to safely hold all kinds of items. Choose a lining fabric that complements your yarn colors. These instructions are designed for rectangular flat and gusseted bags.

Specifications

MATERIALS

Fabric for lining

Interfacing, if a more rigid lining is desired

Scissors or pinking shears

Pins

Ruler or tape measure

Sewing machine (optional)

Needle and thread

NOTE: To add an additional lining of thick interfacing between the knitted fabric and the lining fabric, cut the interfacing as you do the lining fabric, hold it together with the corresponding lining pieces, and sew as instructed.

How to Make the Lining

FLAT RECTANGULAR BAG LINING

1. Cut a piece of lining fabric twice the height of your bag +2" by the width of your bag +1".

2. Fold the fabric in half with RS facing each other along the width. Pin the sides together.

3. Using a sewing machine or a needle and thread, sew side seams, leaving a ½-inch seam allowance on each side.

4. Insert the lining into the bag, WS tog, so that the fold is touching the bottom and the side seams run along the bag's sides.

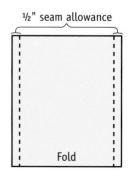

½" seam allowance

Fold

⑤ Reach down into the bag and tack the corners in place. Then tack along each side seam twice, about one-third and two-thirds of the way up.

NOTE: This will keep the lining from pulling down the top of the bag when you put things in it.

⑥ Fold over the top edge of the lining all the way around so that the folded edge runs neatly along the top edge of the bag, about ½ inch down from the edge. Pin in place.

⑦ Using a needle and thread, neatly whipstitch (see page 207) the folded top edge of the lining to the bag.

GUSSETED RECTANGULAR BAG LINING

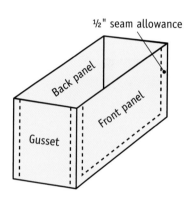

½" seam allowance

① Cut two pieces of lining fabric that are 1 inch longer and wider than your front and back panels (to allow for ½-inch seam allowance).

② Cut a piece of lining fabric that is 1 inch wider than your bag's gusset and 1 inch longer than the entire gusset-base-gusset length.

③ Pin the long edges of the gusset/base strip around three edges (the gusset sides and base) of the panels, with RS facing each other.

④ Using a sewing machine or a needle and thread, sew seams along pinned edges, leaving ½-inch seam allowance.

⑤ Insert the lining into the bag with WS together, matching up corners and seams.

⑥ Reach down into the bag and tack the corners in place. Then tack along each side seam twice, about one-third and two-thirds of the way up.

NOTE: This will keep the lining from pulling down the top of the bag when you put things in it.

⑦ Fold over the top edge of the lining all the way around so that the folded edge runs neatly along the top edge of the bag, about ½ inch down from the edge. Pin in place.

⑧ Using a needle and thread, neatly whipstitch (see page 207) the folded top edge of the lining to the bag.

CHAPTER 14

Easy Knitting Projects

The projects in this chapter introduce you to some basic techniques, without overwhelming you with elaborate shaping, construction, or stitch patterns. It's good to make your first project a short one so that you achieve the satisfaction of finishing something quickly. Be sure to refer to earlier chapters to review how-to information, if necessary.

Easy Horizontal Scarf

You knit this scarf the long way, casting on a lot of stitches onto a long circular needle, and then working back and forth in rows. It knits up very quickly that way, especially at 3 stitches per inch. Because this scarf is knit in simple garter stitch, you should use a yarn that is rich and varied on its own, like this beautiful handspun wool. It's a good idea to test the yarn against your neck to make sure it's soft and not itchy.

Specifications

SIZE
72 inches (not including fringe) × 4 inches

MATERIALS
2 hanks Naturwolle *Black Forest Soft* (100% handspun wool, 110 yd./100 g hank) in red #08

Small amount of accent yarn for fringe (sample used a combination of the scarf yarn and Muench Yarns/Naturwolle *Black Forest Tweed* in yellow T2-08)

Size 13 (9 mm) circular needle, at least 29 inches long

Tapestry needle

Size K (6.5 mm) crochet hook

GAUGE
12 stitches and 22 rows to 4 inches over garter stitch on size 13 (9 mm) needles

How to Make the Easy Horizontal Scarf

SCARF

1 CO 215 sts.

NOTE: Even though you use a circular needle for this scarf, it is worked back and forth in rows.

2 Work in garter st (knit every row) until the scarf is the desired width, making sure you have enough yarn left to BO (that is, at least four times the length of the scarf). (The sample shown was knit to 4 inches in width and used almost two full hanks of Naturwolle Black Forest Soft.)

3 BO sts at an even tension. Cut yarn, leaving a 6-inch tail, and pull tail through last st to secure.

FINISHING

1 Weave in ends.

NOTE: Because a scarf is viewed on both sides, take care to weave in ends as inconspicuously as possible.

2 Block the scarf so that the edges are even. (See pages 164–165.)

3 To make fringe, cut four 12-inch strands of yarn for each bunch of fringe. Add five bunches of fringe to each end of the scarf, using a crochet hook. (See pages 204–205 for instructions on finishing with fringe.)

Easy Baby Booties

This quick and easy project makes a great gift for a new baby. Worked in simple garter stitch with just a little shaping, these booties can be finished in a few hours. Whipstitch detailing and crochet chain ties add the finishing touches. Try yarn a bit thinner or thicker for smaller or larger booties.

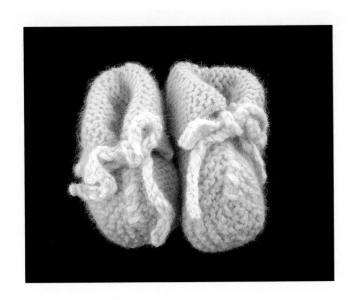

Specifications

SIZE
One size

MATERIALS
2 balls Cascade Yarns *Cloud 9* (50% merino wool/50% angora, 109 yd./50 g ball) in yellow #106

7–8 yd. contrasting lightweight scrap yarn for whipstitch and ties

Size 6 (4 mm) needles

2 stitch markers

Row counter, if desired

Tapestry needle

Size H (5 mm) crochet hook

GAUGE
22 stitches and 40 rows to 4 inches over garter stitch on size 6 (4 mm) needles

How to Make the Baby Booties

BABY BOOTIES (MAKE TWO ALIKE)

NOTE: In this pattern you increase by using the right-slanting make one increase (see page 60).

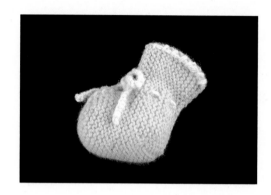

1 CO 42 sts, leaving a 10-inch tail to sew back seam.

2 Knit 2 rows, placing first marker after the 20th st and second marker after the 22nd st on the second row.

3 Next row (RS): Knit to first marker, sl marker, m1, knit to second marker, m1, sl marker, knit to end of row—44 sts.

4 Next row (WS): Knit.

5 Rep steps 3–4 three times to 50 sts, ending with a WS row.

6 Knit 2 rows.

7 Rep step 3—52 sts.

NOTE: You can remove the markers at this point, as they are no longer needed.

8 Knit 11 rows.

9 Next row (RS): K14, m1, k8, m1, k8, m1, k8, m1, k14—56 sts.

10 Knit 1 row.

11 Next row: BO 12 sts, knit to end of row—44 sts.

12 Rep step 11—32 sts.

13 Knit 10 rows.

14 Next row (RS): K1, k2tog, *k2, k2tog; rep from * 6 times, k1—24 sts.

15 Knit 1 row.

16 Next row: K1, k2tog, *k2, k2tog; rep from * 4 times, k1—18 sts.

17 Last row: *K2tog; rep from * to end of row—9 sts.

18 Cut yarn, leaving a 6-inch tail. Thread tail into tapestry needle and pull through remaining 9 sts. Tighten and secure.

FINISHING

1 Turn bootie so that RS are facing each other. Sew back seam from top to heel, using invisible vertical seam (see page 168) and tail left from cast-on.

2 Thread an 8-inch double strand of contrast yarn into tapestry needle and whipstitch (see page 207) instep tog from toe to beg of BO edges.

3 Thread a 12-inch double strand of contrast yarn into tapestry needle and whipstitch cuff edges.

4 Weave in all ends.

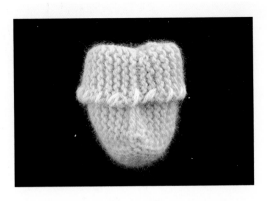

5 Using crochet hook and 48-inch double strand of contrast yarn, crochet a chain (see page 209) approx 18 inches long, leaving a tail of few inches at each end.

6 Thread tail of crochet chain into tapestry needle, and beg at instep edge, weave it in and out of cuff every 1/2–5/8 inches or so, ending at other instep edge.

7 Thread crochet chain tails into tapestry needle and weave them back into chains for a couple inches to conceal them.

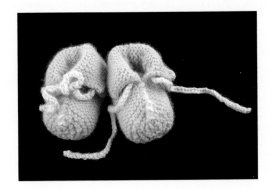

Baby Washcloth Set

M aking these washcloths and mitts allows you to practice stitch patterns without having to worry about shaping at the same time. And the finished set makes a nice gift for a new baby.

Specifications

SIZES
Washcloths: Approx 7 inches × 7 inches

Mitts: Approx 6 inches × 8 inches

MATERIALS
1 ball each Lily *Sugar 'n Cream* (100% cotton, 120 yd./2.5 oz. ball) in lime green #01712 (A), blue #01215 (B), yellow #00010 (C), and pink #00046 (D)

Size 8 (5 mm) needles

Tapestry needle

Size H (5 mm) crochet hook

Cable needle

GAUGE
20 stitches and 26 rows to 4 inches over stockinette stitch on size 8 (5 mm) needles

Pattern Stitches

SSK (LEFT-SLANTING) DECREASE
Sl first st as if to knit and then sl next st as if to knit. Insert left needle into front of slipped sts and knit them together.

How to Make the Baby Washcloth Set

WASHCLOTH IN GARTER STITCH ON BIAS

1. CO 2 sts in A. Knit 1 row.

2. Next row: K1, yo, k1.

3. Next row: K1, yo, knit to end of row.

4. Rep step 3 until there are 40 sts on the needle.

5. Next row: K1, yo, sl1, k2tog, pass slipped st over the k2tog, knit to end of row.

6. Rep step 5 until there are 4 sts on the needle.

7. Ssk, k2tog—2 sts. Cut yarn, leaving a 6-inch tail, pull through rem sts and secure.

8. Weave in ends.

9. Using C, make a crochet chain approx 36 inches long. Weave through eyelets around perimeter of cloth, beg and ending at a corner. Tie in a bow.

WASHCLOTH IN WOVEN STITCH

1. CO 32 sts in B. Knit 1 row.

2. Next row: *K1, k2tog, yo; rep from * to last 2 sts, k2.

3. Next row (RS): Knit.

4. Next row: K3, *p2tog but leave sts on needle, bring yarn to back and k same 2 sts tog and sl them off left needle tog; rep from * to last 3 sts, k3.

5. Next row: K1, k2tog, yo, knit to last 3 sts, yo, k2tog, k1.

6. Next row (WS): K3, p1, *p2tog but leave sts on needle, bring yarn to back and k same 2 sts tog and sl them off left needle tog; rep from * to last 4 sts, p1, k3.

7. Rep steps 3–6 until cloth measures approx 6¾ inches (or is almost square); end with step 4 or step 6.

8. Rep step 2, then knit 1 row.

9. BO knitwise. Weave in ends.

10. Using crochet hook and A, make a crochet chain approx 36 inches long. Weave through eyelets around perimeter of cloth, beg and ending at a corner. Tie in a bow.

CABLED WASH MITT

1. CO 32 sts in D.

2. Knit 1 row.

3. Next row: *K1, k2tog, yo; rep from * to last 2 sts, k2.

4. Next row (RS): K3, [k2, p2] twice, k2, [sl next 2 sts onto cn and hold in front, k2 from left needle, k2 from cn] twice, [p2, k2] twice, k3.

5. Next row (WS): K3, [p2, k2] twice, p10, [k2, p2] twice, k3.

6. Next row: K1, k2tog, yo, [k2, p2] twice, [sl next 2 sts onto cn and hold in back, k2 from left needle, k2 from cn] twice, k2, [p2, k2] twice, yo, k2tog, k1.

7. Next row: Rep step 5.

8. Rep steps 4–7 for patt until cloth measures approx 16 inches.

9. Rep step 3.

10. Knit 1 row.

11. BO knitwise. Weave in ends.

12. Lightly steam on WS to block. Fold mitt in half with WS tog and so the eyelets match up. Using tapestry needle and A, whipstitch mitt sides tog through eyelets.

FAIR ISLE STRIPE WASH MITT

1. CO 29 sts in C.

2. Knit 1 row.

3. Next row: *K1, k2tog, yo; rep from * to last 2 sts, k2. Join B.

NOTE: You will be working with both colors C and B.

4. Next row (RS): K3 in C, k1 in B, *k1 in C, k1 in B; rep from * to last 3 sts, k3 in C.

5. Next row (WS): K3 in C, p1 in B, *p1 in A, p1 in B; rep from * to last 3 sts, k3 in C.

6. Next row: [K1, k2tog, yo, k1] in C, *k1 in B, k1 in C; rep from * to last 3 sts, [yo, k2tog, k1] in C.

7. Next row: K3 in C, p1 in C, *p1 in B, p1 in C; rep from * to last 3 sts, k3 in C.

8. Rep steps 4–5 for patt until cloth measures approx 16 inches, ending with step 5 or 7.

9. Rep step 2.

10. Knit 1 row.

11. BO knitwise. Weave in ends.

12. Lightly steam on WS to block. Fold mitt in half with WS tog and so the eyelets match up. Using tapestry needle and A, whipstitch mitt sides tog through eyelets.

Lacy Cabled Scarf

Don't let the ornate look of this scarf discourage you from trying it. It's a very easy 4-row repeat that combines a feather and fan stitch pattern with a simple 4-stitch cable. After you've worked about 12 rows, you'll likely have the pattern memorized.

Use a soft yarn that feels good on your neck and that works up to a fabric that drapes nicely. If your yarn is soft but the knitting feels tight, try using a needle one or two sizes larger.

Specifications

SIZE
50 inches × 8 inches

MATERIALS
3 balls Cascade Yarns *Cloud 9* (50% merino wool/50% angora, 109 yd./50 g ball) in green #111

Size 7 (4.5 mm) needles

Cable needle

Tapestry needle

GAUGE
18 stitches and 26 rows to 4 inches over pattern stitch on size 8 (5 mm) needles

NOTE: The generic gauge for this yarn is actually 5.5 stitches per inch over stockinette stitch on size 6 (4 mm) needles. Larger needles are used for this project to create a fabric with more drape.

Pattern Stitches

C4F

Sl next 2 sts to cable needle (cn) as if to purl and hold at front of work. Knit the next 2 sts from the left needle. Use the right needle to knit the 2 sts from the cn, starting with the first st slipped onto the cn.

C4B

Sl next 2 sts to cable needle (cn) as if to purl and hold at back of work. Knit the next 2 sts from the left needle. Use the right needle to knit the 2 sts from the cn, starting with the first st slipped onto the cn.

LACY CABLED SCARF STITCH (36 STS)

Row 1 (RS): K6, p2tog twice, [yo, k1] 4 times, p2tog 4 times, [k1, yo] 4 times, p2tog twice, k6.

Rows 2 and 4 (WS): K2, purl to last 2 sts, k2.

Row 3: K2, C4F, k24, C4B, k2.

Rep rows 1–4 for lacy cabled scarf stitch.

How to Make the Lacy Cabled Scarf

SCARF

1. CO 36 sts, leaving a 6-inch tail.

2. Knit 2 rows for border.

3. Beg with row 1, work in lacy cabled scarf stitch until scarf measures 50 inches (or desired length), ending with row 1 of pattern.

4. Knit 2 rows for border.

5. BO sts knitwise, leaving a 6-inch tail.

6. Weave in ends.

7. Block, if desired, and if your yarn's care instructions allow.

Textured Pillow Cover

Making a hand-knit pillow cover is a great way to practice new texture, cable, or color stitch patterns because you don't have to worry about shaping. Be sure to get your gauge correct, though, so that your cover will fit properly onto your pillow form. This pillow cover is worked as two squares that are crocheted together.

Specifications

SIZE
12 inches × 12 inches

MATERIALS
4 balls Dale of Norway *Freestyle* (100% washable wool, 87 yd./50 g ball) in orange #3309 (A) and 1 ball blue #5703 (B)

NOTE: Yarn is used double throughout.

Size 11 (8 mm) needles

Tapestry needle

Size J (6 mm) crochet hook

12 × 12-inch pillow form

GAUGE
12 stitches and 17 rows to 4 inches over Andalusian stitch on size 11 (8 mm) needles with yarn used double

Pattern Stitch

ANDALUSIAN STITCH (ODD NUMBER OF STS)

Row 1 (RS): Knit.

Row 2 (WS): Purl.

Row 3: K1, *p1, k1; rep from * to end of row.

Row 4: Purl.

Rep rows 1–4 for Andalusian stitch.

How to Make the Textured Pillow Cover

PILLOW COVER (MAKE TWO ALIKE)

1 CO 35 sts in double strand A.

2 Beg with row 1, work in Andalusian stitch pattern until piece measures 12 inches, ending with a WS row.

3 BO sts in patt. Cut yarn, leaving a 6-inch tail, and pull tail through last st to secure.

FINISHING

1 Weave in ends.

2 Lightly steam on WS to block and reduce curling.

3 Hold squares tog with WS tog. Work picot crochet (see page 212) in double strand B around three sides to join and embellish as follows: Working left to right, starting at corner and working through both thicknesses at the same time, work 1 single crochet (sc), *ch3, insert the crochet hook back into the same st and pull up loop, yo, and pull yarn through both loops on hook (this re-inserted chain is the picot); sc across next 3 sts; rep from * around three sides. Do not cut yarn or tie off end. Leave loop on st holder.

4 Insert pillow form into cover, taking care not to let edging unravel and making sure the pillow form corners are tucked into the pillow cover corners.

5 Continue picot edging across fourth side to finish. Cut yarn, leaving a 6-inch tail, and pull tail through last st to secure. Thread the end into a tapestry needle and close edging to conceal end.

Cozy Mittens

These mittens are knit in the round on double-pointed needles. The bulky tweed yarn has a homey feel and knits up quickly. The size range covers the whole family. These mittens also go well with the Easy Horizontal Scarf on page 224.

Specifications

SIZES

S (M, L)

Palm circumference: 6.5 (8, 9¼) inches

MATERIALS

1 (1, 2) hanks Muench Yarns/Naturwolle *Black Forest Tweed* (100% handspun wool, 110 yd./100 g hank) in yellow/red tweed #T2-08

Size 10½ (6.5 mm) double-pointed needles

Size 13 (9 mm) double-pointed needles

Stitch marker

Small stitch holder

Tapestry needle

GAUGE

12 stitches and 18 rows to 4 inches over stockinette stitch on size 13 (9 mm) needles

How to Make the Cozy Mittens

MITTEN CUFF

1 With size 10½ needles, CO 20 (24, 28) sts, dividing sts evenly over three dpns.

2 Place marker, join rnd, taking care not to twist sts, and work in St st (knit every rnd) for 4 rnds.

3 Work eyelet rnd: K1 (2, 2), yo, k2tog, [k2 (2, 3), yo, k2tog] twice, [k2 (3, 4), yo, k2tog] twice, k1 (2, 2).

4 Knit 5 rnds.

5 Change to size 13 double-pointed needles, and knit 2 rnds.

SHAPE THUMB GUSSET

NOTE: In this pattern you increase by using the bar increase (see page 58).

1 Next rnd: Inc 1 st in first st of rnd, inc 1 st in next st of rnd, knit to end of rnd—22 (26, 30) sts.

2 Knit 1 (1, 2, 2) rnds.

3 Next rnd: Inc 1 st in first st of rnd, k2, inc 1 st in next st of rnd, knit to end of rnd—24 (28, 32) sts.

4 Knit 1 (1, 2, 2) rnds.

5 Next rnd: Inc 1 st in first st of rnd, k4, inc 1 st in next st, knit to end of rnd—26 (30, 34) sts.

6 Knit 1 (2, 2, 2) rnds.

7 Next rnd: Inc 1 st in first st of rnd, k6, inc 1 st in next st, knit to end of rnd—28 (32, 36) sts.

8 Knit 1 (2, 2, 2) rnds.

9 Next rnd (M and L only): Inc 1 st in first st, k8, inc 1 st in next st—28 (34, 38) sts.

10 All sizes: Knit 0 (1, 2) rnds.

11 Next rnd: Sl first 8 (10, 10) sts onto holder for thumb.

MITTEN BODY

1 Join rnd with rem 20 (24, 28) sts for hand.

2 Knit every rnd until mitten is about 1 inch shorter than desired length.

SHAPE MITTEN TIP

1 Rnd 1: *K2, k2tog; rep from * to end of rnd—15 (18, 21) sts.

2 Rnds 2 and 4: Knit.

3 Rnd 3: *K1, k2tog; rep from * to end of rnd—10 (12, 14) sts.

4 Rnd 5: *K2tog; rep from * to end of rnd—5 (6, 7) sts.

5 Final rnd: *K2tog; rep from * to end of rnd—3 (3, 4) sts.

6 Cut yarn, leaving a 10-inch tail. Pull tail through rem sts, tighten, and fasten.

MITTEN THUMB

NOTE: In this part of the pattern, you pick up stitches. For a refresher on how to do this, see pages 180–183.

1 Divide the 8 (10, 10) thumb sts from the holder evenly over three size 13 dpns. Pick up 2 sts from inside thumb on mitten hand—10 (12, 12) sts.

2 Knit every rnd until thumb is about ¼ inch shorter than desired length.

3 Next 2 rnds: K2tog across all sts—3 sts.

4 Cut yarn, leaving a 6-inch tail, and pull tail through last 3 sts to secure.

CUFF TIES

1 Use accent yarn to crochet two chains (see page 209) approx 10 (12, 14) inches long.

2 Weave ends into chains.

FINISHING

1 Weave in loose ends, using tail at cuff to secure the join of the first rnd, if necessary.

2 Weave chains in and out of eyelets and tie into a knot at the front of the mitten.

NOTE: Instead of chain ties, you can knit garter stitch bands to weave in and out of eyelets. Sew a button to join the ends.

You'll be adept at making bobbles after completing this bag. You knit the tote on large needles with a double strand of yarn. It works up so quickly you can finish it in a weekend, including the felting. The felting creates a dense fabric that can hold keys, wallets, and phones without losing its shape.

Specifications

SIZE

8 inches × 4 inches, not including strap, after felting

MATERIALS

3 skeins elann.com's *Peruvian Highland Wool* (100% wool, 109 yd./50 g skein) in Dusty Teal #4145 (A) and 1 skein each in Peridot #1477 (B) and Slate #3732 (C)

NOTE: A double strand of yarn is used for this pattern.

Size 11 (8 mm) 24-inch circular needle

3 same-color stitch markers, 1 different-color stitch marker

Tapestry needle

¼-inch dome button for center of flower

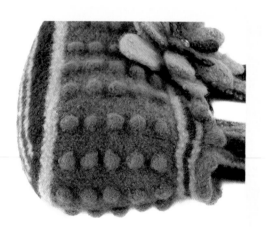

GAUGE

11 stitches and 18 rows to 4 inches over stockinette stitch on size 11 (8 mm) needles with yarn used double

Pattern Stitches

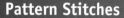

MB (MAKE BOBBLE)

Knit into front, back, front, back, and front (that's five times) of stitch. Then, without turning, pass fourth st over fifth and off, third st over fifth and off, second st over fifth and off, and first st over fifth and off.

How to Make the Felted Tote

BODY

The striped base of the tote is worked back and forth in rows on the circular needle. When that's complete, you pick up stitches around the edges and join the work in the round. The rest of the bag, except for the handles, is worked in the round. All parts of the bag are worked using a double strand of yarn.

① Using the long-tail method, CO 28 sts in a double strand (see page 35) of C.

② Knit 2 rows. Do not cut yarn.

③ Join B and knit 2 rows.

④ Rep last 4 rows five times (24 rows total), running yarn not in use up the side edge (see page 142, step 2). Cut B.

⑤ Knit 3 rows in C (last row is a RS row).

⑥ Place different-colored marker, rotate work clockwise, and with RS facing, use right-hand needle to pick up and knit 13 sts along short edge of base, place marker, pick up and knit 28 sts along long edge of base, place marker, pick up and knit 13 sts along second short edge, place marker—you now have 82 sts on the needle (54 picked-up sts plus the 28 sts that were already on the needle). The different-color marker marks the beg/end of rnd.

⑦ Join rnd and, still using C, knit 2 rnds, sl markers as you go. Cut C.

⑧ Join B. Knit 1 rnd; purl 2 rnds. Cut B.

⑨ Join A. Knit 3 rnds.

⑩ Work bobble rnd: *K2, mb, [k3, mb] twice, k2, sl marker, k1, mb, [k4, mb] five times, k1, sl marker; rep from * once.

⑪ Knit 4 rnds.

⑫ Rep last 5 rnds four times, ending last rep with 2 knit rnds instead of 4.

⑬ Work pleat rnd: *Sl first 3 sts to dpn and hold in front of and parallel to next 3 sts on left needle, [knit the first st on the dpn and the first st on the left needle at the same time (as you would for the three-needle bind-off; see pages 40–41)] three times, k1, sl the next 3 sts to dpn and hold in back of and parallel to next 3 sts on left needle, [knit the first st on the left needle and the first st on the dpn at the same time] twice, sl marker, k28, sl marker; rep from * once—70 sts. Cut A.

⑭ Join B. Knit 1 rnd, purl 1 rnd.

⑮ Join C. Knit 1 rnd, purl 1 rnd.

⑯ Rep step 14. Cut B.

⑰ Join A. Knit 2 rnds.

⑱ Next rnd: *K1, [kfb, k1] three times, sl marker, [k1, kfb] 14 times, sl marker; rep from * once—104 sts.

⑲ Work picot BO: *BO 4, turn and use the knit CO (see page 18) to CO 3 (you now have 4 sts on the right needle), pass the second, third, and fourth sts on the right needle one at a time over the first st and off (you now have 1 st on right needle); rep from * to end of rnd.

⑳ Cut yarn, leaving a 6-inch tail, and pull tail through last st to secure.

HANDLES (MAKE TWO ALIKE)

❶ Using a double strand of C, CO 60 sts.

❷ Purl 1 row, knit 1 row.

❸ Change to B and rep step 2.

❹ Change to A and rep step 2.

❺ Rep step 3.

❻ Change to C and rep step 2.

❼ BO purlwise in C.

FLOWER

❶ Make, felt, and assemble flower as instructed in Chapter 13, on pages 217–218, using B for the main color, A for the second color, and C for the third color. Wait to sew button until later.

FINISHING

❶ Weave in ends.

❷ Handles will curl naturally, with purl side facing out. Sew BO edge of handle to CO edge of handle, leaving 4 inches at each end unsewn.

❸ Sew handle ends flat (not curled) to inside edges of bag, below the picot ruffle, and centered on the front and back panels, with approx 5 inches between the handle ends.

❹ Felt the bag (see pages 176–177 for felting instructions). Shape the bag while wet and stuff it with plastic bags to hold its shape while drying.

❺ Sew button to center of flower and attach to front of bag under handle, as shown in photo on page 239.

Eyelet Hat

This elegant hat is easier to make than it looks. The pattern consists of alternating rounds of stockinette stitch and eyelet-studded reverse stockinette stitch. You work the ribbed brim back and forth in rows and then bind off to create the decorative flaps. From there, you work the rest of the hat in the round on a short circular needle, switching to double-pointed needles during the top shaping. With no seaming necessary, it requires minimal finishing—always a plus!

Specifications

SIZES
Brim circumference: 18 inches (ribbed section)

MATERIALS
2 skeins elann.com *Sonata* (100% mercerized cotton, 115 yd./50 g skein) in Lilac #6399 (MC) and 1 ball in Tarragon #5345 (CC)

Size 7 (4.5 mm) 16-inch circular needle

Size 7 double-pointed needles

Stitch marker

Row counter, if desired

Tapestry needle

GAUGE
20 stitches and 25 rows (or rounds) to 4 inches over stockinette stitch on size 7 (4.5 mm) needles

Pattern Stitches

RIBBED BRIM PATTERN

All rows: *K1, p1; rep from * to end of row.

HAT BODY PATTERN

Rnds 1 and 2: Purl.

Rnds 3: *K2tog, yo; rep from * to end of rnd.

NOTE: Don't forget the last yarn over at the end of rnd 3, or your stitch count will be off!

Rnd 4: Purl.

Rnd 5: *Yo, k2tog; rep from * to end of rnd.

Rnds 6 and 7: Purl.

Rnds 8–11: Knit.

Rep rnds 1–11 for hat body pattern.

How to Make the Eyelet Hat

HAT BRIM

① Using MC, CO 132 sts onto the circular needle.

NOTE: Do not join round. Ribbed portion of hat is worked flat.

② Work ribbed brim patt for 12 rows.

③ Next row (RS): BO first 16 sts in rib, then continue
in rib patt as set to end of row—116 sts.

④ Rep step 3—100 sts.

HAT BODY

① Place marker to note end of round and join sts into a rnd, with RS facing out.

② Beginning with rnd 1, work hat body patt for 30 rnds.

NOTE: Your last round should be rnd 8 of the pattern.

SHAPE TOP

NOTE: In this pattern you decrease by using k2tog and p2tog (see page 65). Switch to the double-pointed needles before the second decrease round because the circular needle will be too long as the hat circumference narrows.

1 Rnd 1: *K8, k2tog; rep from * to end of rnd—90 sts.

2 Rnd 2: Knit.

3 Rnd 3: *K7, k2tog; rep from * to end of rnd—80 sts.

4 Rnd 4: Purl.

5 Rnd 5: *P6, p2tog; rep from * to end of rnd—70 sts.

6 Rnd 6: *K2tog, yo; rep from * to end of rnd.

7 Rnd 7: Purl.

8 Rnd 8: *Yo, k2tog; rep from * to end of rnd.

9 Rnd 9: Purl.

10 Rnd 10: *P5, p2tog; rep from * to end of rnd—60 sts.

11 Rnd 11: Knit.

12 Rnd 12: *K4, k2tog; rep from * to end of rnd—50 sts.

13 Rnd 13: Knit.

14 Rnd 14: *K3, k2tog; rep from * to end of rnd—40 sts.

15 Rnd 15: Purl.

16 Rnd 16: *P2, p2tog; rep from * to end of rnd—30 sts.

17 Rnd 17: *K2tog, yo; rep from * to end of rnd.

18 Rnd 18: Purl.

19 Rnd 19: *Yo, k2tog; rep from * to end of rnd.

20 Rnd 20: Purl.

21 Rnd 21: *P1, p2tog; rep from * to end of rnd—20 sts.

22 Rnd 22: Knit.

23 Rnd 23: *K2tog; rep from * to end of rnd—10 sts.

24 Rnd 24: Rep rnd 23—5 sts.

25 Cut yarn, leaving a 6-inch tail. Pull tail through last 5 sts and secure.

FLOWER

1. Using MC, CO 6 sts.

2. Row 1: *Kfb; rep from * to end of rnd—12 sts.

3. Row 2: Purl.

4. Rep rows 1 and 2 twice—48 sts.

5. Rep row 1 once—96 sts.

6. Knit 1 row.

7. BO loosely knitwise.

8. Roll into a loose spiral to form a rose.

LEAVES (MAKE TWO ALIKE)

1. Using CC, CO 3 sts.

2. (RS) Knit 1 row.

3. Next row: Purl.

4. Next row: [K1, yo] twice, k1—5 sts.

5. Beg with a purl row, work 3 rows in St st.

6. Next row (RS): K2, yo, k1, yo, k2—7 sts.

7. Next row: Rep step 5.

8. Next row: [K1, k2tog] twice, k1—5 sts.

9. Next row: Purl.

10. Next row: K2tog, k1, k2tog—3 sts.

11. Next row: P3tog—1 st.

12. Cut yarn, leaving a 6-inch tail, and pull tail through last st to secure.

FINISHING

1. Weave in all ends.

2. Overlap brim flaps into an upside-down V. Layer the leaves and then the rose on top of the overlapped brim. Using a tapestry needle threaded with MC, sew flower, leaves, and overlapped brim together to secure all.

CHAPTER 15

More Knitting Projects

The knitting projects in this chapter include some techniques that are just beyond the beginner level but are certainly not too difficult for you to handle. These projects offer a good opportunity to try your hand at cables, Fair Isle, textured stitches, beaded knitting, and more involved shaping and finishing techniques. Certain procedures may be difficult to visualize from the instructions alone, but don't give up on a pattern before you've actually put stitches on needles and tried some of the techniques yourself.

Ribbed and Fair Isle Bag

This fun-to-knit bag is made up of two ribbed panels held together by a Fair Isle gusset. It's a good project for practicing color stranding without complicated shaping. The handles are long strips of reverse stockinette stitch that you allow to curl in order to create the tubular effect.

Specifications

SIZE
8½ inches wide × 3 inches deep × 9½ inches high, not including handles

MATERIALS
2 balls each elann.com's *Super Cable Aran* (100% mercerized cotton, 93 yd./50 g ball) in red #3919 (A) and brown #7382 (B)

Size 7 (4.5 mm) needles

Tapestry needle

GAUGE
18 stitches and 24 rows over stockinette stitch on size 7 (4.5 mm) needles

Pattern Stitches

RIBBING STITCH FOR FRONT AND BACK PANELS (46 STS)

Row 1 (RS): K5, p4, *k4, p4; rep from * to last 5 sts, k5.

Row 2 (WS): P5, k4, *p4, k4; rep from * to last 5 sts, p5.

Rep rows 1 and 2 for ribbing stitch.

REVERSE STOCKINETTE STITCH (REV ST ST) FOR HANDLES

Row 1 (RS): Purl.

Row 2: Knit.

Rep rows 1 and 2 for rev St st.

FAIR ISLE PATTERN FOR GUSSET

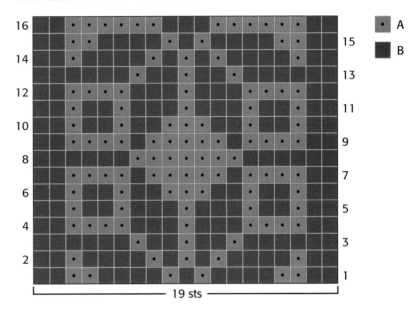

A

B

19 sts

How to Make the Ribbed and Fair Isle Bag

FRONT AND BACK PANELS (MAKE TWO ALIKE)

1. With size 7 needles and A, CO 46 sts.

2. Work in ribbing st until piece measures 8 inches from beg, ending with a WS row.

3. Next row—work eyelets (RS): K3, yo, k2tog, *p4, k2, yo, k2tog; rep from * to last st, k1.

4. Continue with ribbing pattern as established until panel measures 9½ inches from beg, ending with a WS row.

5. Cut yarn and change to yarn B.

6. Next row (RS): Knit.

7. BO purlwise in B.

249

FAIR ISLE GUSSET

1 With size 7 needles and B, CO 19 sts.

2 Join A. Beg with row 1 and using both A and B, work Fair Isle pattern from chart for 127 rows (eight 16-row reps, less 1 row on last rep), ending with row 15 of chart. Cut yarn A.

NOTE: See pages 146–149 for Fair Isle techniques.

3 Next row (WS): Using B, purl.

4 BO knitwise.

HANDLES (MAKE TWO ALIKE)

1 With size 7 needles and B, CO 85 sts.

2 Beg with a purl row, work 6 rows rev St st.

3 BO purlwise.

FINISHING

1 Weave in ends.

2 Lightly steam to block pieces, if desired.

3 Center gusset strip on base of back panel and pin all around. Sew seam with RS tog, reinforcing the top corners with a few extra stitches.

4 Rep step 3 for front panel.

5 Beg at outer eyelets, weave handle ends from RS to WS through first eyelet, from WS to RS through second eyelet, and from RS to WS through third eyelet, so that the two handle ends meet at the middle on the WS. Sew handle ends tog. Rep for second handle.

Beaded Headband

I f you're ready to embellish your knitting with sparkling beads, this is the project for you. Using less than a single skein of yarn and a handful of beads, the headband works up so quickly that you'll want to make two or three to give as gifts.

Specifications

SIZES
One size

MATERIALS
1 ball elann.com's *Luna* (55% viscose/45% cotton, 106 yd./50 g skein) in Moonstone #3706

Size 6 (4 mm) needles

300 size 06 silver-lined glass seed beads

Beading needle and sewing thread

Tapestry needle

Size F (3.75 mm) or G (4 mm) crochet hook

GAUGE
21 stitches and 28 rows to 4 inches over stockinette stitch on size 6 (4 mm) needles

Pattern Stitches

BEADING PATTERN (12 STS)
NOTE: See pages 215–216 for beaded knitting instructions.

Rows 1, 3, and 5 (WS): Purl.

Rows 2 and 4 (RS): P2, *slide 3 beads along working yarn until you hit the right needle, sl3 with yarn held in front (wyif), p2; rep from * once.

NOTE: Slipping the stitches with the yarn holding the beads held in front creates one beaded swag.

Row 6: P2, k8, p2.

Rep rows 1–6 for beading pattern.

How to Make the Beaded Headband

HEADBAND

1 Sl beads onto your yarn, using beading needle and thread.

NOTE: See page 216 to see how this is done.

2 CO 6 sts.

NOTE: No beads are used for the first 8 rows.

3 Row 1 (WS): Purl.

4 Row 2 (RS): P2, knit to last 2 sts, p2.

5 Row 3: Purl.

6 Row 4: P2, m1, knit to last 2 sts, m1, p2—8 sts.

7 Rep rows 3 and 4 twice—12 sts.

8 Beg with row 1, work beading pattern until band measures approx 17 inches, ending with row 5.

9 Next row (RS): P2, k2tog, knit to last 4 sts, k2tog, p2—10 sts.

10 Next row (WS): Purl.

11 Rep last 2 rows twice, ending with a WS row—6 sts.

12 Next row (RS): P2, k2, p2.

13 BO purlwise.

TIES (MAKE TWO ALIKE)

1 Using crochet hook, attach double strand of yarn to tip of headband and chain for 10 (10, 12, 12) inches.

2 Pull yarn through last loop and thread through tapestry needle. Weave end back into chain to conceal.

FINISHING

1 Weave in ends.

2 Gently steam on WS to neaten, if desired.

T his classic men's sleeveless pullover is a good project for practicing cables, shaping techniques, and picking up stitches for the neck and armbands. And there are only two seams to sew—at the shoulders—because the pullover is worked in the round up to the armholes. From there, you divide the stitches in half and work the back and front separately.

Specifications

SIZES

XS (S, M, L, XL)

Finished chest circumference: 38 (42, 44, 46, 48) inches

Back length: 25 (26½, 27, 27½, 28) inches

MATERIALS

4 (4, 5, 5, 6) skeins Valley Yarns *Berkshire* (85% wool/15% alpaca,141 yd./100 g skein) in Stone Blue #38 (MC) and 1 skein in brown #8 (CC)

Size 8 (5 mm) 30- or 36-inch circular needle

Size 9 (5.5 mm) 30- or 36-inch circular needle

Size 8 (5 mm) 16-inch circular needle for working armbands

3 same-color stitch markers, 1 different-color stitch marker

Cable needle

Row counter, if desired

Tapestry needle

GAUGE

16 stitches and 22 rows over stockinette stitch on size 9 (5.5 mm) needles

Pattern Stitches

RIBBING STITCH

All rnds/rows: *K2, p2; rep from * to end of rnd/row.

CABLE PANEL (18 STS)

WORKED IN THE ROUND:

Rnds 1, 2, and 4–10: P2, *k2, p2; rep from * to second cable panel marker.

Rnd 3: *P2, sl next 4 sts onto cn and hold at front of work, k2 from left needle, sl the 2 purl sts from cn back onto left needle, place the cn with 2 knit sts at back of work, p2 from left needle, k2 from cn; rep from * once, p2.

Rep rnds 1–10 for cable panel worked in the round.

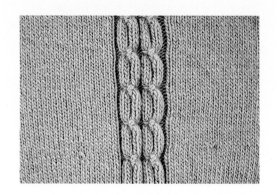

WORKED FLAT IN ROWS:

Rows 1, 5, 7, and 9 (RS): P2, *k2, p2; rep from * to second cable panel marker.

Rows 2, 4, 6, 8, and 10: K2, *p2, k2; rep from * to cable panel marker.

Row 3: *P2, sl next 4 sts onto cn and hold at front of work, k2 from left needle, sl the 2 purl sts from cn back onto left needle, place the cn with 2 knit sts at back of work, p2 from left needle, k2 from cn; rep from * once, p2.

Rep rows 1–10 for cable pattern worked flat in rows.

NOTE: When cable panel divides in half at start of v-neck, work all rows over 9 sts as written above, except in row 3, omit the direction "rep from * once" and end with p1 instead of p2 on one side (left) and begin with p1 instead of p2 on right side.

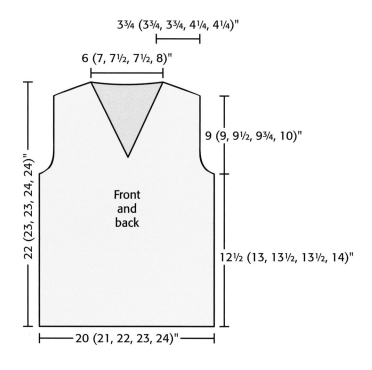

3¾ (3¾, 3¾, 4¼, 4¼)"

6 (7, 7½, 7½, 8)"

9 (9, 9½, 9¾, 10)"

22 (23, 23, 24, 24)"

Front and back

12½ (13, 13½, 13½, 14)"

20 (21, 22, 23, 24)"

How to Make the Cabled Sleeveless Pullover

The sleeveless pullover is worked in the round up to the armholes, at which point the work is divided and worked back and forth in rows.

LOWER BODY

1 With size 8 circular needle and MC, CO 160 (168, 176, 184, 192) sts. Place different-color marker to note beg/end of rnd, and join in rnd.

2 Work ribbing stitch for 6 rnds. Cut MC.

3 Join CC and knit 1 rnd.

4 Work ribbing stitch in CC for 3 rnds. Cut CC.

5 Rejoin MC and knit 1 rnd.

6 Work ribbing stitch for 6 rnds. Change to size 9 circular needle.

7 Rnd 1—place markers and beg cable patt: K80 (84, 88, 92, 96), place first marker to indicate side seam; k31 (33, 35, 37, 39), place second marker to mark beg of cable panel on pullover front; work rnd 1 of cable panel over next 18 sts, place third marker to mark end of cable panel; k31 (33, 35, 37, 39) sts, slip different-color marker at end of rnd.

8 Rnd 2: K80 (84, 88, 92, 96), sl marker, k31 (33, 35, 37, 39), sl marker, work rnd 2 of cable panel over next 18 sts, sl marker, k31 (33, 35, 37, 39) sts to different-color marker at end of rnd.

9 Continue as established, working vest in St st while maintaining the 18 sts between markers on pullover front in cable panel until pullover measures 15½ (16, 17, 17¼, 17½) inches from CO edge.

UPPER BODY: BACK

1 Divide back and front and shape armholes: BO 6 (6, 7, 7, 8) sts, knit to first marker, turn and put the 80 (84, 88, 92, 96) unworked sts for front (with cable panel) onto spare needle to be worked later.

NOTE: The pullover is worked back and forth in rows—still using the circular needle—from this point, starting with the back. Make a note of last cable row worked.

2 Next row (WS): BO 6 (6, 7, 7, 8) sts, purl to end of row—68 (72, 74, 78, 80) sts.

3 Next row (RS): K2, ssk, knit to last 4 sts, k2tog, k2—66 (70, 72, 76, 78) sts.

4 Next row: Purl.

5 Rep last 2 rows six times—54 (58, 60, 64, 66) sts.

6 Continue without further shaping until armholes measure 9 (9, 9½, 9¾, 10) inches, ending with a WS row.

7 Shape shoulders: BO 7 (7, 7, 8, 8) sts beg next 2 rows, then 8 (8, 8, 9, 9) sts beg next 2 rows—24 (28, 30, 30, 32) sts.

8 BO rem back neck sts.

UPPER BODY: FRONT

1 Sl the 80 (84, 88, 92, 96) sts for front back onto size 9 needle, ready to beg a RS row.

2 Maintaining cable panel over center 18 sts, beg shaping armholes as for back: BO 6 (6, 7, 7, 8) sts beg next 2 rows—68 (72, 74, 78, 80) sts.

NOTE: From here, the cable panel separates into two 9-st panels that run alongside the v-neck shaping.

3 Next row—divide neck and continue armhole shaping (RS): K2, ssk, knit to marker, work cable panel over next 9 sts (see note under Cable Panel on page 254), turn; sl rem 34 (36, 37, 39, 40) sts for right upper front onto holder or spare needle to be worked later.

NOTE: You should now have 33 (35, 36, 38, 39) sts on the needle for the left front.

4 Next row (WS): Work cable panel over first 9 sts, sl marker, purl to end of row.

5 Next row—beg neck shaping and continue armhole shaping (RS): K2, ssk, knit to 4 sts before marker, k2tog, k2, sl marker, work cable patt over last 9 sts—31 (33, 34, 36, 37) sts.

6 Rep last 2 rows five times—21 (23, 24, 26, 27) sts.

7 Rep step 4 once more, ending with a WS row.

8 Next row—continue shaping neck only (RS): Knit to 4 sts before marker, k2tog, k2, sl marker, work cable panel over last 9 sts—20 (22, 23, 25, 26) sts.

9 Next row (WS): Work cable panel over first 9 sts, sl marker, purl to end of row.

10 Rep last 2 rows to 15 (15, 15, 17, 17) sts.

11 Work without further shaping, maintaining 9-st cable panel at neck edge, until armhole measures 9 (9, 9½, 9¾, 10) inches, ending with a WS row.

12 Next row (RS): BO 7 (7, 7, 8, 8) sts, work in patt to end of row—8 (8, 8, 9, 9) sts.

13 Next row (WS): Purl.

14 BO rem sts.

15 Sl the 34 (36, 37, 39, 40) sts for right upper front onto size 9 needle, ready to work a RS row.

16 Next row (RS): Work cable panel over first 9 sts, sl marker, knit to last 4 sts, k2tog, k2—33 (35, 36, 38, 39) sts.

17 Next row (WS): Purl to marker, sl marker, work cable panel over last 9 sts.

18 Next row—beg neck shaping and continue armhole shaping (RS): Work cable panel over first 9 sts, sl marker, k2, ssk, knit to last 4 sts, k2tog, k2—31 (33, 34, 36, 37) sts.

19 Rep last 2 rows five times—21 (23, 24, 26, 27) sts.

20 Rep step 17 once more, to end with a WS row.

21 Next row—continue to shape neck only (RS): Work cable panel over first 9 sts, sl marker, k2, ssk, knit to end of row—20 (22, 23, 25, 26) sts.

22 Next row (WS): Purl to marker, sl marker, work cable panel over last 9 sts.

23 Rep steps last 2 rows to 15 (15, 15, 17, 17) sts.

24 Work without further shaping, maintaining 9-st cable panel at neck edge, until armhole measures 9 (9, 9½, 9¾, 10) inches, ending with a RS row.

25 Next row (WS): BO 7 (7, 7, 8, 8) sts, work in patt to end of row—8 (8, 8, 9, 9) sts.

26 Next row (RS): Work in cable patt to end of row.

27 BO rem sts.

FINISHING

1 Weave in ends.

2 Block pullover to measurements shown on page 254 but do not block ribbing.

3 Sew shoulder seams.

4 Work armbands: Beg at base of armhole with RS facing, use 16-inch size 8 circular needle and MC to pick up and knit 38 (38, 40, 41, 42) sts evenly to shoulder seam, then pick up and knit same number of sts back down to base of armhole—76 (76, 80, 80, 84) sts total.

5 Place marker, join sts in rnd, and work in ribbing stitch for 2 rnds. Drop MC.

6 Join CC and knit 1 rnd, then work 1 rnd B in ribbing stitch. Cut CC.

7 Pick up MC and knit 1 rnd, then work 2 rnds in ribbing stitch. BO in rib patt.

8 Rep steps 4–7 for second armband.

9 Work neckband: With RS facing and beg at base of V on right front, use longer size 8 needle and MC to pick up and knit 36 (36, 38, 39, 40) sts up to right shoulder seam, then pick up and knit 24 (28, 28, 30, 32) sts along back neck, then 36 (36, 38, 39, 40) sts back down left front neck to base of V—96 (100, 104, 108, 112) sts.

NOTE: Neckband is worked back and forth in rows.

10 Work ribbing stitch for 2 rows. Drop MC.

11 Join CC, purl 1 row, then work 2 rows ribbing stitch. Cut CC.

12 Pick up MC, knit 1 row, then work 2 rows ribbing stitch. BO in rib patt.

13 Overlap left front neckband edge over right front neckband edge at base of V and sew in place.

14 Weave in rem ends.

15 Lightly steam pullover again, including seams, but taking care not to block the elasticity out of the edgings.

Striped Sweater and Hat for Babies and Kids

K nit in a simple stripe pattern, this sweater has minimal shaping. Inset pockets and an easy-to-work shawl collar provide a little challenge—which you should be up for at this point. The matching hat has you working color segments in intarsia but without a lot of the fuss.

The instructions here include sizes ranging from 6 months to 10 years.

Specifications

SIZES (SEE PATTERN SCHEMATIC ON NEXT PAGE)
Sweater: 6 mos. (1–2 yrs., 3–4 yrs., 5–6 yrs., 7–8 yrs., 9–10 yrs.)

Finished chest circumference: 22 (26, 29, 32, 35, 38) inches

Back length: 10 (12, 14, 15, 16, 18) inches

Sleeve length: 6½ (8, 10, 12, 13, 14) inches

Hat circumferences: XS (S, M, L)

Brim circumferences: 15½ (17, 18½, 20) inches

GAUGE
18 stitches and 24 rows to 4 inches over stockinette stitch on size 7 (4.5 mm) needles

MATERIALS
2 (2, 2, 3, 3, 4) balls Mission Falls *1824 Cotton* (100% cotton, 84 yd./50 g ball) in Chili #207 (A), 1 (2, 2, 3, 3, 3) ball(s) in Lemongrass #305 (B), 1 (1, 2, 2, 2, 3) balls in Sky #403 (C), and 1 (1, 1, 2, 2, 2) balls in Ebony #100 (D)

Size 6 (4 mm) needles

Size 7 (4.5 mm) needles

Size 6 (4 mm) circular needle, at least 20 inches long, for working trim

5 stitch holders

Size 6 (4 mm) double-pointed needles (for grafting shoulder seams)

Row counter, if desired

Tapestry needle

Three ⅝- to ¾-inch buttons for the first three sizes; five ⅝- to ¾-inch buttons for the remaining three sizes

Size G (4–4.25 mm) crochet hook

Pattern Stitches

STRIPE PATTERN

Over stockinette stitch, work stripe patt as
follows:

> 12 rows in A
> 12 rows in B
> 12 rows in C

Rep these 36 rows for stripe patt.

NOTE: If you don't want to have to weave in so many
ends, you can carry the yarns alternately up the side as
you go (see page 142, step 2).

SSK (LEFT-SLANTING) DECREASE

Sl first st as if to knit and then sl next st as if to knit. Insert
left needle into front of slipped sts and knit them together.

K2TOG TBL (THROUGH BACK OF LOOP)

Insert the right needle from front to back into the back of
the next 2 sts on the left needle. Knit the 2 sts together
as 1 st.

P2TOG TBL

Insert the right needle from back to front into the back of
the next 2 sts on the left needle. Purl the 2 sts together
as 1 st.

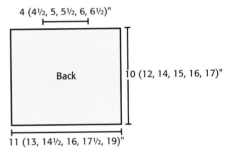

4 (4½, 5, 5½, 6, 6½)"

Back

10 (12, 14, 15, 16, 17)"

11 (13, 14½, 16, 17½, 19)"

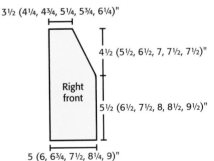

3½ (4¼, 4¾, 5¼, 5¾, 6¼)"

4½ (5½, 6½, 7, 7½, 7½)"

Right
front

5½ (6½, 7½, 8, 8½, 9½)"

5 (6, 6¾, 7½, 8¼, 9)"

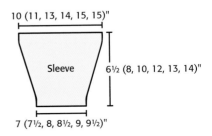

10 (11, 13, 14, 15, 15)"

Sleeve

6½ (8, 10, 12, 13, 14)"

7 (7½, 8, 8½, 9, 9½)"

How to Make the Striped Sweater

BACK

1. With size 6 needles and D, CO 50 (58, 66, 72, 78, 86) sts.

2. Knit 8 (8, 10, 12, 12, 12) rows.

3. Change to size 7 needles and A, and, beg with a knit row, work in St st and stripe patt for 4½ (5½, 6⅓, 6¾, 7¼, 7¾) stripes—approx 10 (12, 14, 15, 16, 17) inches from beg.

4. Put first 16 (19, 22, 24, 26, 28) sts on spare needle or holder for one shoulder, put center 18 (20, 22, 24, 26, 30) sts on holder for neck, and put rem 16 (19, 22, 24, 26, 28) sts onto third holder for second shoulder, leaving a long enough tail to graft shoulder tog later.

POCKET LININGS (MAKE TWO ALIKE)

1. With size 7 needle and D, CO 11 (12, 13, 15, 16, 17) sts.

2. Work in St st for 2½ (2¾, 3, 3¼, 3½, 3¾) inches. Put sts onto holder.

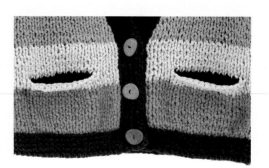

LEFT FRONT

1. With size 6 needles and D, CO 22 (27, 30, 34, 37, 40) sts.

2. Knit 8 (8, 10, 12, 12, 12) rows.

3. Change to size 7 needles and A, and, beg with a knit row, work in St st and stripe patt until you have completed 15 (15, 17, 17, 19, 19) rows of stripe patt (not including garter st hem).

4. Place pocket (WS): P5 (7, 8, 9, 10, 11), BO 11 (12, 13, 15, 16, 17) sts, purl to end of row.

5. Next row (RS): K6 (8, 9, 10, 11, 12), k11 (12, 13, 15, 16, 17) sts from holder for pocket lining with RS facing, k5 (7, 8, 9, 10, 11).

6. Continue working stripe patt until left front measures 5½ (6½, 7½, 8, 8½, 9½) inches from beg, ending with a WS row.

7 Shape neck (RS): Knit to last 2 sts, k2tog—21 (26, 29, 33, 36, 39) sts.

8 Dec 1 st at the end of every fourth row (as established in step 7) 4 (7, 5, 9, 10, 11) times—17 (19, 24, 24, 26, 28) sts.

9 Dec 1 st at the end of every eighth row 1(0, 2, 0, 0, 0) time(s)—16 (19, 22, 24, 26, 28) sts.

10 Cont without further shaping until left front is same length as back and ends with the same number of rows.

11 Put shoulder sts onto spare needle or holder for later.

RIGHT FRONT

1 Work as for left front through step 3.

2 Place pocket (WS): P6 (8, 9, 10, 11, 12), BO 11 (12, 13, 15, 16, 17) sts, purl to end of row.

3 Next row (RS): K5 (7, 8, 9, 10, 11), k11 (12, 13, 15, 16, 17) sts from holder for pocket lining with RS facing, k6 (8, 9, 10, 11, 12).

4 Work from here until piece measures 5½ (6½, 7½, 8, 8½, 9½) inches from beg, ending with a WS row.

5 Shape neck (RS): Ssk, knit to end of row—21 (26, 29, 33, 36, 39) sts.

6 Dec 1 st at beg of every fourth row 4 (7, 5, 9, 10, 11) times.

7 Dec 1 st at beg of every eighth row 1 (0, 2, 0, 0, 0) time(s)—16 (19, 22, 24, 26, 28) sts.

8 Cont without further shaping until right front is same length as back and ends with the same number of rows.

9 Put shoulder sts onto spare needle or holder for later.

SLEEVES (MAKE TWO ALIKE)

1 With size 6 needles and D, CO 31 (34, 36, 38, 40, 43) sts.

2 Work in garter stitch (knit every row) for 1 (1, 2, 2, 3, 3) inches.

3 Change to size 7 needles and A and work first 2 rows stripe patt.

NOTE: You might want to use a row counter to keep track of inc rows.

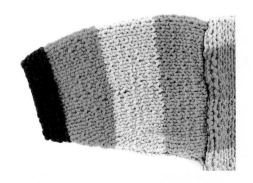

4 Next row—begin sleeve shaping (RS): Inc 1 st each end of row—33 (36, 38, 40, 42, 45) sts.

⑤ Inc 1 st each end every fourth row 5 (5, 9, 9, 13, 9) times, maintaining stripe patt—43 (46, 56, 58, 68, 63) sts.

⑥ Inc 1 st each end every eighth row 1 (2, 1, 2, 0, 3) time(s), maintaining stripe patt—45 (50, 58, 62, 68, 69) sts.

⑦ Work without further shaping until sleeve measures approx 6½ (8, 10, 12, 13, 14) inches from beg, end with at least 3 rows of one stripe.

⑧ BO firmly but not tightly, using same color as final stripe.

GRAFT SHOULDER SEAMS

Before working the trim, you need to join the shoulders. Use the three-needle bind-off method to graft shoulder seams, as described here. (See pages 40–41 for more information.)

① With RS tog, place the 16 (19, 22, 24, 26, 28) sts from the left front shoulder onto a size 6 dpn and do the same for the 16 (19, 22, 24, 26, 28) sts from the left back shoulder; then hold the needles parallel to one another.

② Insert a third dpn into the first st on the first needle as if to knit, then into the first st on the second needle as if to knit, and knit the 2 sts as 1 st, using the same color yarn as the sts on the needles.

③ Rep step 2; there should now be 2 sts on the right needle.

④ Pass the first st on the right needle over the second and off.

⑤ Rep steps 3 and 4, knitting the corresponding sts of each shoulder together and binding off as you go, until 1 st rem on the right needle.

⑥ Cut yarn, pull it through the last st, and secure.

⑦ Rep steps 1–6 for the right shoulder.

WORK TRIM

The button band, collar, and buttonhole band are worked simultaneously in garter stitch, using a long circular needle so that you can pick up all the stitches. The shawl collar is shaped with a simple version of short-rowing (see pages 74–77) that doesn't involve wrapping stitches. For these short rows, you simply knit partway across the row, turn, and work back in the other direction. This way, you widen the trim only for the length of the shawl collar.

1. With size 6 circular needle and D, beg with RS facing at lower edge of right front, pick up and k20 (24, 28, 30, 32, 34) sts up right front to beg neck shaping, then pick up and knit 21 (25, 29, 31, 33, 35) sts up to shoulder seam, then k18 (20, 22, 24, 26, 30) sts from holder for back neck, then pick up and knit 21 (25, 29, 31, 33, 35) sts down left neck, then pick up and knit 20 (24, 28, 30, 32, 34) sts down to lower left edge—100 (118, 136, 146, 156, 168) sts total.

2. Knit 1 (1, 1, 3, 3, 3) rows.

3. Row 1 (RS)—beg shawl collar shaping: K68 (80, 91, 98, 105, 114), turn.

4. Row 2: K36 (42, 46, 50, 54, 60), turn.

5. Row 3: K38 (44, 48, 52, 56, 62), turn.

6. Row 4: K40 (46, 50, 54, 58, 64) turn.

7. Continue shaping collar as established, completing an additional 2 sts at end of each short row, until you get to 60 (70, 82, 86, 94, 100) sts, turn.

8. Next row (RS): Knit. (This takes you to the hem of the left front.)

9. Next row (WS): Knit. (This takes you to the right front hem.)

NOTE: If you are making the sweater for a girl, work buttonhole row as specified in step 10 and skip step 11. If the sweater is for boy, skip step 10 and work the buttonhole row as specified in step 11.

10. Work buttonhole row/girls' sweater: K2 (2, 2, 2, 2, 3), *yo, k2tog, k6 (8, 10, 11, 5, 5)*; rep from * to * 1 (1, 1, 1, 3, 3) time(s), yo, k2tog, knit to end of row.

11. Work buttonhole row/boys' sweater: K80 (94, 108, 116, 124, 135), *k2tog, yo, k6 (8, 10, 11, 5, 5)*; rep from * to * 1 (1, 1, 1, 3, 3) time(s), k2tog, yo, k2 (2, 2, 2, 2, 3).

12. Knit 3 rows.

13. BO loosely knitwise.

FINISHING

1. Weave in ends, except for those that can be used to sew seams.

2. Attach sleeves: With RS tog, pin sleeve caps to armholes, with shoulder seam centered, and backstitch in place.

3. Lightly steam entire sweater on WS to block, including seams and pocket linings.

4. Sew side and sleeve seams, using the backstitch seam or invisible vertical seam (see pages 167–168).

5. Whipstitch pocket linings in place (see page 207). Steam again.

6. Sew buttons opposite buttonholes, using thread to match D.

How to Make the Matching Hat

You work the hat back and forth in rows and then sew the back seam. You start by knitting the ear flaps and then work them into the garter stitch brim. From there, you knit the color segments, which are gradually narrowed to shape the crown of the hat.

EAR FLAPS (MAKE TWO ALIKE)

1 With size 6 needle and D, CO 4 sts.

2 Knit 2 rows.

3 Next row—begin ear flap shaping (RS): K1, m1, knit to last st, m1, k1—6 sts.

4 Knit 3 rows.

5 Rep last 4 rows 5 (6, 7, 8) times—16 (18, 20, 22) sts.

6 Knit 3 rows.

7 Cut yarn, leaving a 6-inch tail, and sl sts to holder.

HAT BODY

1 With size 6 needle and D, CO 8 (9, 10, 11) sts, k16 (18, 20, 22) sts from holder for first ear flap, CO 21 (21, 24, 24) more sts using knit cast-on (see page 18), k16 (18, 20, 22) sts from holder for second ear flap, CO 8 (9, 10, 11) more sts using knit cast-on—69 (75, 84, 90) sts.

2 Knit 8 (10, 10, 12) rows. Cut yarn D, leaving a tail.

3 Beg color block segments (RS): K23 (25, 28, 30) in A, k23 (25, 28, 30) in B, k23 (25, 28, 30) in C.

4 Next row (WS): P23 (25, 28, 30) in C, p23 (25, 28, 30) in B, p23 (25, 28, 30) in A, twisting yarns together at color changes to prevent holes.

NOTE: See pages 156–157 for more on intarsia knitting.

5 Rep last 2 rows 4 (4, 6, 6) times more, taking care to twist yarns on WS when changing color to prevent holes.

6 Shape crown (RS): Using A, k2tog tbl, k19 (21, 24, 26), k2tog; change to B, k2tog tbl, k19 (21, 24, 26), k2tog; change to C, k2tog tbl, k19 (21, 24, 26), k2tog—63 (69, 78, 84) sts.

7 Work 3 rows without shaping, maintaining color segments.

8 Next row (RS): Using A, k2tog tbl, k17 (19, 22, 24), k2tog; using B, k2tog tbl, k17 (19, 22, 24), k2tog; using C, k2tog tbl, k17 (19, 22, 24), k2tog—57 (63, 72, 78) sts.

9 Work 3 rows without shaping, maintaining color segments.

10 Next row (RS): Dec in each color segment as set—51 (57, 66, 72) sts.

11 Next row (WS): Purl, maintaining color segments.

12 Dec at the beg and end of each color segment *every* RS row 4 times (dec 6 sts total per dec row)—27 (33, 42, 48) sts.

13 Next row (WS): Using C, p2tog, p5 (7, 10, 12), p2tog tbl; using B, p2tog, p5 (7, 10, 12), p2tog tbl; using A, p2tog, p5 (7, 10, 12), p2tog tbl—21 (27, 36, 42) sts.

14 Dec at the beg and end of each color segment *every* row (with k2tog and k2tog tbl on RS and p2tog and p2tog tbl on WS) 2 (3, 5, 6) times—9 (9, 6, 6) sts.

15 Next row: K3tog (p3tog, p2tog, k2tog) in C; k3tog (p3tog, p2tog, k2tog) in B; k3tog (p3tog, p2tog, k2tog) in A—3 sts.

16 Cut yarn A, leaving a long enough tail to sew back seam, pull through rem sts, and tighten.

TIES (MAKE TWO ALIKE)

1 Using 4 mm crochet hook and D, attach yarn to tip of earflap and chain for 10 (10, 12, 12) inches.

2 Pull yarn through last loop and thread through tapestry needle. Weave end back into chain to conceal.

FINISHING

1 Sew back seam.

2 Weave in ends.

3 Use D threaded in a tapestry needle to sew straight lines across color breaks up to top of hat, as pictured.

This small vintage-look wool headband is packed with lessons for you: It has shaping for the ear coverings, a Fair Isle stripe in four colors, and crochet trim. Try new color schemes and make headbands for the whole family.

Specifications

SIZES
Circumference: 17 (18, 19½, 20½) inches

MATERIALS
1 skein each Brown Sheep *Nature Spun* (100% wool/245 yd./100 g skein) in gray tweed (A), light blue (B), red (C), gold (D), and lime green (E)

NOTE: This project is great for using up leftover yarn. The yarn specified comes in high-yardage skeins—much more than you need for this project—so search through your stash for yarn that matches the gauge before buying.

Size 6 (4 mm) needles

Stitch holder

Tapestry needle

Size F (3.75 mm) crochet hook

GAUGE
20 stitches and 24 rows to 4 inches over stockinette stitch on size 6 (4 mm) needles

Pattern Stitches

FAIR ISLE CHART

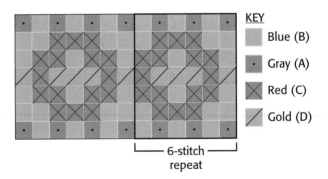

6-stitch repeat

KEY

Blue (B)

Gray (A)

Red (C)

Gold (D)

How to Make the Fair Isle Winter Headband

HEADBAND

1. With A, CO 85 (91, 97, 103) sts.

2. Beg with a knit row, work 8 rows St st.

3. Beg with row 1, work all 7 rows of Fair Isle patt from chart. Cut all yarns except A.

4. Beg with a purl row, work 3 rows St st in A.

5. Next row (RS): BO 10 (10, 11, 11) sts, work next 17 (19, 20, 21) sts and then sl them onto holder, BO 31 (33, 35, 39) sts, knit to end of row.

6. Next row (WS): BO 10 (10, 11, 11) sts, purl to end.

7. Beg with a knit row, work 2 rows St st on first earflap.

8. Next row—beg shaping flap (RS): *K2, skp, knit to last 4 sts, k2tog, k2.

9. Next row (WS): Purl.

10. Rep last 2 rows until 7 (9, 10, 9) sts rem, ending with a WS row.

11. Next row (RS): *K2tog; rep from *, end k1 (1, 0, 1)—4 (5, 5, 5) sts.

12. Next row (FIRST SIZE ONLY): K2tog twice, pass first st on right needle over second—1 st.

13. Next row (ALL OTHER SIZES): K2tog twice, past first st on right needle over second, k1, pass first st on right needle over second—1 st.

14. Cut yarn, pull through rem st, and tighten.

15. Sl the 17 (19, 20, 21) sts for second earflap onto needle, ready to work a RS row.

16. Rep steps 7–14 for second earflap.

FINISHING

1. Weave in ends.

2. Lightly steam to neaten and block.

3. Sew back seam.

4. With crochet hook and E, and beg at back seam, single crochet around perimeter of headband and steam again.

Women's Pullover with Big Cable

K nit in soft super-bulky yarn, this pullover is fun and quick to knit. Plus, you'll like the way the thick yarn magnifies the honeycomb cable that runs up the center of the pullover. It's not a complicated cable to create, and as most of the sweater is worked in stockinette stitch, it's a great project for someone new to cables.

Specifications

SIZES

S (M, L)

Finished chest circumference: 44 (52, 62) inches

Back length: 27 (28, 29) inches

Sleeve length: 18 (18½, 19) inches

NOTE: This sweater is meant to have an oversized fit.

GAUGE

9 stitches and 13 rows over stockinette stitch on size 15 (10 mm) needles

MATERIALS

10 (11, 12) balls Reynolds *Blizzard* (65% alpaca/35% acrylic, 66 yd./100 g hank) in pink #641

Size 13 (9 mm) needles

Size 15 (10 mm) needles

Size 13 double-pointed needles or 16-inch circular needle

2 stitch markers

Cable needle

Row counter, if desired

2 large stitch holders

Tapestry needle

Pattern Stitches

BOBBLE RIB FOR SLEEVES (MULT OF 5 STS PLUS 2)

Rows 1 and 5 (RS): P2, *k3, p2; rep from * to end of row.

Rows 2 and 4 (WS): K2, *p3, k2; rep from * to end of row.

Row 3—bobble row: P2, *k1, mb (k into front, back, front, back, and front of next st), k1, p2; rep from * to end of row.

Rep rows 1–5 for bobble rib.

HONEYCOMB CABLE PANEL (20 STS)

Row 1 (RS): P2, k16, p2.

Rows 2, 4, 6, and 8 (WS): K2, p16, k2.

Row 3 (cable row): P2, *sl next 2 sts to cn and hold at back, knit the next 2 sts from left needle, knit the 2 sts from cn; sl next 2 sts to cn and hold at front, knit next 2 sts from left needle, knit the 2 sts from cn; rep from * once, p2.

Row 5: P2, k16, p2.

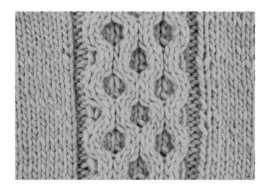

Row 7 (cable row): P2, *sl next 2 sts to cn and hold at front, knit next 2 sts from left needle, knit the 2 sts from cn; sl next 2 sts to cn and hold at back, knit next 2 sts from left needle, knit the 2 sts from cn; rep from * once, p2.

Rep rows 1–8 for honeycomb cable panel.

How to Make the Sweater

BACK

1. With size 13 needles, CO 50 (60, 70) sts.

2. Row 1 (RS): [P2, k3] three (four, five) times across first 15 (20, 25) sts, place marker, work row 1 of cable panel over next 20 sts, place marker, [k3, p2] three (four, five) times across rem 15 (20, 25) sts.

3. Row 2 (WS): [K2, p3] three (four, five) times across first 15 (20, 25) sts, sl marker, work row 2 of cable panel over next 20 sts, sl marker, [p3, k2] three (four, five) times across rem 15 (20, 25) sts.

④ Cont as established, working 20-st cable panel centered between markers with ribbing on either side, for 4 more rows.

⑤ Change to size 15 needles.

⑥ Next row (RS): K15 (20, 25), sl marker, work row 7 of cable panel, sl marker, k15 (20, 25).

⑦ Next row (WS): P15 (20, 25), sl marker, work row 8 cable panel, sl marker, p15 (20, 25) sts.

⑧ Cont as established, working cable panel centered between markers with St st on either side, until back measures 19 inches from beg, ending with a WS row.

⑨ Beg armhole shaping: BO 3 (4, 5) sts beg next 2 rows—44 (52, 60) sts.

⑩ Next row (RS): K2, ssk, work in patt as established to last 4 sts, k2tog, k2—42 (50, 58) sts.

⑪ Next row (WS): P2, p2tog, work in patt established to last 4 sts, ssp, p2—40 (48, 56) sts.

⑫ Rep last 2 rows three (four, five) times—34 (40, 46) sts.

⑬ Rep step 10—32 (38, 44) sts.

⑭ Next row (WS): Purl to marker, sl marker, work cable panel as established, sl marker, purl to end of row.

⑮ Rep last 2 rows one (two, three) time(s)—30 (34, 38) sts.

⑯ Work without further shaping, maintaining patt as set, until back measures 26 (27, 28) inches from beg, ending with a WS row.

⑰ Shape shoulders: Maintaining cable patt, BO 2 (2, 3) sts beg next 4 rows, then BO 2 (3, 3) sts beg foll 2 rows—18 (20, 20) sts.

⑱ Next row (RS): BO all sts in patt.

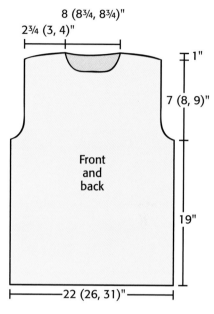

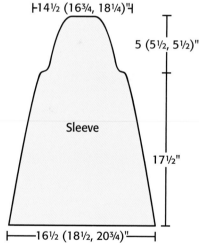

FRONT

1 Work as for back until front measures 26 (27, 28) inches from beg, ending with a WS row.

NOTE: At this point, you should have 30 (34, 38) sts on needles for front. The neck and shoulders are shaped one side at a time.

2 Next row (RS): BO 2 (2, 3) sts, knit to marker, p2tog, BO center 16 sts—1 cable st rem on right needle— p2tog, pass the rem cable st over the p2tog, sl marker, knit to end of row. You should now have 4 (6, 7) sts for left shoulder and 6 (8, 10) sts for right shoulder. Put left shoulder sts on holder while you work the right shoulder only.

3 Next row (WS): BO 2 (2, 3) sts, purl to marker, k1—4 (6, 7) sts.

4 Next row (RS): Ssk, knit to end of row—3 (5, 6) sts.

5 Next row (FIRST SIZE ONLY): BO 2 sts, purl to end of row—2 sts. Skip to step 7.

6 Next row (SECOND AND THIRD SIZES ONLY): BO (2, 3) sts, purl to last 2 sts, p2tog—3 sts.

7 Next row (ALL SIZES): Knit.

8 BO rem 2 (3, 3) sts.

9 Sl the 4 (6, 7) left shoulder sts back to size 15 needle and rejoin yarn to left neck edge, ready to work a WS row.

10 Next row (WS): K1, purl to end of row.

11 Next row: BO 2 (2, 3) sts, knit to last 2 sts, k2tog—1 (3, 3) sts.

12 Next row (SECOND AND THIRD SIZES ONLY): P2tog, purl to end of row—2 sts.

13 BO rem 1 (2, 2) sts.

SLEEVES (MAKE TWO ALIKE)

1 With size 13 needle, CO 37 (42, 47) sts.

2 Beg with row 1, work bobble rib for sleeves for 5 rows.

3 Change to size 15 needles and beg with a purl row, work in St st for 9 rows.

NOTE: You might want to use a row counter from this point to keep track of decrease rows. Decrease rows are worked as follows: K2, ssk, knit to last 4 sts, k2tog, k2.

4 Next row—beg sleeve shaping (RS): K2, ssk, knit to last 4 sts, k2tog, k2—35 (40, 45) sts.

5 Cont in St st, dec 1 st each end as established in step 4 every 12th row one (one, two) time(s)—33 (38, 41) sts.

6 Continue without further shaping until sleeve measures 17½ inches from beg, ending with a WS row.

7 Begin sleeve cap shaping: BO 3 (4, 5) sts beg next 2 rows—27 (30, 31) sts.

8 Next row (RS) K2, ssk, knit to last 4 sts, k2tog, k2—25 (28, 29) sts.

9 Next row: Purl.

10 Rep last 2 rows six (seven, seven) times, ending with a WS row—13 (14, 15) sts.

11 BO 2 sts beg next 2 rows, then BO 2 (2, 3) sts beg foll 2 rows—5 (6, 5) sts.

12 BO rem sts.

FINISHING

1 Weave in ends.

2 Block pieces to measurements shown on page 271.

3 Sew shoulder seams using backstitch seam or the invisible horizontal seam (see pages 166–169 for seaming techniques).

4 Pick up sts for neckband: Beg at right shoulder seam with RS facing, use size 13 circular needle or dpns to pick up and k18 (20, 20) sts across back neck to left shoulder seam, pick up and k6 sts down left front neck shaping to beg of BO front neck sts, pick up and k16 sts across BO cable sts, and pick up and k6 sts up right front neck to right shoulder—46 (48, 48) sts.

5 Place marker and join sts in rnd.

6 Next rnd: Knit, increasing 2 (0, 0) sts (1 at each shoulder seam)—48 (48, 48) sts.

7 Next rnd—work neckband: *K2, p2; rep from * to end of rnd.

8 Rep last rnd until neckband measures 3 inches. Work in St st (knit every rnd) for an additional 1½ inches. BO loosely knitwise using size 15 needle.

9 Center sleeves on shoulder seams, set in and pin in place, and sew sleeves onto sweater using a combination of the vertical-to-horizontal seam and the invisible horizontal seam.

10 Lightly steam seams.

11 Sew side and sleeve seams using the invisible vertical seam (see page 168).

12 Weave in rem ends.

13 Steam entire sweater, including seams, again.

Toe-Up Socks

Although it's not as common as the top-down method, you can make socks from the toe up. Setting up the toe stitches takes a little ingenuity, but once you master it with the first sock, the second will come easily. The benefit of working socks this way is that you can try them on as you go and customize the fit more easily and accurately than with the top-down method.

Specifications

SIZES
Approximate foot circumference: 8 inches

MATERIALS
2 hanks Classic Elite *Lush* (50% angora/50% wool, 124 yd./50 g hank) in Granny Smith #4481

Size 8 (5 mm) double-pointed needles

1 split-ring marker to fit your needle size

Tapestry needle

Row counter, if desired

GAUGE
16 sts and 20 rounds to 4 inches in stockinette stitch on size 8 needles

Pattern Stitches

INSTEP AND LEG PATTERN
Rnd 1: *K3, p2, k3; rep from * to end of rnd.

Rnds 2 and 4: Knit.

Rnd 3: *P1, k6, p1; rep from * to end of rnd.

How to Make the Socks

Make two of these fun toe-up socks exactly the same.

MAKE THE TOE

1 Using 1 dpn, CO 20 sts. Do not divide sts onto 3 or 4 dpn or work in the round yet.

2 Row 1: *Sl1, k1; rep from * to end of row.

3 Row 2: Rep row 1.

4 Divide the sts between two dpns: Holding the dpn with the sts on it in your left hand and two more dpns in your right hand, alternately slip the knit stitches onto one needle and the sl sts onto the other needle until you have 10 sts parallel to each other on each of the two dpns. Place a marker onto the needle opposite the working yarn, for beg of rnd. Now you are ready to shape the toe.

NOTE: The toe is worked in the round, with stitches held on two dpns, using a third dpn as the working needle. Be sure to start with the knit side out, bumpy side in.

5 Rnd 1: *K1 (to join rnd), m1, knit to last st on first needle, m1, k1; on second needle, k1, m1, knit to last st, m1, k1—24 sts.

6 Rnd 2: Knit.

7 Rep last 2 rnds until you have 32 sts.

MAKE THE FOOT

1 Using three dpns, divide the sts so that 16 sts are on the first needle and 8 sts each are on the second and third needles.

NOTE: The first 16 sts of the rnd are the instep sts.

2 Work the stitch pattern over the 16 instep sts and knit the rem 16 sts for sole until sock is approx 2 inches shorter than the desired foot length.

3 Arrange the sts to prepare for heel shaping: Put the first 16 stitches, for the instep, onto a holder or loose strand of scrap yarn. Place the rem 16 sts for the heel onto a second needle.

MAKE THE HEEL

The short-row heel is worked back and forth in rows.

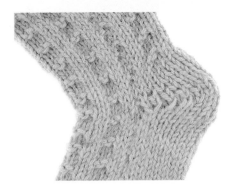

1 Row 1: K15, bring yarn to front, sl1 purlwise to right needle, turn.

2 Row 2: Sl1 (the unworked st from the last row) purlwise wyif to right needle, purl to last st, bring yarn to back, and sl1 to the right needle, turn.

NOTE: You have now wrapped 1 st on each end.

3 Row 3: Sl1 wyib, knit to the st before the wrapped st, bring yarn to front, sl1 purlwise to right needle, turn.

4 Row 4: Sl1 wyif, purl to the st before the wrapped st, bring yarn to back, sl1 to the right needle, turn.

5 Rep rows 3 and 4 until you have 5 wrapped sts on each end and 6 unwrapped sts in the middle, ready to work a RS row.

6 Next row—beg back of heel: Sl1 to complete wrap, knit to the first wrapped st, [insert the right needle knitwise into both the wrap and the wrapped st, knit the wrap and the wrapped st as 1 st], bring yarn to front of work, sl1 (the next wrapped st), turn. (This last slipped st will now have 2 wraps.)

7 Next row: Sl1 (the st with 2 wraps), purl to the first wrapped st, [insert the right needle from back to front through the back loop of the wrap, lift the wrap, and place it onto the left needle with the wrapped st, purl the wrap and the st as 1 st], bring yarn to back, sl1.

8 Rep last 2 rows but pick up both wraps and knit or purl them together with their accompanying st, until you have worked all sts and have 16 unwrapped sts and are ready to beg a knit row.

9 Knit across the heel sts once more so that you're ready to rejoin the rnd.

MAKE THE LEG AND CUFF

① Sl 8 heel sts onto a second dpn. Place the instep sts back onto a dpn. Join rnd and again begin working all 32 sts in patt from where you left off in the rnd.

NOTE: If a gap occurs where the heel and instep sts meet, pick up 1 st between the two. Then decrease back to 32 sts in the next rnd.

② Work until sock leg is 4 inches for an ankle sock, 6 inches for a midcalf sock, or 8½ inches for a knee sock, minus the cuff.

③ Next rnd—work cuff: P1, k2, *p2, k2; rep from * to last st, p1.

④ Rep last rnd until cuff measures approx 4 inches.

⑤ Last rnd: P1, *k2, CO 1 st using backward-loop CO, p2, M1; rep from * to last 3 sts, k2, M1, p1—47 sts.

NOTE: For an even looser cuff edge, use a needle two or three sizes larger for the bind-off.

⑥ BO loosely in rib patt, except sl each M1 as you BO instead of working it.

FINISHING

① Weave in ends.

② Block socks using sock blockers to match the size of your socks, or, if your yarn's care instructions allow, lightly steam to block, taking care not to block ribbing.

CHAPTER 16

Modifiable Patterns for Hats, Socks, and Mittens

Some knitters like to follow patterns down to the last detail, without making any changes. Other knitters like to alter patterns: They choose a different yarn than a pattern specifies, omit a collar, use an alternate stitch pattern, or add embellishments. This chapter provides modifiable knitting patterns for hats, socks, and mittens in multiple gauges, sizes, shapes, and stitch patterns—allowing you to create your own unique styles without having to tackle too much complicated math.

Hats

Hats look more complicated than they are, and they're quicker to make than most scarves. The hats here are knit in the round from the brim up on double-pointed needles, eliminating an unsightly back seam and minimizing finishing.

Using the master pattern, these hats are easy to customize: Simply change the brim style; shape the crown a little differently; or add a pompom, tassel, or topknot. The variations that follow are just a few to get you started.

BRIM TREATMENTS

Here are four brim styles that are easy to do but result in completely different styles. The rolled brim is the easiest because it's worked in stockinette stitch. For the hats master pattern, you can work the ribbed brim in single (1 × 1) rib, or, if your stitch count is divisible by 4, in double (2 × 2) rib. You can double the length of the brim if you prefer to fold it over.

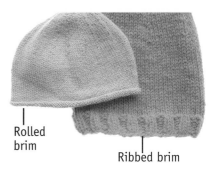

Rolled brim

Ribbed brim

The hemmed brim is folded under at the turning row. The hemmed brim shown here uses a picot hem, which has a tiny scalloped edge, but you can also follow the instructions for a simple purled turning row. Don't be put off by the earflaps—they're knit right on to the brim and are easy to make.

Seed stitch brim with earflaps

Hemmed brim

SHAPING TREATMENTS

After you have completed your brim and knit your hat body to the desired length, choose one of several shapings to finish the crown of your hat. The square top is the easiest because it requires no shaping at all. You can leave the top square after finishing or sew the corners together as shown; for a completely different look, attach cords to the corners and tie them together. The rounded top is achieved by working a short series of decrease rounds. The yarn is then cut, and the tail is pulled through the few remaining stitches, cinched tight, and fastened off.

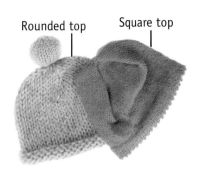

Rounded top   Square top

The pointed top is worked and finished almost like the rounded top, but over many more rounds. To make a long, pointed hat like the stocking cap shown, you work decrease rounds separated by a larger number of non-decrease rounds.

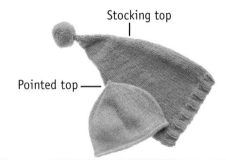

Stocking top

Pointed top

EMBELLISHMENTS

You can decorate your hats all kinds of ways. Try pompoms, tassels, crochet chains, knitted cords, loops, or balls. Sew a pompom to the top for a traditional look or attach it to the front, off to one side, for a chic style. Finish the top with a length of knitted cord and then form the cord into a knot or loop, or sew a pompom to the end of the cord. Crochet chains also work well as hat ties and pompom or tassel holders. The knitted ball is a fun embellishment—you can make one big one or a cluster of small ones to sew to your hat top.

Hat: Master Pattern

With this one master pattern, you can create countless hat styles, in many shapes, sizes, and stitch patterns. The size range covers the whole family, and the gauges include yarns from sport weight to bulky.

Specifications

SIZES

XXS (XS, S, M, L)

Brim circumference: 14 (16, 18, 20, 22) inches

MATERIALS

Desired yarn, in the amount specified in Table 1

1 set of double-pointed needles in size needed to obtain gauge

1 set of double-pointed needles one or two sizes smaller than size needed to obtain gauge (for edgings)

Stitch marker to fit your needle size

Tapestry needle

Pompom maker (optional)

Table 1. Approximate Yardage for Hat	
Gauge (in Stockinette Stitch)	**Approximate Yardage**
2 sts/in.	85–150 yd.
3 sts/in.	100–175 yd.
4 sts/in.	125–225 yd.
5 sts/in.	150–250 yd.
6 sts/in.	175–275 yd.
7 sts/in.	200–325 yd.

NOTES ON THE SAMPLES

The pink rolled-brim hat has a round top and is embellished with a knitted ball.

The orange stocking cap brim is worked in 2 × 2 rib, and the top is embellished with a matching pompom.

The brim and earflaps of the green hat are worked in seed stitch. The top has round shaping and is embellished with a knitted cord loop. The pompom ties attached to the earflaps are knitted cord.

The blue pointed hat with a rolled brim has a loose pompom sewn to the front.

The purple hat brim is hemmed with a picot folding ridge, and the top is square.

How to Make the Hats

CAST ON: ALL STYLES

1 CO sts for your size and gauge, according to Table 2, dividing sts as evenly as possible over three or four dpns.

NOTE: If you want a firm, elastic brim, you might want to cast on using needles a size or two smaller than the size you use to work the rest of the hat. For example, a seed stitch brim will likely require needles two sizes smaller, so the brim doesn't end up larger than the body. Ribbed brims can be worked in the same needles as the body, or you can go down a size to ensure lasting elasticity. You can use a needle one size smaller for the rolled brim and for the section of the hemmed brim that gets folded under.

2 Place marker (pm) and join rnd, taking care not to twist sts.

3 Go to the directions for the desired brim style under "Work the Brim," below.

Table 2. Cast On for Hat			
Gauge	**No. of Sts to CO**	**Gauge**	**No. of Sts to CO**
2 sts/in.	28 (32, 36, 40, 44) sts	5 sts/in.	70 (80, 90, 100, 110) sts
3 sts/in.	42 (48, 54, 60, 66) sts	6 sts/in.	84 (96, 108, 120, 132) sts
4 sts/in.	56 (64, 72, 80, 88) sts	7 sts/in.	98 (112, 126, 140, 154) sts

WORK THE BRIM

ROLLED BRIM

This brim can be worked over any number of stitches, and it results in a fun and casual style that looks good on hat-wearers of all ages.

1 Knit all rnds, sl marker beg every rnd, until piece measures 1½ inches from CO edge.

2 Go to "Work the Body: All Styles," page 285.

RIBBED BRIM

You work this brim over an even number of stitches. If your stitch count is a multiple of 4 sts, you can work it as 2 × 2 rib, as shown.

① *K1, p1; rep from * to end of rnd.

② Rep last rnd, sl marker beg every rnd, until brim measures 1 (1, 1½, 1½, 2) inch(es) from CO edge.

NOTE: If you want a folded ribbed brim, work until brim measures 2½ (2½, 3, 3, 4) inches.

③ Go to "Work the Body: All Styles," on the next page.

HEMMED BRIM

This brim works best in yarns no thicker than 4 sts per inch.

① Knit all rnds, sl marker beg every rnd, until piece measures 1 (1¼, 1¼, 1½, 1½) inch(es) from CO edge.

② Purl next rnd to form folding ridge.

NOTE: For a picot hem like the one shown here, work the folding ridge (step 2) as an eyelet row by repeating [k2tog, yo] around.

③ Go to "Work the Body: All Styles," on the next page.

SEED STITCH BRIM

You work this brim over an even number of stitches. Because seed stitch can create a loose fabric, you should work this brim using needles a size or two smaller than the ones you use for the body.

① *K1, p1; rep from * to end of rnd.

② *P1, k1; rep from * to end of rnd.

③ Rep last 2 rnds, sl marker beg every rnd, until piece measures 1 (1¼, 1¼, 1½, 1½) inch(es) from CO edge.

④ Go to "Work the Body: All Styles," on the next page.

WORK THE BODY: ALL STYLES

1 Change to larger needles if smaller needles were used for the brim and knit every rnd until piece measures 4 (4½, 5, 6, 7) inches from CO edge or folding ridge. If using a folded ribbed brim, measure from where the brim will fold.

NOTE: If you're making a rounded or short pointed hat, try the hat on the wearer, and if you can barely see the top of the wearer's head, it is time to start the top shaping.

2 Go to the directions for the desired top shaping, under "Work the Top Shaping," below.

WORK THE TOP SHAPING

At this point, you can decide to make the top of your hat rounded, pointed, elongated, or square. Follow the directions for your desired style.

SQUARE TOP SHAPING

1 Work until piece measures 7 (7½, 8, 9, 10) inches from CO edge or folding ridge. If using the folded ribbed brim, measure from where the brim will fold.

2 Starting at beg of rnd, put first half of sts onto one or two dpns and put second half of sts onto one or two dpns. Using a third or fifth dpn, work three-needle bind-off across top (see pages 40–41).

3 Go to the finishing instructions for your style, under "Finish the Hat," page 288.

ROUNDED TOP, POINTED TOP, AND STOCKING CAP: BEGIN SHAPING

1 Work first dec rnd: *K5 (6, 7, 8, 9), k2tog; rep from * to end of rnd. You should have rem the number of sts specified for your size and gauge in Table 3.

Table 3. Number of Stitches Remaining After First Decrease Round		
Gauge	**No. of Sts Rem**	**No. of Sts to Dec**
2 sts/in.	24 (28, 32, 36, 40) sts	4 sts
3 sts/in.	36 (42, 48, 54, 60) sts	6 sts
4 sts/in.	48 (56, 64, 72, 80) sts	8 sts
5 sts/in.	60 (70, 80, 90, 100) sts	10 sts
6 sts/in.	72 (84, 96, 108, 120) sts	12 sts
7 sts/in.	84 (98, 112, 126, 140) sts	14 sts

2 Without decreasing, work the number of rnds specified for your size, gauge, and top style in Table 4.

3 Work second dec rnd: *K4 (5, 6, 7, 8), k2tog; rep from * to end of rnd. You should have rem the number of sts specified for your size and gauge in Table 5.

4 Go to the directions for final shaping for your style.

Table 4. Number of Rounds to Work Even After Decrease Round for Tops

Gauge	Rounded Top	Short Pointed Top	Stocking Cap
2 sts/in.	1 rnd	1 rnd	5 rnd
3 sts/in.	1 rnd	1 rnd	6 rnd
4 sts/in.	2 rnd	2 rnd	7 rnd
5 sts/in.	2 rnd	2 rnd	8 rnd
6 sts/in.	3 rnd	3 rnd	9 rnd
7 sts/in.	3 rnd	3 rnd	10 rnd

Table 5. Number of Stitches Remaining After Second Decrease Round

Gauge	No. of Sts Rem	No. of Sts to Dec
2 sts/in.	20 (24, 28, 32, 36) sts	4 sts
3 sts/in.	30 (36, 42, 48, 54) sts	6 sts
4 sts/in.	40 (48, 56, 64, 72) sts	8 sts
5 sts/in.	50 (60, 70, 80, 90) sts	10 sts
6 sts/in.	60 (72, 84, 96, 108) sts	12 sts
7 sts/in.	70 (84, 98, 112, 126) sts	14 sts

ROUNDED TOP: FINAL SHAPING

1 Continue to dec every rnd the same number of sts per rnd evenly, as established, until you have rem the number of sts specified for your gauge in Table 6.

2 K2tog to end of rnd.

3 For hats that are 2, 3, or 4 sts per inch: If you are finishing the top with a knitted cord stem, loop, or knot, transfer rem sts to smaller dpn and knit cord to desired length per instructions on page 206; otherwise, skip ahead to step 4.

For hats that are 5, 6, or 7 sts per inch: K2tog to end of rnd before beginning knitted cord or continuing to step 4.

4 Cut yarn, leaving a 10-inch tail. Pull through rem sts and secure.

5 Go to the finishing instructions for your style, under "Finish the Hat," page 288.

Table 6. Number of Stitches Remaining After Decreasing Every Round, as Established

Gauge	No. of Sts Rem	Gauge	No. of Sts Rem
2 sts/in.	12 sts	5 sts/in.	20 sts
3 sts/in.	12 sts	6 sts/in.	24 sts
4 sts/in.	16 sts	7 sts/in.	28 sts

Short Pointed Top and Stocking Cap: Final Shaping

1 Continue to dec the same number of sts evenly per rnd as established for your gauge and work the same number of non-decrease rnds between dec rnds as specified for your gauge and style in Table 4, until you have the number of sts specified for your gauge in Table 6.

2 Again work the number of non-decrease rnds specified for your gauge and style in Table 4.

3 K2tog to end of rnd.

4 Rep steps 2 and 3. You will have rem the number of sts specified for your gauge in Table 7.

5 K2tog to end of rnd.

NOTE: For an odd number of stitches, k2tog as many times as possible and then knit the remaining stitch.

6 Rep step 5 until you have 1 st rem.

7 Cut yarn, leaving a 10-inch tail. Pull through rem st and secure.

8 Go to the finishing instructions for your style, under "Finish the Hat," on the next page.

Table 7. Number of Stitches Remaining After All Decrease Rounds for Pointed Top	
Gauge	**No. of Sts Rem**
2 sts/in.	2 sts
3 sts/in.	3 sts
4 sts/in.	4 sts
5 sts/in.	5 sts
6 sts/in.	6 sts
7 sts/in.	7 sts

FINISH THE HAT

You finish each of the hats a little differently. Go to the instructions for the style you're making.

FINISH HAT: ALL STYLES

1 Weave in ends.

NOTE: If you're making the earflap hat, mark the join of the rnd with a safety pin. This will be the center back of the hat.

2 Lightly steam to block, if your yarn's care instructions allow.

3 Embellish as desired. (See Chapter 13.)

4 If you are making a hemmed brim hat, go to "Hemmed Brim: Further Finishing," below. If you are making a seed stitch brim with earflaps, go to "Seed Stitch Brim with Earflaps: Further Finishing," below.

HEMMED BRIM: FURTHER FINISHING

1 Fold brim to the inside along folding ridge and pin in place.

2 Whipstitch CO edge neatly to backs of sts, ensuring that sewing sts don't show on the RS and that hat doesn't pucker.

3 Weave in ends and lightly steam hem to neaten it.

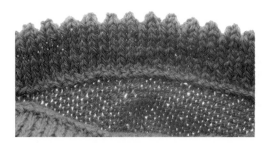

Hemmed brim

SEED STITCH BRIM WITH EARFLAPS: FURTHER FINISHING

1 Holding hat upright with join of rnd (the back of the hat) facing, place marker for left earflap: Beg at the join, measure 1¾ (2, 2¼, 2½, 2¾) inches along brim to the left and mark with a safety pin. Place a second safety pin 3 (4, 4, 4, 5) inches to the left of the first safety pin.

Seed stitch brim with ear flaps

2 With hat upside-down and with RS facing, use smaller needle to pick up and knit the number of sts specified for your size and gauge in Table 8 along CO edge between safety pins for left earflap.

3 Turn and knit this first WS row.

4 Next row (RS)—Beg seed stitch: *K1, p1; rep from * to end of row.

5 Next row (WS): *P1, k1; rep from * to end of row.

6 If you are working at 6 or 7 sts per inch gauge, rep steps 4 and 5.

7 Shape flap—Row 1 (RS): P2tog, *k1, p1; rep from * to last 2 sts, k2tog.

8 Row 2 (WS): *K1, p1; rep from * to end of row.

9 Row 3: K2tog, *p1, k1; rep from * to last 2 sts, p2tog.

10 Row 4: *P1, k1; rep from * to end of row.

11 Rep rows 1–4 until you have the number of stitches shown for your gauge in Table 9.

12 To finish flap without knitted cord tie, cut yarn, leaving a 10-inch tail. Pull tail through rem sts and secure. Skip to step 14 for right earflap.

NOTE: It is not recommended to make the ties if the hat is for an infant.

13 To work a knitted cord tie on the flap, sl rem sts onto smaller dpn and work knitted cord to length desired (10 inches for child, 12 inches for adult). Attach pompom to end. See page 206 for knitted cord instructions and pages 200–201 for pompom instructions.

14 Work right earflap as for left, only place markers at the same measurements to the right of the join and pick up sts working from first to second safety pin.

Table 8. Number of Stitches to Pick Up for Earflap	
Gauge	**No. of Sts to Pick Up**
2 sts/in.	6 (8, 8, 8, 10) sts
3 sts/in.	8 (12, 12, 12, 14) sts
4 sts/in.	12 (16, 16, 16, 20) sts
5 sts/in.	16 (20, 20, 20, 24) sts
6 sts/in.	18 (24, 24, 24, 30) sts
7 sts/in.	20 (28, 28, 28, 34) sts

Table 9. Number of Stitches Remaining After Shaping Earflap	
Gauge	**No. of Sts Rem After Shaping Earflap**
2 sts/in.	2 sts
3 sts/in.	2 sts
4 sts/in.	4 sts
5 sts/in.	4 sts
6 sts/in.	6 sts
7 sts/in.	6 sts

You can leave the crown of your hat unadorned, or you can decorate it. Just a few options are pompoms, tassels, buttons, knots, and loops. For a colorful finish, try using a contrasting color or colors for the finishing touch.

POMPOMS AND TASSELS

You can sew pompoms and tassels tightly to the top singly or in groups. Or, for a more whimsical look, you can attach them with a crocheted chain so they dangle. For babies' and children's hats, attaching two pompoms or tassels like ears can have a cute effect. (For instructions on making pompoms and tassels, see pages 200–203.)

CROCHET CHAINS

You can use crochet chains to attach pompoms and tassels if you want them to swing. You can also crochet ties to earflap hats, kerchiefs, and baby bonnets. Crochet chain loops produce a playful look, and if you use many loops, they can look like a braided pompom. (For instructions on making a crochet chain, see page 209.)

KNITTED CORD

A cute option is to create a topknot, stem, or loop. You do this by knitting the few stitches remaining after shaping as a knitted cord. It's easy to do and requires less finishing than attaching a separate embellishment. You can also knit cords onto earflaps and baby bonnets for firm, durable ties. Just remember to keep the cords on baby apparel short, to avoid danger. (For instructions on making a knitted cord, see page 206.)

KNITTED BALL

Here is a decoration that you don't see very often. Like pompoms, knitted balls can be sewn to hat tops singly or in clusters. If you knit very small balls and cluster them, they can look like berries. A ball is knit separately, filled with polyester stuffing, and then sewn to the top. (For instructions on making a knitted ball, see page 219.)

BUTTONS

When you want to decorate a hat with something other than a pompom or tassel—or if you don't have a lot of yarn left—try sewing a button to that spot. Using a contrasting thread can create an eye-catching touch. Sew buttons in a cluster, as shown, or overlap a small button on a larger button for added detail.

Socks

Most knitters love to make socks. Socks are quick to knit—even when knit in fine yarn—and they're very portable, so you can have them with you all the time. Socks make wonderful gifts. They can be long or short, plain or patterned, thick or thin. Socks don't require a lot of yarn; just a ball or two should do it.

Before you choose a sock pattern and the yarn to go with it, you should take a moment to consider a few things. Who will wear the socks? What yarns would work best for the socks? What needles are required for that yarn? Will the socks be worn with shoes or as slippers? The answers to these questions should help determine what style sock to knit and what yarn to choose.

TYPES OF SOCKS

Socks can range from highly practical to frivolous, depending on the yarn and stitch pattern used to knit them. Using a sparkly, hairy, or variegated yarn will liven up the plainest sock pattern. You can also adjust the leg length from knee-high to ankle length, depending on your preference. Embroidering initials, flowers, or emblems onto the side of the leg can personalize a very plain pair of socks. Most of the socks in this chapter are fairly practical, though the lacier ones are ornamental, too.

THE BEST YARNS FOR SOCKS

How the socks you are making will be worn should help determine what type of yarn to use. If you are knitting socks to be worn with shoes, choose yarn that is very durable but not too thick. Yarns specifically manufactured and labeled as sock yarns are good for this purpose because these yarns are usually thin and spun with wool that has been reinforced with nylon. If you are making socks for lounging, look for yarns that are soft to the touch and provide warmth. In all cases, choose yarns that have elasticity because the socks will stretch with wear; yarns that have no elasticity will produce socks that stretch out and never regain their original shape.

TYPES OF NEEDLES FOR SOCK KNITTING

The socks in this chapter are knit on sets of four double-pointed needles. Some knitters like metal double-pointed needles because the slippery metal enables them to knit faster; others prefer wood or bamboo because the needles don't slide and fall out of the work when it is turned or stored. Plastic double-pointed needles are usually lightweight and less expensive than the other two types.

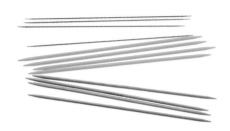

SOCK SIZES

The master sock pattern in this chapter covers the range of sizes shown in Table 10. You measure both the circumference and length of the foot of the wearer to determine which set of instructions to follow. You can adjust the length to suit the wearer.

Table 10. Sock Sizes		
Sock Size	Approx. Foot Circumference at Widest Point	Approx. Foot Length from Tip of Big Toe Diagonally to End of Heel
XS	5 in.	4 to 6½ in.
S	6 in.	6½ to 7½ in.
M	7 in.	7½ to 8½ in.
L	8 in.	8½ to 10 in.
XL	9 in.	10 to 11½ in.

TIP

Faux Fair Isle Socks

You don't have be an expert knitter to create vibrant socks in eye-catching stripes and color patterns. You can knit any of the sock styles that follow in self-patterning yarn. This is yarn that has been dyed in several colors at measured intervals along the strand. Knitting with self-patterning yarn produces these fun stripes and almost Fair Isle–looking color patterns. The added element of surprise makes knitting with these yarns exciting.

Socks: Master Pattern

You can turn out countless pairs of socks with this master pattern. The sizes range from toddler to men's XL, and the gauges run from 4 stitches per inch to 7 stitches per inch.

Specifications

SIZES

XS (S, M, L, XL)

Approximate foot circumference: 5 (6, 7, 8, 9) inches

Approximate foot length: 4–6½ (6½–7½, 7½–8½, 8½–10, 10–11½) inches

Table 11. Approximate Yardage for Socks

Gauge (in Stockinette Stitch)	Approximate Yardage
4 sts/in.	100–350 yd.
5 sts/in.	125–400 yd.
6 sts/in.	125–450 yd.
7 sts/in.	150–550 yd.

MATERIALS

Desired yarn, in the amount specified in Table 11

1 set of double-pointed needles in size needed to obtain gauge

1 set of double-pointed needles in size one size smaller than size needed to obtain gauge (for hemmed cuff)

Split-ring markers to fit your needle size

Cable needle (for cabled leg styles)

2 stitch holders

Tapestry needle

NOTES ON THE SAMPLES

The gray diagonal rib socks have a 2 × 2 ribbed cuff, a heel stitch flap, and star toe shaping. The diagonal rib is carried onto the instep and up to the beginning of the toe shaping.

The red marl round cable socks have a 2 × 2 ribbed cuff, a heel stitch flap, and wedge toe shaping.

The pink lace socks have a picot hemmed cuff and a stockinette stitch heel flap. The lace pattern is carried onto the instep up to the beginning of the wedge toe shaping.

The pale green socks are knit in an allover 2 × 2 rib and have a heel stitch flap and wedge toe shaping.

The reverse stockinette stitch stripe gray marl socks have a 2 × 2 ribbed cuff, a heel stitch flap, and star toe shaping.

How to Make the Socks

When making socks, you have a number of options: cuff stitch, leg stitch, heel stitch, and toe shaping. Because these socks are worked from the top down, stitch patterns will be upside-down. If you want to apply your own color pattern or motif, remember to work it upside-down. You make two socks exactly the same.

CAST ON

1 CO the number of sts specified for your size and gauge in Table 12.

NOTE: It is important to cast on loosely so that the socks pull on easily. If necessary, use a needle two or three sizes larger for casting on.

2 Divide sts evenly onto three dpns (use the fourth as the working needle), place marker (pm), and join rnd, taking care not to twist sts.

3 Go to the directions for the desired cuff style under "Make the Cuff," below.

Table 12. Cast On for Socks	
Gauge	**No. of Sts to CO**
4 sts/in.	24 (24, 28, 32, 36) sts
5 sts/in.	28 (32, 36, 40, 44) sts
6 sts/in.	32 (36, 44, 48, 56) sts
7 sts/in.	36 (44, 48, 56, 64) sts

NOTE: Be sure your stitch count is compatible with the stitch pattern you choose. Most of the leg patterns are worked on a multiple of 4 stitches and will work with all the stitch counts in Table 12. However, there are a few that can be worked only on a multiple of 8 stitches.

MAKE THE CUFF

1 × 1 RIBBED CUFF (EVEN NO. OF STS)

This easy rib is one of the most common cuff styles, and it works well with just about any leg pattern.

1 *K1, p1; rep from * to end of rnd.

2 Rep step 1, sl marker beg every rnd, until cuff measures 1 (1, 1¼, 1¼, 1½) inch(es) or desired length.

3 Go to the directions for the desired leg style under "Make the Leg," on the next page.

Easy Ribbed Socks

A sock with a 1 × 1 or 2 × 2 ribbed cuff and leg has a handsome look and a nice, snug fit. For this type of sock, you continue the rib as established until the sock measures 2½ (3, 4, 5, 6) inches from the CO row for ankle socks or 4 (5, 6, 7, 8) inches for mid-calf-length socks. Then you go to the heel directions.

2 × 2 Ribbed Cuff (Mult of 4 Sts)

This rib produces a very elastic cuff. It works well with leg stitch patterns that are worked over a multiple of 4 stitches.

① *K2, p2; rep from * to end of rnd.

② Rep step 1, sl marker beg every rnd, until cuff measures 1 (1, 1¼, 1¼, 1½) inch(es) or desired length.

③ Go to the directions for the desired leg style under "Make the Leg," below.

Hemmed Cuff (Any No. of Sts)

This type of cuff looks pretty, but it doesn't hug the leg like the ribbed cuff. It's great for fancy and delicate ankle socks.

① Using needles one size smaller than the needles needed to obtain gauge, knit all rnds, sl marker beg every rnd, until piece measures 1 (1¼, 1¼, 1½, 1½) inch(es) from CO edge.

② Switch to needles needed to obtain gauge. Purl next rnd to form folding ridge.

NOTE: For a picot hem, as shown in the photo here, work the folding ridge as an eyelet row by repeating [k2tog, yo] around.

③ Knit all rnds until piece measures 1 (1¼, 1¼, 1½, 1½) inch(es) from CO edge.

④ Go to the directions for the desired leg style under "Make the Leg," below.

MAKE THE LEG

Stockinette Stitch Leg (Any No. of Sts)

This pattern, which is worked over any number of stitches, is a good basic pattern that can be used with any yarn and works especially well with variegated yarns.

① Knit every rnd until sock measures 2½ (3, 4, 5, 6) inches from CO row for ankle sock or 4 (5, 6, 7, 8) inches for midcalf-length sock.

② Go to "Divide for the Heel," page 299.

Reverse Stockinette Striped Leg (Any No. of Sts)

This pattern, which can be worked over any number of stitches, produces fun ridges.

1 Knit 4 rnds.

2 Purl 2 rnds.

3 Rep steps 1 and 2 until sock measures 2½ (3, 4, 5, 6) inches from CO row for ankle sock or 4 (5, 6, 7, 8) inches for midcalf-length sock.

4 Go to "Divide for the Heel," page 299.

Lace Leg (Mult of 8 Sts)

This pretty pattern works best in yarns no thicker than 5 sts per inch.

1 Rnd 1: *P2, yo, k2tog, p2, [k second st then first st on left needle and sl both sts off needle tog]; rep from * to end of rnd.

2 Rnds 2 and 4: *P2, k2; rep from * to end of rnd.

3 Rnd 3: *P2, k2tog, yo, p2, [k second st then first st on left needle and sl both sts off needle tog]; rep from * to end of rnd.

4 Rep rnds 1–4 until sock measures 2½ (3, 4, 5, 6) inches from CO row for ankle sock or 4 (5, 6, 7, 8) inches for midcalf-length sock.

NOTE: Make a note of which row of the pattern you worked last if you want to continue the pattern on the instep stitches after the heel and gusset shaping.

5 Go to "Divide for the Heel," page 299.

DIAGONAL RIB LEG (MULT OF 4 STS)

This pattern works well with the 2 × 2 ribbed cuff.

① Rnds 1 and 2: *K2, p2; rep from * to end of rnd.

② Rnds 3 and 4: P1, *k2, p2; rep from * to last 3 sts, k2, p1.

③ Rnds 5 and 6: *P2, k2; rep from * to end of rnd.

④ Rnds 7 and 8: K1, *p2, k2; rep from * to last 3 sts, p2, k1.

⑤ Rep rnds 1–8 until sock measures 2½ (3, 4, 5, 6) inches from CO row for ankle sock or 4 (5, 6, 7, 8) inches for midcalf-length sock.

NOTE: Make a note of which row of the pattern you worked last if you want to continue the pattern on the instep stitches after the heel and gusset shaping.

⑥ Go to "Divide for the Heel," on the next page.

ROUND CABLED LEG (MULT OF 8 STS)

This pattern looks great on socks for a man, woman, or child. The reverse stockinette stitch background offsets the cable nicely.

① Rnd 1: *P2, [sl next st onto cable needle (cn) and hold at back of work, knit next st on needle, then knit st from cn], [sl next st onto cn and hold at front of work, knit next st on needle, then knit st from cn], p2; rep from * to end of rnd.

② Rnds 2 and 4: *P2, k4, p2; rep from * to end of rnd.

③ Rnd 3: *P2, [sl next st onto cn and hold at front of work, knit next st on needle, then knit st from cn], [sl next st onto cn and hold at back of work, knit next st on needle, then knit st from cn], p2; rep from * to end of rnd.

④ Rep rnds 1–4 until sock measures 2½ (3, 4, 5, 6) inches from CO row for ankle sock or 4 (5, 6, 7, 8) inches for midcalf-length sock.

NOTE: Make a note of which row of the pattern you worked last if you want to continue the pattern on the instep stitches after the heel and gusset shaping.

⑤ Go to "Divide for the Heel," below.

DIVIDE FOR THE HEEL

You must divide the stitches to work the heel. You put aside half the stitches for the instep and work the other half back and forth in rows to shape the heel. Here's how you do it.

① Starting at the beg of the rnd, knit the number of sts specified for your size and gauge in Table 13.

② Turn and purl across the sts you knit in step 1. Set aside needle from which sts were purled.

③ Do not turn. Using same needle, continue across beg/end of rnd (marker) to purl across the same number of sts on the third needle as you did in step 1. Half your total sock sts will be on one needle. These are the heel sts. Check Table 14 to ensure that you have the correct number of heel sts for your size and gauge.

④ Put rem sts (these will be the instep) onto holders, if desired; if your needles aren't slippery, leave them on the dpn(s).

⑤ Go to the directions for the desired heel flap, under "Make the Heel Flap," on the next page.

Table 13. Divide for Heel	
Gauge	No. of Sts to Knit
4 sts/in.	6 (6, 7, 8, 9) sts
5 sts/in.	7 (8, 9, 10, 11) sts
6 sts/in.	8 (9, 11, 12, 14) sts
7 sts/in.	9 (11, 12, 14, 16) sts

Table 14. Total Number of Heel Stitches	
Gauge	No. of Sts for Heel
4 sts/in.	12 (12, 14, 16, 18) sts
5 sts/in.	14 (16, 18, 20, 22) sts
6 sts/in.	16 (18, 22, 24, 28) sts
7 sts/in.	18 (22, 24, 28, 32) sts

MAKE THE HEEL FLAP

STOCKINETTE STITCH HEEL FLAP

This heel flap is worked in stockinette stitch. It is flat but not as strong as a heel flap worked in heel stitch. You can reinforce it with thread later.

1 Beg with a knit row (RS), work in St st for the number of rows specified for your size and gauge in Table 15.

2 Go to "Turn the Heel," on the next page.

Table 15. Number of Rows to Work for Heel Flap	
Gauge	**No. of Rows to Work for Heel Flap**
4 sts/in.	12 (12, 14, 16, 18) rows
5 sts/in.	14 (16, 18, 20, 22) rows
6 sts/in.	16 (18, 22, 24, 28) rows
7 sts/in.	18 (22, 24, 28, 32) rows

NOTE: The heel flap should be approximately square.

HEEL STITCH FLAP

This flap is worked in a slip 1, knit 1 pattern that produces a sturdy heel.

1 Row 1 (RS): *Sl1 purlwise wyib, k1; rep from * to end of row.

2 Row 2: Sl1 purlwise wyif, purl to end of row.

3 Rep rows 1 and 2 until you have worked the number of rows specified for your size and gauge in Table 15.

NOTE: Use a row counter to keep track of rows. The heel flap should be approximately square.

4 Go to "Turn the Heel," on the next page.

I am worried that my knit socks will wear at the heels, ruining all my hard work. What can I do to reinforce the heel?

You should reinforce the heel if your yarn is not already strengthened with nylon. Here's what you do:

1. When you start the heel flap, carry a strand of matching polyester sewing thread or very fine yarn along with your knitting yarn.

2. Work the heel flap to the end, carrying along the thread. Break it off after step 1 of the gusset instructions, after you have worked halfway across the heel sts.

TURN THE HEEL

To make the angle that joins the leg to the foot, you must turn the heel. The instructions look more complicated than they really are. Read carefully as you work and you'll have a beautifully turned heel in no time.

① **Row 1 (RS):** Knit half the heel stitches in the row, k2, sl1 purlwise wyib, k1, psso, k1, turn work without finishing row.

② **Row 2 (WS):** Sl1 purlwise wyif, p5, p2tog, p1, turn work again without finishing row.

③ **Row 3:** Sl1 purlwise wyib, knit across to 1 st before the gap caused by turning, sl1 purlwise wyib, k1, psso, k1, turn.

④ **Row 4:** Sl1 purlwise wyif, purl to 1 st before turning gap, p2tog, p1, turn.

⑤ Rep rows 3 and 4, sl first st beg every row, and working tog the 2 sts, as established, on each side of the turning gap, until all sts have been worked into the center and there are no more gaps, ending with a WS row.

NOTE: For the 12-stitch heel and on the last decrease row(s) of the other sizes, you may not have enough stitches to end the row with a k1 or p1. End these rows with the decrease.

⑥ After turning the heel, you should have rem the number of heel sts specified for your size and gauge in Table 16.

Table 16.Number of Heel Stitches Remaining After Turning	
Gauge	**No. of Heel Sts Rem After Turning**
4 sts/in.	8 (8, 10, 10, 12) sts
5 sts/in.	10 (10, 12, 12, 14) sts
6 sts/in.	10 (12, 14, 14, 16) sts
7 sts/in.	12 (14, 14, 16, 18) sts

MAKE THE GUSSET

① With RS facing you, use an empty needle to knit halfway across heel sts, placing split-ring marker on last st worked, if necessary.

NOTE: This is the same point where the rnd ended and began when you were working the leg.

② Using another empty needle (this will be called needle #1), knit across rem heel stitches; then, using the same needle, pick up and knit the number of stitches specified for your size and gauge in Table 17 (on the next page) along right edge of heel flap. You will have on needle #1 the number of stitches specified for your size and gauge in the third column of Table 17.

NOTE: The number of stitches picked up along the edge corresponds to the number of slipped edge stitches along the side of the heel flap.

③ Using another empty needle, work across the instep sts from their needle or holder. (This set of sts will be on needle #2.)

Table 17. Number of Stitches to Pick Up Along Right Edge of Heel Flap		
Gauge	No. of Sts to Pick Up Along Right Edge of Heel Flap	Total No. of Sts on Needle #1 at This Point
4 sts/in.	6 (6, 7, 8, 9) sts	10 (10, 12, 13, 15) sts
5 sts/in.	7 (8, 9, 10, 11) sts	12 (13, 15, 16, 18) sts
6 sts/in.	8 (9, 11, 12, 14) sts	13 (15, 18, 19, 22) sts
7 sts/in.	9 (11, 12, 14, 16) sts	15 (18, 19, 22, 25) sts

4 Using a fourth needle, pick up and knit the number of sts specified for your size and gauge in Table 18 along left edge of heel flap. Then, using the same needle, knit across the first half of the heel sts to marker. (These picked-up sts and heel sts will be on needle #3.) You should now have all sts on three needles, ready to beg first rnd of foot; the third column of Table 18 shows the total number of sts you should have at this point.

NOTE: You should have the same number of stitches (one-quarter the total number of stitches) on needles #1 and #3 and half the stitches on needle #2.

Table 18. Number of Stitches to Pick Up Along Left Edge of Heel Flap		
Gauge	No. of Sts to Pick Up Along Left Edge of Heel Flap	Total No. of Sts at This Point
4 sts/in.	6 (6, 7, 8, 9) sts	32 (32, 38, 42, 48) sts
5 sts/in.	7 (8, 9, 10, 11) sts	38 (42, 48, 52, 58) sts
6 sts/in.	8 (9, 11, 12, 14) sts	42 (48, 58, 62, 72) sts
7 sts/in.	9 (11, 12, 14, 16) sts	48 (58, 62, 72, 82) sts

SHAPE THE GUSSET

1 Rnd 1: Knit to last 3 sts of needle #1, k2tog, k1; knit across instep sts on needle #2; on needle #3, k1, ssk, knit to end of rnd. You have decreased 2 sts for gusset.

2 Rnd 2: Knit.

3 Rep rnds 1 and 2 until you have the number of sts specified for your size and gauge in Table 19.

Table 19. Total Number of Stitches After Gusset Shaping	
Gauge	No. of Sts Rem After Gusset Shaping
4 sts/in.	24 (24, 28, 32, 36) sts
5 sts/in.	28 (32, 36, 40, 44) sts
6 sts/in.	32 (36, 44, 48, 56) sts
7 sts/in.	36 (44, 48, 56, 64) sts

WORK THE FOOT

You can work the foot in stockinette stitch as described here, or, if you worked the leg in one of the pattern stitches, you can continue in that pattern, on the instep stitches only, down to the beginning of the toe shaping.

1 Knit all rnds without decreasing, until foot (from heel back) measures approx 2¾–5¼ (5–6, 5¾–6¾, 6½–8, 7¾–9¼) inches, depending on the size of the foot you're knitting for.

NOTE: If none of the foot lengths is suitable for your needs, work until foot measures approximately 1¼ (1½, 1¾, 2, 2¼) inches shorter than desired total foot length.

2 Go to the directions for the desired toe shaping under "Shape the Toe," below.

SHAPE THE TOE

STAR TOE SHAPING

This toe shaping is achieved by knitting 2 stitches together 4 times evenly around. It results in a nice round toe that requires no extra finishing.

NOTE: You can reinforce the toe by carrying along with your yarn a strand of polyester sewing thread.

1 Place a split-ring marker halfway across the stitches on needle #2, dividing them in half.

2 Rnd 1: Knit to last 2 sts on needle #1, k2tog; knit to last 2 sts before marker on needle #2, k2tog; knit to last 2 sts on needle #2, k2tog; knit to last 2 sts on needle #3, k2tog—4 sts dec.

3 Rnd 2: Knit.

4 Rep rnds 1 and 2 until you have rem the number of sts specified for your size and gauge in Table 20.

5 Rep rnd 1 every rnd until 8 sts rem.

6 Cut yarn, leaving an 8-inch tail. Thread tail through rem sts and tighten.

NOTE: For a longer toe, work more non-decrease rounds between decrease rounds. For a shorter toe, begin working decrease round every round earlier than specified above.

7 Go to "Finish the Sock," on the next page.

Table 20. Number of Stitches Remaining After Toe Shaping	
Gauge	**No. of Sts Rem After Toe Shaping**
4 sts/in.	12 (12, 16, 16, 16) sts
5 sts/in.	16 (16, 16, 20, 20) sts
6 sts/in.	16 (16, 20, 24, 28) sts
7 sts/in.	16 (20, 24, 28, 32) sts

WEDGE TOE SHAPING

This toe shaping results in a rounded, fitted toe.

NOTE: You can reinforce the toe by carrying along with your yarn a strand of polyester sewing thread.

1 Rnd 1: Knit to last 3 sts on needle #1, k2tog, k1; on needle #2: k1, ssk, knit to last 3 sts, k2tog, k1; k1, ssk, knit to end of needle #3. You have decreased 4 sts.

2 Rnd 2: Knit.

3 Rep rnds 1 and 2 until you have rem the number of sts specified for your size and gauge in Table 20.

4 Rep rnd 1 every rnd until 8 sts rem.

5 Graft rem sts using Kitchener st (see pages 170–171) or cut yarn, leaving an 8-inch tail, thread tail through rem sts, and tighten.

6 Go to "Finish the Sock," below.

FINISH THE SOCK

1 Weave in ends.

2 Block socks using sock blockers to match the size of your socks, or, if your yarn's care instructions allow, lightly steam to block, taking care not to mash stitch patterns.

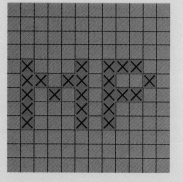

TIP

As long as sock legs are worked in stockinette stitch, you can embroider initials onto them in duplicate stitch.

1. Chart the initial(s) onto graph paper.

2. Frame the area where you want the initials to be with safety pins.

3. Thread a tapestry needle with a long strand of a contrast color yarn.

4. Work the initial(s) in duplicate stitch (see page 208) within the frame, starting at the lower-right corner.

M ittens are easy—they're basically a tube for the hand with a smaller tube coming off for the thumb. Fit is not crucial with mittens, so they make excellent gifts for people of all ages.

Mittens come in all shapes and sizes and can be knit in all kinds of yarn. You can add a personal touch by choosing from one of the many cuff styles presented here. Hand coverings ideally should be warm and soft, but aside from that, they can be colorful, playful, or completely practical.

CUFF TREATMENTS

Here are a few basic cuff options that work well for mittens. The ribbed cuff is the most common, probably because the elasticity of the stitch pattern helps keep the mitten on the hand. For this master pattern, you can work the ribbed cuff in single (1 × 1) rib, or, if your stitch count is divisible by four, in double (2 × 2) rib. You can double the cuff length if you prefer to fold it over for added warmth or a different look.

Reverse
stockinette
stitch stripe
cuff

Ribbed
cuff

Seed stitch cuff

Here are some playful cuff treatments. The loop stitch cuff requires a little extra yarn, but the result is worth it. You can also work your cuff in a novelty yarn like the one shown here for added texture and color. Just be sure to choose a novelty yarn that is warm and not itchy to the sensitive skin on the underside of the wrist.

Loop stitch cuff   Novelty yarn cuff

THE THUMB

There are a few different ways to work a thumb. Some mitten patterns involve increasing along one side to form a gusset. The master pattern in this chapter uses a thumb that requires no added shaping to the body and lies flat when the mitten or glove is off the hand. To work this thumb, you slip a thumb's width worth of stitches onto a holder and cast on the same number of stitches in their place—much as you work a buttonhole—and continue knitting until the rest of the mitten or glove is finished. Then you slip the stitches from the holder back to the needle, pick up the same number of stitches plus a couple more around the edge of the thumbhole, and knit the thumb in the round to the desired length. Working the body of a mitten or glove in a repeating stitch or color pattern is easier when this type of thumb is used. You can also have a little fun and knit this type of thumb in an accent color.

Thumb

MITTEN TIP TREATMENTS

After you have worked the cuff and knit the body of the mitten to the desired length, you can shape the tip as either a rounded tip or a pointed tip. The rounded tip is achieved by working a short series of decrease rounds and then pulling the cut tail through the last remaining stitches, cinching it tight, and fastening it off.

Rounded tip

You make a pointed tip by working decreases on opposite sides of every round until you have only one or two stitches left. You then cut the yarn, pull the tail through the last remaining stitch or stitches, and pull it tight.

Pointed tip

Mittens: Master Pattern

You can use this master pattern to knit mittens for the whole family, from toddlers to adult men. Choose from several different cuff treatments or create your own. Instructions for rounded-tip mittens and pointed-tip mittens are presented together: Simply follow the instructions for the style of your choice.

Specifications

SIZES

XS (S, M, L, XL)

Hand circumference: 5 (6, 7, 8, 9) inches

MATERIALS

Desired yarn, in the amount specified in Table 21

10–20 yd. of second color yarn (B) for two-color cuff styles

1 set of double-pointed needles in size needed to obtain gauge

1 set of double-pointed needles one size smaller than size needed to obtain gauge (for some cuff edgings)

Stitch marker to fit your needle size

Tapestry needle

Right mitten

Mitten body
5(6, 7, 8, 9)"
circumference

Mitten tip: 1(1¼, 1½, 1¾, 2)"

Thumb circumference:
2 (2½, 2½, 3, 3½)"

Mitten body:
3–3¾ (3½–4¼,
4–4¾, 4½–5¾,
5½–6¾)"

Thumb before shaping:
1¼ (½, 1¾, 2, 2¼)"

Body below thumb:
1¼–1¾ (1½–2, 1¾–2½,
2–3, 2¾–3¾)"

Cuff: variable lengths

Table 21. Approximate Yardages for Mittens	
Gauge (in Stockinette Stitch)	Mittens: Approximate Yardage
3 sts/in.	50–175 yd.
4 sts/in.	75–225 yd.
5 sts/in.	75–250 yd.
6 sts/in.	100–300 yd.
7 sts/in.	100–375 yd.

NOTES ON THE SAMPLES

The light yellow mittens have a rounded top and loop stitch cuff.

The small lime mittens are worked with a reverse stockinette stitch stripe cuff and have a rounded tip; the thumb is worked in the second color. The mitten chain is a twisted cord made from the two colors.

The light brown mittens with the striped ribbed cuff are worked with a 2 × 2 striped ribbed cuff and have a pointed tip.

How to Make the Mittens

CAST ON

1. Using smaller needles, loosely CO sts for your size and gauge, according to Table 22, dividing sts as evenly as possible onto three dpns.

2. Place marker (pm) and join rnd, taking care not to twist sts.

3. Go to the directions for the desired cuff style under "Make the Cuff," below.

Table 22. Cast On for Mittens

Gauge	No. of Sts to CO
3 sts/in.	16 (18, 22, 24, 28) sts
4 sts/in.	20 (24, 28, 32, 36) sts
5 sts/in.	26 (30, 36, 40, 44) sts
6 sts/in.	30 (36, 42, 48, 54) sts
7 sts/in.	36 (42, 48, 56, 64) sts

MAKE THE CUFF

The cuff gives your mittens character, and because there is no shaping to interrupt your knitting, you can have fun with it. Following are some of the possibilities.

1 × 1 RIBBED CUFF (EVEN NO. OF STS)

This basic rib can be worked over any even number of stitches. It provides a nice elastic cuff.

1. Rnd 1: *K1, p1; rep from * to end of rnd.

2. Rep rnd 1, sl marker beg every rnd, until cuff measures 1½–2 (2–2½, 2¼–2½, 2½–3, 3–3¼) inches or desired length.

3. Go to "Make the Body Below the Thumb Opening," page 311.

Striped 2 × 2 Ribbed Cuff (Mult of 4 Sts)

You can work this as 2 × 2 rib if your stitch count is divisible by 4. Choose a contrast color (B) that looks nice with the main color (A). Or, you can omit the color change instructions and work a one-color 2 × 2 rib.

1 Rnd 1: Using A, *K2, p2; rep from * to end of rnd.

2 Rep rnd 1, sl marker beg every rnd, for 3 more rnds.

3 Change to B and knit 1 rnd.

4 Still using B, work rib as set in step 1, for 2 more rnds.

5 Change back to A and knit 1 rnd.

6 Work rib for 3 rnds.

7 Rep steps 3–6.

8 Go to "Make the Body Below the Thumb Opening," page 311.

Checkered Pattern Cuff (Even No. of Sts)

This fun cuff uses two colors, A and B. You cast on in A.

1 Knit 1 rnd, sl marker beg every rnd.

2 Purl 1 rnd.

3 Beg check patt—Rnd 1: *K1 in A, k1 in B; rep from * to end of rnd.

4 Rnd 2: *K1 in B, k1 in A; rep from * to end of rnd.

5 Rep rnds 1 and 2 until cuff measures approx 1½–2 (2–2½, 2¼–2½, 2½–3, 3–3¼) inches from CO edge, ending with rnd 1.

6 Go to "Make the Body Below the Thumb Opening," page 311.

Leaf Pattern Cuff (Mult of 4 Sts)

This cuff, which must be worked over a multiple of 4 stitches, uses two colors, A and B. You cast on in A.

1 Purl 2 rnds in A, sl marker beg every rnd.

2 Knit 2 rnds in B.

3 Knit 1 rnd in A.

4 Knit 1 rnd in B.

5 Beg leaf patt—Rnds 1 and 7: *K1 in B, k3 in A; rep from * to end of rnd.

6 Rnds 2 and 6: *K3 in A, k1 in B; rep from * to end of rnd.

7 Rnds 3 and 5: *K2 in A, k1 in B, k1 in A; rep from * to end of rnd.

8 Rnd 4: *K2 in B, k1 in A, k1 in B; rep from * to end of rnd.

9 After completing all 7 rnds of patt, knit 1 rnd in B.

10 Knit 1 rnd in A.

11 Knit 2 rnds in B.

12 Knit 1 rnd in A.

13 Purl 2 rnds in A.

14 Go to "Make the Body Below the Thumb Opening," on the next page.

Novelty Yarn Cuff (Any No. of Sts)

This simple garter stitch cuff works well with hairy or fuzzy yarns.

1 Rnd 1: Knit.

2 Rnd 2: Purl.

3 Rep rnds 1 and 2, sl marker beg every rnd, until cuff measures 1½–2 (2–2½, 2¼–2½, 2½–3, 3–3¼) inches or desired length.

4 Go to "Make the Body Below the Thumb Opening," on the next page.

Loop Stitch Cuff (Any No. of Sts)

This cuff is fun to work and produces a fun and fashionable accent to girls' and women's mittens. It uses the following stitch:

loop 1: Knit into next st but don't drop it off the needle. Bring the yarn to the front, between the needles, and loop it over your thumb, then bring it between the needles to the back. Knit into the st again, this time bringing it up and off the left needle. You will have 2 sts on the right needle. Pass the first st over the second and off. This secures the loop.

1 Rnd 1: Purl.

2 Rnd 2: *Loop 1; rep from * to end of rnd.

3 Rep rnd 2 until cuff measures 1½–2 (2–2½, 2¼–2½, 2½–3, 3–3¼) inches from CO edge or desired length.

4 Go to "Make the Body Below the Thumb Opening," below.

MAKE THE BODY BELOW THE THUMB OPENING

1 Change to larger needles and knit every rnd (or work in desired stitch patt) for 1¼–2 (1½–2¼, 1¾–2¾, 2–3¼, 2¾–4) inches.

NOTE: These measurements are approximate. For the most accurate fit, try mitten on a hand that is close in size to that of the intended wearer. The thumb opening should be placed at the crook of the thumb.

2 Go to "Make the Thumb Opening," on the next page.

MAKE THE THUMB OPENING

① K1 at beg of rnd, then sl the number of sts indicated for your size and gauge in Table 23 onto a holder or safety pin.

② CO the same number of sts as specified in Table 23 to the right (working) needle, using backward-loop cast-on (see page 15), and knit to end of rnd.

③ Go to "Make the Body Above the Thumb Opening," below.

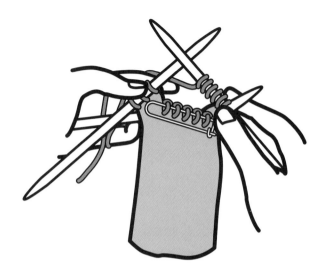

Table 23. Number of Stitches to Put on Holder for Thumb Opening

Gauge	No. of Sts to Put on Holder for Thumb Opening
3 sts/in.	3 (4, 4, 5, 5) sts
4 sts/in.	4 (5, 5, 6, 7) sts
5 sts/in.	5 (7, 7, 8, 9) sts
6 sts/in.	6 (7, 7, 9, 11) sts
7 sts/in.	7 (9, 9, 11, 12) sts

MAKE THE BODY ABOVE THE THUMB OPENING

① Knit every rnd until body of mitten measures approx 3–3¾ (3½–4¼, 4–4¾, 4½–5¼, 5½–6¼) inches from top of cuff/beg of body.

NOTE: These measurements are approximate. For the most accurate fit, begin tip shaping above tip of pinky.

② Go to desired mitten tip shaping under "Shape the Mitten," below.

SHAPE THE MITTEN

There are two basic styles of mitten tips: rounded and pointed. If you use the rounded style, you work both mittens the same. If you use the pointed style, you end up with a left and a right mitten, and you shape their tips slightly differently.

ROUNDED MITTEN TIP SHAPING

1 Work dec rnd as specified for your size and gauge in Table 24. You should have rem the number of sts indicated for your size and gauge in the third column of Table 24.

2 Next rnd: Knit.

Table 24. First Decrease Round for Rounded-Tip Mitten

Gauge	Work Dec Rnd	No. of Sts Rem After First Dec Rnd
3 sts/in.	*K2, k2tog; rep from * to last 0 (2, 2, 0, 0) sts, k0 (2, 2, 0, 0).	12 (14, 17, 18, 21) sts
4 sts/in.	*K2, k2tog; rep from * to end of rnd.	15 (18, 21, 24, 27) sts
5 sts/in.	*K2, k2tog; rep from * to last 2 (2, 0, 0, 0) sts, k2 (2, 0, 0, 0).	20 (23, 27, 30, 33) sts
6 sts/in.	*K2, k2tog; rep from * to last 2 (0, 2, 0, 2) sts, k2 (0, 2, 0, 2).	23 (27, 32, 36, 41) sts
7 sts/in.	*K2, k2tog; rep from * to last 0 (2, 0, 0, 0) sts, k0 (2, 0, 0, 0).	27 (32, 36, 42, 48) sts

3 Work dec rnd as specified for your size and gauge in Table 25. You should have rem the number of sts indicated for your size and gauge in the third column of Table 25.

4 Next rnd: Knit.

5 Next rnd: *K2tog; rep from * to end of rnd.

6 If you have 7 or fewer sts rem, skip to step 8. Otherwise, knit 1 rnd.

7 Rep steps 5–6 until you have 7 or fewer sts.

NOTE: If you have an odd number of stitches, k2tog around to last stitch and knit the remaining stitch.

8 Cut yarn, leaving a 6-inch tail. Pull through rem sts and secure.

9 Go to "Work the Thumb," page 315.

NOTE: For a photo of a rounded mitten tip, see page 306.

Table 25. Second Decrease Round for Rounded Tip Mitten

Gauge	Work Dec Rnd	No. of Sts Rem After Second Dec Rnd
3 sts/in.	*K1, k2tog; rep from * to last 0 (2, 2, 0, 0) sts, k0 (2, 2, 0, 0).	8 (10, 12, 12, 14) sts
4 sts/in.	*K1, k2tog; rep from * to end of rnd.	10 (12, 14, 16, 18) sts
5 sts/in.	*K1, k2tog; rep from * to last 2 (2, 0, 0, 0) sts, k2 (2, 0, 0, 0).	14 (16, 18, 20, 22) sts
6 sts/in.	*K1, k2tog; rep from * to last 2 (0, 2, 0, 2) sts, k2 (0, 2, 0, 2).	16 (18, 22, 24, 28) sts
7 sts/in.	*K1, k2tog; rep from * to last 0 (2, 0, 0, 0) sts, k0 (2, 0, 0, 0).	18 (22, 24, 28, 32) sts

POINTED MITTEN TIP: RIGHT MITTEN SHAPING

1. Arrange the sts on the three needles as shown in Table 26 to prepare for shaping. Needle #1 is the one that begins the rnd. The stitches on needles #1 and #2 form the palm.

2. Rnd 1: Ssk the first 2 sts on needle #1; knit to last 2 sts on needle #2, k2tog; ssk the first 2 sts on needle #3, knit to last 2 sts on needle #3, k2tog—4 sts dec.

3. Rnd 2: Knit.

4. Rep rnds 1 and 2—4 more sts dec.

5. Rep rnd 1 until 4 or 6 sts rem.

6. Cut yarn, leaving a 6-inch tail. Pull through rem sts and secure.

7. Go to "Work the Thumb," on the next page.

Table 26. Arrangement of Stitches on Three dpns for Right Mitten			
Gauge	No. of Sts on Needle #1	No. of Sts on Needle #2	No. of Sts on Needle #3
3 sts/in.	4 (4, 5, 6, 7) sts	4 (5, 6, 6, 7) sts	8 (9, 11, 12, 14) sts
4 sts/in.	5 (6, 7, 8, 9) sts	5 (6, 7, 8, 9) sts	10 (12, 14, 16, 18) sts
5 sts/in.	6 (7, 9, 10, 11) sts	7 (8, 9, 10, 11) sts	13 (15, 18, 20, 22) sts
6 sts/in.	7 (9, 10, 12, 13) sts	8 (9, 11, 12, 14) sts	15 (18, 21, 24, 27) sts
7 sts/in.	9 (10, 12, 14, 16) sts	9 (11, 12, 14, 16) sts	18 (21, 24, 28, 32) sts

POINTED TIP: LEFT MITTEN SHAPING

1. Arrange the sts on the three needles as indicated in Table 27 (on the next page) to prepare for shaping. Needle #1 is the one that begins the rnd. The sts on needles #1 and #3 form the palm.

2. Rnd 1: Knit to last 2 sts on needle #1, k2tog; ssk first 2 sts on needle #2, knit to last 2 sts on needle #2, k2tog; ssk the first 2 sts on needle #3, knit to end—4 sts dec.

3. Rnd 2: Knit.

4. Rep rnds 1 and 2—4 more sts dec.

5. Rep rnd 1 until 4 or 6 sts rem.

6. Cut yarn, leaving a 6-inch tail. Pull through rem sts and secure.

7. Go to "Work the Thumb" on the next page.

Table 27. Arrangement of Stitches on Three dpns for Left Mitten			
Gauge	No. of Sts on Needle #1	No. of Sts on Needle #2	No. of Sts on Needle #3
3 sts/in.	4 (4, 5, 6, 7) sts	8 (9, 11, 12, 14) sts	4 (5, 6, 6, 7) sts
4 sts/in.	5 (6, 7, 8, 9) sts	10 (12, 14, 16, 18) sts	5 (6, 7, 8, 9) sts
5 sts/in.	6 (7, 9, 10, 11) sts	13 (15, 18, 20, 22) sts	7 (8, 9, 10, 11) sts
6 sts/in.	7 (9, 10, 12, 13) sts	15 (18, 21, 24, 27) sts	8 (9, 11, 12, 14) sts
7 sts/in.	9 (10, 12, 14, 16) sts	18 (21, 24, 28, 32) sts	9 (11, 12, 14, 16) sts

WORK THE THUMB

1 Join yarn and use a dpn to knit across the thumb sts from the holder.

2 Using a second dpn, pick up and knit 1 st at left side of thumb opening, then pick up and knit from the top of the thumb opening half the number of sts that were on holder for the thumb earlier (refer to Table 23, page 312).

NOTE: If the number of stitches on the holder for the thumb was an odd number, pick up 1 stitch fewer than half.

3 Using a third dpn, pick up and knit the remaining sts around the top of the thumb opening—half the number of sts that were on the holder, plus 1 at the side of the thumb opening. You should have on your three dpns the number of sts indicated for your size and gauge in Table 28.

4 Pm and join rnd.

5 Knit every rnd until thumb measures approx 1¼ (1½, 1¾, 2, 2¼) inches, or to midpoint of the thumbnail.

6 Work dec rnd as specified for your size and gauge in Table 29 (on the next page).

7 Knit 1 rnd.

8 Next rnd: *K2tog; rep from * to end of rnd.

NOTE: If you have an odd number of stitches, k2tog around to last stitch and knit the remaining stitch.

9 Rep last 2 rnds until you have 4 or 3 sts rem.

10 Cut yarn, leaving a 6-inch tail. Pull through rem sts and secure.

11 Go to "Finish the Mittens" on the next page.

Table 28. Number of Thumb Stitches	
Gauge	No. of Thumb Sts
3 sts/in.	8 (10, 10, 12, 12) sts
4 sts/in.	10 (12, 12, 14, 16) sts
5 sts/in.	12 (16, 16, 16, 20) sts
6 sts/in.	14 (16, 16, 20, 24) sts
7 sts/in.	16 (20, 20, 24, 26) sts

Table 29. First Decrease Round for Tip of Thumb		
Gauge	Work Dec Rnd	No. of Sts Rem After Dec Rnd
3 sts/in.	*K2, k2tog; rep from * to last 0 (2, 2, 0, 0) sts, k0 (2, 2, 0, 0).	6 (8, 8, 9, 9) sts
4 sts/in.	*K2, k2tog; rep from * to last 2 (0, 0, 2, 0) sts, k2 (0, 0, 2, 0).	8 (9, 9, 11, 12) sts
5 sts/in.	*K2, k2tog; rep from * to end of rnd.	9 (12, 12, 12, 15) sts
6 sts/in.	*K2, k2tog; rep from * to last 2 (0, 0, 0, 0) sts, k2 (0, 0, 0, 0).	11 (12, 12, 15, 18) sts
7 sts/in.	*K2, k2tog; rep from * to last 0 (0, 0, 0, 2) sts, k0 (2, 0, 0, 2).	12 (15, 15, 18, 20) sts

FINISH THE MITTENS

1 Weave in yarn ends, stitching up holes at beg of thumb if necessary.

2 Lightly steam to block, if yarn's care instructions allow.

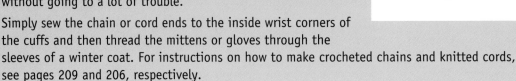

TIP

No More Lost Mittens

It would be a shame if one of the mittens you lovingly knit were to fall out of a pocket into the snow and get lost. You can join a pair of mittens or gloves with a mitten chain to ensure that this doesn't happen. Mitten chains can be worked as crocheted chains or knitted cords—and they're not necessarily just for children. If you make a chain in matching and contrast colors, you can add a lively twist to your plain old mittens or gloves, without going to a lot of trouble.

Simply sew the chain or cord ends to the inside wrist corners of the cuffs and then thread the mittens or gloves through the sleeves of a winter coat. For instructions on how to make crocheted chains and knitted cords, see pages 209 and 206, respectively.

Reference Materials

This appendix provides lots of useful charts—including extensive body measurements charts, yarn yardage charts, and more. Use it when you want to alter an existing knitting pattern or design your own hand-knits.

Measurement Charts

Included here are measurement charts for infants (sizes 3 to 24 months), children (sizes 2 to 16), women (sizes X-Small to 5X), and men (sizes Small to XX-Large). We've also included a head circumference measurement chart, which covers infants (preemies, babies, and toddlers), children, and adults (both women and men). Measurements are given in both inches and centimeters. For more information about standard measurements, check out the Web site www.yarnstandards.com from the Craft Yarn Council of America.

Babies' Sizes					
Baby's Size (not age):	3 months	6 months	12 months	18 months	24 months
Chest					
Inches	16	17	18	19	20
Centimeters	40.5	43	45.5	48	50.5
Center Back Neck to Cuff					
Inches	10½	11½	12½	14	18
Centimeters	26.5	29	31.5	35.5	45.5
Back Waist Length					
Inches	6	7	7½	8	8½
Centimeters	15.5	17.5	19	20.5	21.5
Across Back (Shoulder to Shoulder)					
Inches	7¼	7¾	8¼	8½	8¾
Centimeters	18.5	19.5	21	21.5	22
Sleeve Length to Underarm					
Inches	6	6½	7½	8	8½
Centimeters	15.5	16.5	19	20.5	21.5

Children's Sizes								
Size	2	4	6	8	10	12	14	16
Chest								
Inches	21	23	25	26½	28	30	31½	32½
Centimeters	53	58.5	63.5	67	71	76	80	82.5
Center Back Neck-to-Cuff								
Inches	18	19½	20½	22	24	26	27	28
Centimeters	45.5	49.5	52	56	61	66	68.5	71
Back Waist Length								
Inches	8½	9½	10½	12½	14	15	15½	16
Centimeters	21.5	24	26.5	31.5	35.5	38	39.5	40.5
Across Back (Shoulder to Shoulder)								
Inches	9¼	9¾	10¼	10¾	11¼	12	12¼	13
Centimeters	23.5	25	26	27	28.5	30.5	31	33
Sleeve Length to Underarm								
Inches	8½	10½	11½	12½	13½	15	16	16½
Centimeters	21.5	26.5	29	31.5	34.5	38	40.5	42

Measurement Charts *(continued)*

Women's Sizes									
Size	**X-Small**	**Small**	**Medium**	**Large**	**IX**	**2X**	**3X**	**4X**	**5X**
Bust									
Inches	28–30	32–34	36–38	40–42	44–46	48–50	52–54	56–58	60–62
Centimeters	71–76	81–86	91.5–96.5	101.5–106.5	111.5–117	122–127	132–137	142–147	152–158
Center Back Neck to Cuff									
Inches	27–27½	28–28½	29–29½	30–30½	31–31½	31½–32	32½–33	32½–33	33–33½
Centimeters	68.5–70	71–72.5	73.5–75	76–77.5	78.5–80	80–81.5	82.5–84	82.5–84	84–85
Back Waist Length									
Inches	16½	17	17¼	17½	17¾	18	18	18½	18½
Centimeters	42	43	43.5	44.5	45	45.5	45.5	47	47
Across Back (Shoulder to Shoulder)									
Inches	14–14½	14½–15	16–16½	17–17½	17½	18	18	18½	18½
Centimeters	35.5–37	37–38	40.5–42	43–44.5	44.5	44.5	45.5	47	47
Sleeve Length to Underarm									
Inches	16½	17	17	17½	17½	18	18	18½	18½
Centimeters	42	43	43	44.5	44.5	45.5	45.5	47	47

Men's Sizes

Size	Small	Medium	Large	X-Large	XX-Large
Chest					
Inches	34–36	38–40	42–44	46–48	50–52
Centimeters	86–91.5	96.5–101.5	106.5–111.5	116.5–122	127–132
Center Back Neck to Cuff					
Inches	32–32½	33–33½	34–34½	35–35½	36–36½
Centimeters	81–82.5	83.5–85	86.5–87.5	89–90	91.5–92.5
Back Hip Length					
Inches	25–25½	26½–26¾	27–27¼	27½–27¾	28–28½
Centimeters	63.5–64.5	67.5–68	68.5–69	69.5–70.5	71–72.5
Across Back (Shoulder to Shoulder)					
Inches	15½–16	16½–17	17½–18	18–18½	18½–19
Centimeters	39.5–40.5	42–43	44.5–45.5	45.5–47	47–48
Sleeve Length to Underarm					
Inches	18	18½	19½	20	20½
Centimeters	45.5	47	49.5	50.5	52

Head Circumference

	Infant/Child				Adult	
	Preemie	Baby	Toddler	Child	Woman	Man
Inches	12	14	16	18	20	22
Centimeters	30.5	35.5	40.5	45.5	50.5	56

Perfecting the Fit

You can design hand-knits or alter knitting patterns to fit any body type. Creating a perfectly fitting garment isn't as difficult as it might seem. It's mostly a matter of taking accurate measurements, determining ease, and calculating stitch counts based on the measurements. Here we look at how to perfect the fit of a sweater, which is probably the most demanding garment to design.

Taking Body Measurements

To ensure a good fit when designing a sweater—or knitting from a pattern, for that matter—you need to take detailed body measurements. Here's how:

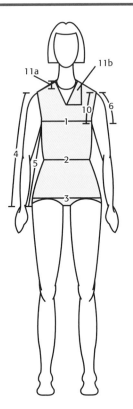
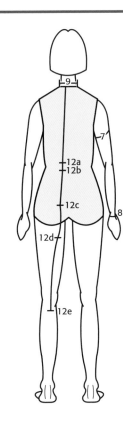

1. Measure the bust or chest by placing the tape measure around the fullest part of the chest, at the underarm.

2. For the waist, measure around the smallest part of the torso.

3. For the hip, measure around the fullest part of the lower torso.

4. Measure for sleeve length by placing the tape measure at the edge of the shoulder and extending down (with arm held straight at side) to the wrist.

5. Measure from the underarm to the wrist to obtain a measurement for where to begin the sleeve cap shaping.

6. If you're designing a short-sleeved sweater, take the same measurements as in steps 4 and 5, only end at the point on the upper arm where you want the sleeve to fall.

7. Measure the circumference of the upper arm.

8. Measure the circumference of the wrist.

9. Measure the circumference of the neck (or the width of the back of the neck).

10. Measure the armhole depth from the top of the shoulder down the front to the base of the underarm.

11. Also take some neck shaping measurements: For a rounded neck, begin at the neck where the shoulder meets it and measure straight down to where you want the bottom of the rounded part to be. Do the same for a v-neck.

⑫ Don't forget to measure the length along the back to best suit your sweater style:

a. For a cropped or shrug-like sweater, measure above the waist.

b. For a short sweater, measure at the waist.

c. For a hip-length sweater, measure at the hip.

d. For a fingertip-length jacket or tunic, measure at the thigh where the fingertips fall.

e. For a long coat, measure anywhere from the knee down.

Calculating Ease

Some of your knitted measurements should be a few inches larger than the actual body measurements, or the garment will be too tight. The difference between body measurements and knit measurements is called *ease*.

Things to consider when calculating ease are whether the sweater will be worn over a shirt or other clothing and whether you're aiming toward a tight or tailored fit or a more loose and boxy fit. You can use the table below as a guideline.

What Size to Knit?					
Chest Size	**Finished Measurements**				
	Tight Fit	**Tailored Fit**	**Normal Fit**	**Loose Fit**	**Oversized Fit**
21–22 in.	20 in.	22 in.	24 in.	26 in.	27–28 in.
23–24 in.	22 in.	24 in.	26 in.	28 in.	29–30 in.
25–26 in.	24 in.	26 in.	28 in.	30 in.	31–32 in.
27–28 in.	26 in.	28 in.	30 in.	32 in.	33–34 in.
29–30 in.	28 in.	30 in.	32 in.	34 in.	35–36 in.
31–32 in.	30 in.	32 in.	34 in.	36 in.	37–38 in.
33–34 in.	32 in.	34 in.	36 in.	38 in.	39–40 in.
35–36 in.	34 in.	36 in.	38 in.	40 in.	41–42 in.
37–38 in.	36 in.	38 in.	40 in.	42 in.	43–44 in.
39–40 in.	38 in.	40 in.	42 in.	44 in.	45–46 in.
41–42 in.	40 in.	42 in.	44 in.	46 in.	47–48 in.
43–44 in.	42 in.	44 in.	46 in.	48 in.	49–50 in.
45–46 in.	44 in.	46 in.	48 in.	50 in.	51–52 in.
47–48 in.	46 in.	48 in.	50 in.	52 in.	53–54 in.
49–50 in.	48 in.	50 in.	52 in.	54 in.	55–56 in.

Determining Yarn Yardage

When you're ready to design your own sweater or alter an existing knitting pattern, it can be difficult to calculate exactly how much yarn you need. Certain stitch patterns—such as highly textured stitches and cables—require more yarn than others, and yarn use can vary from knitter to knitter. You can do a fairly accurate estimate by using the method described here; however, it is always advisable to purchase an extra ball or two in the correct dye lot.

Calculating Yardage

To estimate the yarn needed for a sweater, you need to knit a 4-inch-square swatch in the stitch pattern that will be used for the sweater. You also need to calculate the area of each sweater piece, based on your schematic. Here's how you do that:

1. Multiply the width of the back of the sweater by the length and then multiply this number by 2. For example, if your sweater width is 20 inches and length is 23 inches, you multiply 20 × 23 to get 460 square inches for one piece. You multiply 460 × 2 to get 920 square inches total for the back and front.

2. Add the width of the sleeve at the cuff to the width of the sleeve at the cap's widest point; divide the result by 2 and multiply that number by the length of the sleeve. Multiply this new number by 2 to determine the total square inches for both sleeves. For example, if the width of the sleeve at the cuff is 10 inches and the width of the cap is 17 inches, you add 10 + 17 to get 27. Divide 27 ÷ 2 to get 13.5. Multiply 13.5 by the length of the sleeve, 18 inches, and you get 243 square inches for one sleeve. Multiply 243 × 2 to get 486 square inches total for both sleeves.

3. Add together the results from steps 1 and 2. This is approximately the total number of square inches for your sweater. Using the example, if you add 920 + 486, you get 1,406 square inches total for the sweater.

4. Determine the area of your swatch by multiplying the width by the length. Divide the result of step 3 by the area of your swatch. For example, if your swatch is 4 inches square, the area of the swatch is 16 square inches. You divide 1,406 ÷ 16 to get approximately 89.

5. Unravel the swatch and measure how many yards were used to knit it. Let's say it took 17 yards to knit the swatch.

5

6. Multiply the result from step 4 by the result from step 5 to determine the approximate yardage needed for your sweater. For example, you would multiply 89 × 17 to determine that you need approximately 1,513 yards of yarn for the sweater.

Using Yarn Yardage Charts

The method described on the previous page is good if you have yarn already but you're not sure if it is enough to knit an item. For a more general estimate, use the charts below as guides to the yardage needed.

Vest: Yarn Weights, Sizes, and Approximate Yardages

| Yarn Weight | Baby/Child Finished Chest | | | | | Adult Finished Chest | | |
	24 in.	28 in.	32 in.	36 in.	40 in.	44 in.	48 in.	52 in.
Bulky	200 yd.	300 yd.	400 yd.	500 yd.	600 yd.	700 yd.	800 yd.	900 yd.
Worsted	250 yd.	350 yd.	500 yd.	600 yd.	700 yd.	800 yd.	900 yd.	1,000 yd.
Sport	300 yd.	450 yd.	600 yd.	750 yd.	850 yd.	950 yd.	1,050 yd.	1,150 yd.
Fingering	450 yd.	600 yd.	750 yd.	950 yd.	1,100 yd.	1,250 yd.	1,450 yd.	1,650 yd.

Pullover/Cardigan: Yarn Weights, Sizes, and Approximate Yardages

| Yarn Weight | Baby/Child Finished Chest | | | | | Adult Finished Chest | | |
	24 in.	28 in.	32 in.	36 in.	40 in.	44 in.	48 in.	52 in.
Bulky	375 yd.	525 yd.	725 yd.	925 yd.	1,100 yd.	1,300 yd.	1,500 yd.	1,750 yd.
Worsted	500 yd.	700 yd.	1,000 yd.	1,250 yd.	1,400 yd.	1,600 yd.	1,800 yd.	2,000 yd.
Sport	600 yd.	800 yd.	1,100 yd.	1,400 yd.	1,650 yd.	1,900 yd.	2,100 yd.	2,300 yd.
Fingering	750 yd.	1,100 yd.	1,500 yd.	1,750 yd.	2,150 yd.	2,500 yd.	2,750 yd.	3,000 yd.

Hat: Yarn Weights, Sizes, and Approximate Yardages

| Yarn Weight | Finished Circumference | | | | |
	14 in.	16 in.	18 in.	20 in.	22 in.
Bulky	60 yd.	85 yd.	100 yd.	125 yd.	150 yd.
Worsted	75 yd.	125 yd.	175 yd.	225 yd.	250 yd.
Sport	125 yd.	175 yd.	225 yd.	250 yd.	275 yd.
Fingering	150 yd.	200 yd.	250 yd.	300 yd.	325 yd.

Socks: Yarn Weights, Sizes, and Approximate Yardages

| Yarn Weight | Foot Length | | | | | | |
	4 in.	5 in.	6½ in.	8 in.	9½ in.	10½ in.	11½ in.
Bulky	85 yd.	100 yd.	125 yd.	150 yd.	175 yd.	225 yd.	250 yd.
Worsted	125 yd.	175 yd.	225 yd.	250 yd.	300 yd.	350 yd.	400 yd.
Sport	125 yd.	175 yd.	225 yd.	275 yd.	325 yd.	375 yd.	450 yd.
Fingering	150 yd.	200 yd.	250 yd.	325 yd.	400 yd.	475 yd.	550 yd.

Changing the Body Shape

You might want to change the body shape of a particular sweater design by shaping the waist of an otherwise boxy sweater. Here are a couple of easy ways to tailor a pattern to a more fitted look.

EASY WAIST SHAPING

A quick and easy way to give a sweater a more flattering silhouette is to work some ribbing at the waistline. For this approach, omit ribbing at the hem and work an edge that doesn't gather, like seed stitch or garter stitch. Work up to just before where the waist falls and then work in ribbing for 1½ to 3 inches.

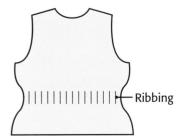

TAILORED WAIST SHAPING

You can work a tailored waistline into the body of a sweater by using a series of gradual decreases from the cast-on edge to the waist, followed by the same number of gradual increases from the waist to the armhole. The general rule is to decrease 4 inches total for a tailored waist: Decrease 2 inches worth of stitches on the back and 2 inches on the front. (For a cardigan, decrease 2 inches on the back and 1 inch on each side edge of the front pieces.)

To work such a waist, you cast on according to your pattern and work a non-gathering edging for about an inch. Then you begin decreasing, as determined by the following calculations:

1 Calculate for your gauge how many stitches you need to decrease for the back: 2 (inches) × stitch gauge. (For example, if your stitch gauge is 4 stitches per inch, you decrease 8 stitches for the waist.)

2 The stitches are decreased at each end of the decrease rows, so divide the result in step 1 by 2 to determine how many decrease rows to work to the waist. For this example, 8 divided by 2 is 4, so you work 4 decrease rows.

3 Subtract 1 inch from the body length from cast-on edge to armhole. (The actual waist after the decreases and before the increases is worked even for about 1 inch.) So, if the body length is 11 inches, the result for this step is 10.

4 Multiply the result from step 3 by your row gauge and divide that result by 2 to determine how many rows to work for the body sections above and below the 1 inch of waist. For example, your result in step 3 is 10. If your gauge is 6 rows per inch, the total body length less the 1 inch of waist takes 60 rows. Therefore, you need 30 rows below and above the waist.

5 Divide the result from step 4 by the result from step 2 to determine how many rows should be worked between decrease/increase rows. For example, 30 divided by 4 is 7.5, so you need to work decreases about every 7 or 8 rows.

After you work the waist even for about an inch, you work the same number of increase rows as decrease rows—at the same interval—up to the armhole. You should finish with the same number of stitches that you started with.

Altering Sleeves

Adjusting sleeve length and shape is not as clear-cut as simply adding length to straight knitting. However, when you understand how to calculate length and width based on your row and stitch gauge, you can work out a new length or shape without too much trouble.

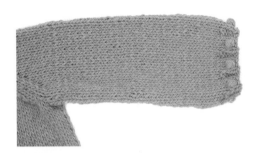

Adjusting Sleeve Length

One way to lengthen a sleeve is to simply knit a longer cuff. By the same token, knitting a shorter cuff, or omitting the cuff altogether, is an easy way to shorten a sleeve.

To add length to a sleeve above the cuff, you use your row gauge to determine how many additional rows are needed to reach the desired length and then work those additional rows, evenly spaced, between increase rows. To subtract length above the cuff, you use your row gauge to determine how many rows need to be eliminated to reach the desired length and then omit those rows periodically between increase rows.

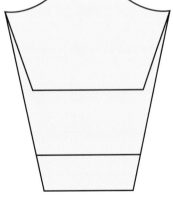

For substantially shorter sleeves, such as three-quarter-length sleeves, you need to cast on more stitches at the cuff to accommodate the larger circumference of the forearm. An easy way to work a three-quarter sleeve is to subtract the length you want from your pattern's sleeve length and then begin at that point in the pattern, casting on the number of stitches that are expressed at that point in the instructions. (For example, if the original sleeve begins with a cast-on number of 44 at the cuff, and after working and shaping for 4 or 5 inches—which is about where three-quarter-length sleeves would begin—the stitch count is 50, you would begin your three-quarter sleeves by casting on 50 stitches.) That way, you don't have to rewrite the shaping instructions.

Adjusting Sleeve Shape

Most knitting patterns include sleeves that are shaped traditionally, gradually widening from the cuff up to the cap. You can change this in a number of ways, such as by creating fashionable kimono or bell-shaped sleeves.

KIMONO SLEEVE

One easy way to alter both the length and the shape of a sleeve is to make a straight sleeve like the one shown here. This produces a kimono-like sleeve, which is attractive on womens' coats and sweaters.

To make this adjustment, you go to the sleeve instructions in your pattern and find the number of stitches you're supposed to end up with after performing all the increases before the sleeve cap begins. You cast on that number and work straight to where the cap shaping should begin, for the length desired, and shape the cap as written. It's easy to adjust the length of a kimono sleeve because there is no shaping in that section of the sleeve.

BELL SLEEVE

You can alter a sleeve's shape to create bell sleeves. The key is to not disrupt the length too much and to maintain the sleeve cap's width and shaping so that it will still fit in the armhole. Bell sleeves are often a little longer than standard sleeves, so that they cover the wrist and a portion of the back of the hand.

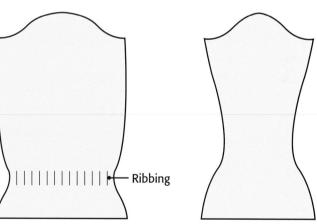

Ribbing

The best way to calculate the adjustments for a bell sleeve is to draw out the sleeve on graph paper and calculate stitch and row counts, decreases, and increases based on size, stitch gauge, and row gauge. There is no rule or formula because sizes, gauges, and style preferences vary greatly. A very easy way to create a bell sleeve look is to work the kimono sleeve as instructed above, adding a 2-inch ribbing, or an eyelet row and tie, that gathers the sleeve about 2 to 3 inches above the cast-on row for a baby or child or 4 to 6 inches above the cast-on row for an older child or woman.

Another approach to making a nice bell sleeve is to cast on twice as many stitches as your pattern indicates to cast on. You work a non-gathering edging for 1 inch and then decrease gradually—over about 2 to 5 inches of length—back to the cast-on number specified in your pattern. From here, you make the sleeve as written in your pattern, except that you decrease the number of rows between increase rows, to compensate for the added length of the bell.

Index